FORWARD AIR BASES in EUROPE FROM D-DAY TO THE BALTIC

This book is dedicated to the men and women of 2nd TAF.
They made it work – whatever their rank or role.

FORWARD AIR BASES in EUROPE FROM D-DAY TO THE BALTIC

SUPPORTING THE ALLIED ADVANCE

TREVOR STONE

AIR WORLD

FORWARD AIR BASES IN EUROPE FROM D-DAY TO THE BALTIC
Supporting the Allied Advance

First published in Great Britain in 2023 by
Air World
An imprint of
Pen & Sword Books Ltd
Yorkshire – Philadelphia

Copyright © Trevor Stone, 2023

ISBN 978 1 39901 081 8

The right of Trevor Stone to be identified as Author of this work has been asserted by him in accordance with the Copyright, Designs and Patents Act 1988.

A CIP catalogue record for this book is available from the British Library.

All rights reserved. No part of this book may be reproduced or transmitted in any form or by any means, electronic or mechanical including photocopying, recording or by any information storage and retrieval system, without permission from the Publisher in writing.

Typeset by SJmagic DESIGN SERVICES, India.

Printed and bound in the UK by CPI Group (UK) Ltd.

Pen & Sword Books Ltd incorporates the imprints of Air World,
After the Battle, Pen & Sword Archaeology, Atlas, Aviation, Battleground, Discovery,
Family History, History, Maritime, Military, Naval, Politics, Social History, Transport,
True Crime, Claymore Press, Frontline Books, Praetorian Press, Seaforth Publishing
and White Owl.

For a complete list of Pen & Sword titles please contact

PEN & SWORD BOOKS LIMITED
George House, Units 12 & 13, Beevor Street, Off Pontefract Road,
Barnsley, South Yorkshire, S71 1HN, England
E-mail: enquiries@pen-and-sword.co.uk
Website: www.pen-and-sword.co.uk

or
PEN AND SWORD BOOKS
1950 Lawrence Rd, Havertown, PA 19083, USA
E-mail: uspen-and-sword@casematepublishers.com
Website: www.penandswordbooks.com

Contents

List of Maps and Figures vi
Acknowledgements vii
Preface viii
Glossary and Definitions xii
Introduction xv

PART 1: THE PATH TO NORMANDY 1
Chapter 1   A New Air Force 2
Chapter 2   Planning for D-Day 11
Chapter 3   The Support Plan 19

PART 2: THE JOURNEY 39
Chapter 4   A Foothold on the Continent 40
Chapter 5   Developing the Bridgehead 58
Chapter 6   Crossing the Start Line – Breakout from Normandy 91
Chapter 7   Logistics at Breaking Point – The Autumn Crisis 120
Chapter 8   Over the Rhine and into the Reich 142

APPENDICES 161
Appendix I   Timeline of Key Dates and Events – June 1944 to May 1945 162
Appendix II   Channel Ports used by the Allies – Key Data 164
Appendix III   Alphabetical Listing of 2nd TAF Support Units 1944 to 1945 166
Appendix IV   Composition of 2nd TAF in February 1945 185
Appendix V   Roll of Honour and Awards to 2nd TAF Support Personnel 190

Notes and References 197
Bibliography 214
Index 219

List of Maps and Figures

Maps

1. The Normandy Lodgement Area. 13
2. Final Layout of the Rear Maintenance Area in Normandy. 82
3. North-west Europe Ports Utilised by the British, 1944 to 1945. 116
4. 2nd TAF Airfields (in use and under construction)
   1 December 1944. 132

Figures

1. Miles Travelled and Tonnage Carried by No.309 Supply and Transport Column August 1944 to May 1945. 101
2. Air Freight carried by Dakotas of No.46 Group – Scheduled and Special Services 13 September to 19 November 1944. 113
3. 2nd TAF Average Aircraft Strength and Availability June to September 1944 119
4. Air Freight carried by Dakotas of No.46 Group – Scheduled Services and Selected Dates January to April 1945. 152

Acknowledgements

The Normandy campaign in 1944 has always held a fascination for me, particularly the support of air power. The idea for this book emerged from a dissertation that I submitted for a degree in military history with the University of Buckingham in 2018. I was most fortunate to have Professor Gary Sheffield as my supervisor and I learned much from him. His advice, knowledge and wise council were greatly appreciated.

    A dissertation is one thing but turning it in to a more readable book is quite a different matter. I could not have done this without the support of the publisher, Pen & Sword. From the outset, my experience with them has been superb. My commissioning editor, Martin Mace, himself a highly experienced author, was a great help. His flexibility and guidance – even with my woefully inadequate estimates of timescales – was most welcome! I must also extend thanks to Ed Paice of EDesign Graphic Design Consultancy, whom I have known for many years, for the excellent maps and diagrams. He did much work to produce these in a more contemporary way, which I think makes them easier to engage with than some of the more traditional styles. The support of Lee Barton from the RAF's Air Historical Branch, in providing photographic illustrations, is acknowledged.

    Whilst the lion's share of the factual content came from research in various archives, some of the content came from veterans (or their families), fellow historians and researchers, several of whom kindly gave me permission to use their material. Particular thanks are extended to Mike Fenton, John Haywood, Neil Huband, Tim Knight, Jim Payne and Geoff Slee.

    Last, but no means least, I could not have completed this project without the patience and support of my wife, Lynne. Not only did she keep me on track, but quietly endured the many hours I spent isolated in my study on this, my third book. She also acted as a great sounding board for my ideas and commented on the developing manuscript from a reader's perspective. When the work was complete, she was also a much-valued proofreader. I cannot say how much that has been appreciated.

Preface

This book examines how Royal Air Force tactical air power was supported, during and after the invasion of Northern Europe in June 1944. It focuses on 2nd Tactical Air Force (2nd TAF), from its part in the days following the invasion, during the breakout from Normandy in early August 1944, through to the entry into Germany in 1945. The official story took some time to emerge after the war. Indeed, the biographer of Air Marshal Sir Arthur Coningham, 2nd TAF's commander throughout the campaign, commented that he (Coningham) 'made no attempt to compose his own overall account of the years 1941–1945 and foresaw that the RAF would prove slow to publish detailed narratives matching those written by soldiers who, naturally, paid little attention to the deeds of airmen'.[1]

Coningham was right and it took nearly a decade for these deeds to receive attention from the Air Ministry's historians, albeit these were not commercially published. It was the impressive, four volume work by the two Christophers (Shores and Thomas) in the 2000s that really tackled the subject, although from an operational perspective.[2]

The story of the RAF's European tactical air force is a fascinating one. Its origins lay in the highly successful Desert Air Force during the campaign in North Africa during 1941 and 1942. The nature of the desert war was highly dynamic and demanded flexibility and mobility, from both the RAF and General (later Field Marshal) Sir Bernard Montgomery's Eighth Army. This warfare called for close cooperation between air and ground forces. As described by the popular historical writer Philip Guedalla: 'Desert life, it seemed, had taught the RAF to be nomadic'.[3] And so it had. The experience of what was the RAF's first tactical air force laid the foundations for a second such force and enabled it to hold its own in north-west Europe during 1944 and 1945.

Formed and initially based in the United Kingdom, 2nd TAF was able to support Operation *Overlord* from the British Isles, but soon moved its headquarters and flying squadrons to France after the D-Day landings. It then consolidated its new basing and built-up the supplies it needed to support the developing ground campaign. Once Montgomery's Twenty-First Army Group was finally on the move after the long, hard-fought battles to seize the important city of Caen and its environs in late July 1944, the RAF started its journey through France, the Low Countries and into Germany. During the early days in France, many of the forward air bases were just temporary airstrips, created on farmland using the resourceful expertise

PREFACE

of the airfield construction engineers of both the army and air force. As the advance progressed, many former enemy occupied airfields were pressed into service after their previous occupiers were put to flight by the Allies as they advanced towards the German frontier. By and large, much of the supplies, equipment and ground crew had to be moved by road, which led to a long supply chain, stretching back to the United Kingdom. Although some captured enemy resources were reused, the RAF's flying squadrons had to take everything with them to keep their aircraft flying and combat effective. The ground support organisation had to be highly mobile. The story of how this was done is not well understood and rarely features in the popular narratives.

By the time the Allied advance had reached Belgium, the planners expected that the capture of the inland port of Antwerp would enable them to bring in vitally needed supplies further north on the Continent. It did not work out as planned. Although the city and its port were captured in September 1944, the route to the sea along the river Scheldt was still controlled by German forces. It took nearly three months until they were ousted, and the port opened for business. Until then, resupply was some 300 miles by road from Normandy with the RAF largely reliant on the army for transporting its needs. For an air force needing large volumes of fuel and ammunition, demand soon began to outpace the rate of supply. Several emergency measures were put in place to keep the aircraft operational and saw the RAF resorting to the use of heavy bombers to fly in supplies. Even when Antwerp was up and running, supplying the tactical air force remained a hand-to-mouth affair right through until the enemy's surrender in May 1945. The whole drive to defeat Nazi Germany was nearly undone by the practicalities of the Allies logistical effort, both for land and air forces. In the end, miraculously, it worked, but it was a close-run thing.

Based on new and original research in the United Kingdom's National Archives, this book takes a detailed look at the support of British tactical air power in the European campaign. From the safety and comfort of your armchair, it takes you on a journey, from the conference rooms of the planning teams, across the Normandy beaches to the hinterland of Nazi Germany. It tells the story of how the ground crews kept the aircraft flying and how the many challenges were overcome. It was a long journey from the shores of the United Kingdom through to that momentous day on 8 May 1945 when so many celebrated the end of nearly six years of war in Europe. It was a journey that covered many roads, many bridges and, most significantly, numerous forward air bases on the Continent. It is a compelling story.

There were many organisations that supported 2nd TAF. Several of them had a starring role, others less so. What is important is that it was a team effort, and all played their part well. It is not possible to recount all their stories in detail because for many there is little surviving information in the archives. Several units were formed just for this part of the war and disbanded soon after they had served their purpose. Some feature more frequently in the story and perhaps steal the show. Hopefully, I have captured the majority, even if it is a passing mention or description. Where possible, references have been included to other books or sources to aid further research or more detailed reading on specific aspects.

FORWARD AIR BASES IN EUROPE FROM D-DAY TO THE BALTIC

Comment also needs to be made about terminology. In L.P. Hartley's novel *The Go Between*, he opens the book with the memorable line 'The past is a foreign country: they do things differently there'. Hartley's sentiment reminds us, that even just over seventy-five years ago, things were quite different, especially the use of the English language. At that time, the *RAF War Manual* defined the support which this book examines as administration. In the twenty-first century this term implies clerical work. What was administration or administrative is of course much wider than this and covers what is now more commonly referred to as military logistics. The full definition is reproduced in the glossary, which follows this preface. Details from many of 2nd TAF's Operational Record Books have been used throughout the text and many of them contain acronyms or expressions, which are not defined or explained. In such cases, and elsewhere, I have included amplifying comment within square brackets.

In researching the account, I found that I had a much closer link with the story than I realised. As a newly commissioned officer in the RAF's Supply Branch back in the early 1980s, I was posted to the RAF station at Laarbruch in the then West Germany. The country was still divided into two independent nations following the immediate post-war Allied occupation. Life on the Continent was still very much in the menacing shadow of the Cold War. The Berlin Wall, the symbolic but divisive apparatus of the Eastern Bloc, was still six years from its fall. Laarbruch, situated close to the Dutch-German border in north-west Germany, was one of the RAF's major flying bases and was just being equipped with the new Tornado aircraft. Unlike many army and RAF bases in Germany at the time which had been repurposed, Laarbruch was a new-build airfield and had not used any of the former Third Reich military infrastructure. It did, though, have an interesting claim to fame in that the main maintenance hangar had been built, largely using a relocated Nazi aircraft manufacturing hangar, which had originally been constructed in the mid-1930s at Bremen, North Germany.

The new airfield, though, had been built on the site of a former 2nd TAF advanced landing ground, set out by army engineers, and used for just a few months in preparation for the final push across the river Rhine in early 1945. Known as Airfield B.100 Goch (the largest nearby town), its main runway had been laid using the innovative interlocking perforated steel planking known as Marston Mat. The airstrip was only used during March and April 1945, and was home to RAF and Royal Canadian Air Force squadrons operating Auster, Typhoon and Spitfire aircraft. Towards the end of my career in the RAF I became the first honorary historian of what then had become the RAF's Logistics Branch and Trades and accompanied several RAF units on battlefield tours to Normandy to speak to them about the RAF's ground support during D-Day and thereafter. Both connections with the story seemed to have subconsciously prompted me to research and record a missing part of 2nd TAF's epic endeavours.

Just after the unconditional surrender of German forces in May 1945, British Prime Minister Winston Churchill, wrote a letter of thanks to the commander of 2nd TAF. He commented:

PREFACE

> Now that Germany has been well and truly defeated, I wish to express to you, on behalf of His Majesty's Government, the deep sense of gratitude felt by all our people for the glorious part which has been played by the Second Tactical Air Force ... The Nation will not forget the decisive part which your officers, airmen and airwomen have made to the victory.[4]

Today, commemorations of wartime events have become more broad brush, and the decisive part played by 2nd TAF has become less well known. The story of how they were supported concerns a very different group of men and women from the more famous and applauded aircrews. The experience of the ground crews is replete with many examples of sacrifice, ingenuity, courage and commitment. Many of them would have said (and indeed did), with typical modesty, that it was just a job that needed to be done and that they just got on and did it. That they did, but their part deserves more attention than it has received to date. This is their story, and I am pleased to have given them a voice in the historiography.

Trevor Stone,
Brampton, Cambridgeshire,
2023

Glossary

Commonly used acronyms in the text and supporting notes

AHB	Air Historical Branch
AM	Air Ministry
AOC	Air Officer Commanding
C-in-C	Commander-in-Chief
CO	Commanding Officer
Fw	Focke-Wulf (German aircraft manufacturer)
Ju	Junkers (German aircraft manufacturer)
Me	Messerschmitt (German aircraft manufacturer)
NCO	Non-Commissioned Officer
ORB	Operational Record Book (referred to as War Diary in the main narrative)
RAF	Royal Air Force
RAFVR	Royal Air Force Volunteer Reserve
RCAF	Royal Canadian Air Force
TAF	Tactical Air Force
TNA	The National Archives (United Kingdom)

DEFINITIONS

Administrative Services	The *RAF War Manual* defines the most important of these as: Accommodation, food, and water supply. Preparation and maintenance of landing grounds. Fuel and ammunition supply. Facilities and equipment for the day-to-day repair and maintenance of aircraft. Ground equipment in connection with night flying, armament, photography, wireless and navigation. Ground inter-unit communication. Medical facilities. Anti-gas and anti-aircraft defence. Parks and depots for supply and repair of reserve aircraft.

GLOSSARY

	The ground organisation and network of inter-communications which are essential for coordinating the air and the ground components of an air defence scheme for a theatre of operations.[1]
Bridgehead	Various definitions exist for this term, but it is best described as a strategically significant location, at the end of a bridge or other water crossing in the battle area, which an enemy might wish to defend or capture. It is also an area in which men, *materiel* (see definition below) and supplies are accumulated prior to further operations.
Combined Operations	During the Second World War, the term 'combined' was used when two or more of the three United Kingdom's armed services worked together.
D-Day	Although the term D-Day is commonly associated with the Allied invasion of Europe in June 1944, the term is a much wider-used military convention used to denote the actual day that an operation commences. Days prior to that are referred to as D-minus (or -) 1, 2, 3 etc. and days after as D-plus (or +) 1, 2, 3 etc. The actual time that an operation commences is referred to as H-Hour.
Joint Operations	During the Second World War, the term joint was used to refer to operations or work conducted with other Allied nations.
Landing Ships	A whole range of specialist landing ships were developed during the Second World War and formed a vital part of the cross-Channel transport for D-Day and thereafter. Amongst the commonest used were the: Landing Craft Vehicle Personnel or the famous Higgins Boats; Landing Craft Assault; Landing Craft Infantry (or Landing Ship Infantry) and the ubiquitous Landing Ship Tank. Whilst this was (and remains) the preferred style in official and more formal academic texts, this convention has been slightly modified throughout the main narrative and the acronyms avoided for ease of reading.
Line(s) of Communication	This was defined by the RAF as 'The system of communication in a theatre of war between the bases and railhead, both inclusive, along which the requirements of the force are transported'.[2] Throughout the campaign this was largely maintained by the army and used to denote the route between the rear area and forward areas.

FORWARD AIR BASES IN EUROPE FROM D-DAY TO THE BALTIC

Lodgment Area	This term applies to a bridgehead when it has been established and enlarged, serving as a base from which to conduct a breakout and mount future operations into enemy held territory.
Materiel	This spelling, with an 'e' at the end rather than an 'a', relates to the specific equipment and supplies required by a military force. Derived from the French matériel, the term seems to have gained more widespread usage after the Second World War. It does, however, provide a useful collective term for the myriad items required to provide support for a military force. To avoid any confusion, where the term is used in this book it is shown in italics.
Munitions	A generic term which encompasses explosives, bombs, small arms ammunition and pyrotechnics.
Order of Battle	Essentially this is a listing which shows the hierarchical organisation, command structure, strength and disposition of equipment and people within the formations or units of a military force.
Petrol, Oil and Lubricants	A collective term which encompasses: Aviation fuel. Aircraft engine lubricating oils. Motor transport fuel (80 Octane). Motor transport lubricants. Kerosene. Derv (Diesel Engined Road Vehicles) fuel oil. Petroleum spirit: undyed for use in catalytic heaters; all generating and charging sets; small pump sets; outboard engines and small propulsion units on motorboats or barges; similar type petrol engines on signal and engineer equipment (this fuel was not permitted to be used for motor transport vehicles and cookers).[3] *For simplicity and ease of reading, the more generic term 'fuel(s)' is used throughout the main narrative.*
Radio Telephony	Communication messages broadcast over open radio waves.
Stores	Air force *materiel* other than supplies.[4]
Supplies	Food, forage, fuel, petrol, oil, light, disinfectants, and medical comforts.[5]
Wireless Telegraphy	Communication messages sent using Morse code.

Introduction

Whilst the focus of this book is the support of 2nd TAF after the breakout from Normandy in mid-1944, there is an important background to the story and the content is therefore divided into two parts. Part one starts in the inter-war period with the uncertain and somewhat turbulent relationships between the RAF and the army regarding the role of air power. Despite this faltering start, the RAF formed an Army Cooperation Command in 1940 although this had been disbanded by the time of Operation *Overlord*. It was the campaign in the deserts of North Africa during 1941 and 1942 that forged the role of tactical air power, and this paved the way for the formation of a new air force – 2nd TAF. Coincidentally, the desert force was an important part in the defeat of Field Marshal Erwin Rommel's Africa Korps, the same commander who had been placed in charge of the German forces opposing the Allied landings in 1944. From the very beginning of the planning for *Overlord*, a tactical air force was a key component of the order of battle.

The narrative then moves on to examine certain aspects of the planning for *Overlord* and how the RAF developed its Administrative Plan for the forthcoming campaign. This work was the key to success for the campaign and the path to Normandy involved a vast range of experts in numerous specialisations. It was a path which was paved with lessons learned, notably, the first, albeit disastrous foray into amphibious warfare, at Dieppe in August 1942 and then the more successful invasions of North Africa in November 1942, Sicily in July 1943 and then mainland Italy later in September 1943.[1] All of these enabled the Allies to fine-tune how they operated. It also gave them valuable inter-operating experience of land, sea and air forces, as well as with other nations. All of this shaped what was to follow in north-west Europe in 1944.

With this important background established time is then taken to consider the challenges of meeting the RAF's campaign plan from a support perspective and what the various organisations were to meet the operational deployment of 2nd TAF in the highly mobile environment of the long journey north from France into Germany.

With the scene set, Part Two, commencing with Chapter Four – A Foothold on the Continent – starts the journey. Many of the official histories produced just

FORWARD AIR BASES IN EUROPE FROM D-DAY TO THE BALTIC

after the war divided the campaign into four phases and these have been used as a framework to guide the story through the remaining chapters:

Phase I
6 June – 25 July 1944
The initial landing on the beaches of up to the breakout from the bridgehead.

Phase II
26 July – 26 September 1944
Breakout from the bridgehead in Normandy and the advance through France and Belgium up to the airborne operation, which resulted in the first capture of Arnhem (Operation *Market Garden*).

Phase III
27 September 1944 – 14 January 1945
The period from Operation *Market Garden*, up to and including the defeat of the enemy spoiling offensive in the Ardennes.

Phase IV
15 January – 8 May 1945
The period from the crossing of the Meuse (operations *Veritable* and *Grenade*) to the crossing of the Rhine (Operation *Plunder*) and the final disruption and pursuit.[2]

Prior to Phase I though, there was a preliminary period, which is generally considered to be from 1 April to 5 June 1944. Broadly speaking, this was intended to achieve air superiority – a factor considered to be the 'principal prerequisite for the successful assault of Europe from the West'. Indeed, it would become the 'cardinal point of air planning'. This period included an extensive range of operations against the enemy that set out to dislocate lines of communication; disrupt radar and radio facilities; attack military bases; harass coastal shipping; attack airfields; conduct air reconnaissance; protect the assembly of Allied assault forces and attacks on the V-1 flying bomb production and launch sites.[3]

D-Day on 6 June 1944, marked the beginning of Phase I. After a nail-biting build up, the Allies successfully put ashore an invasion force on the Normandy beaches. This enabled a foothold to be established on the Continent. This assault phase, codenamed Operation *Neptune*, was launched across a front of five landing beaches with the first troops stepping ashore at 06.30 hours. The landings had been preceded just after midnight with the bombing of coastal batteries between Cherbourg and Le Havre by British and Canadian aircraft. The aerial assault was resumed half an hour before the landing craft came ashore, with some 1,000 American heavy bombers hitting a range of coastal targets. In parallel with this vital softening up of the German defences, just before 01.00 hours, pathfinder troops of the British 6th Airborne Division landed on the eastern flank of the landing areas, followed

INTRODUCTION

by paratroopers of the United States 82nd Airborne Division and 101st Airborne Division on the western flank. This preceded the main airborne landings: at around 02.00 hours the British dropped its parachutists east of the Orne river, capturing their initial objectives the bridges over the river Orne and Canal de Caen à la Mer. The Americans dropped their leading units near the village of Sainte-Mère-Église.[4]

It was during this phase of the operation that 2nd TAF landed much of its support personnel and equipment. The move of their flying squadrons from the many temporary bases in southern England to Normandy began in earnest on D+4. Despite the vast numbers of men, machines and equipment that were flowing from the United Kingdom to Normandy, it took, on average, just ten to twelve days for a complete squadron move to take place, from packing of equipment, to landing in France and onward transit. In the initial stages of the landings, the RAF used its specialist beach squadrons to unload stores, supplies and vehicles across the open beaches and located these in temporary inland concentration areas or supply dumps as they were colloquially known.[5]

The build-up of RAF personnel was rapid and by 20 June 1944, 13,000 men and 3,200 vehicles had been disembarked. They were unable to achieve their key objective, to take the city of Caen, quickly enough, which meant that the time spent in the bridgehead (the duration of Phase I) was longer than anticipated. Situated on the Orne river, the city was approximately 9 miles from the coast and the planners had envisaged that it would be captured on D-Day itself. Securing this historic city, dating back to the reign of William the Conqueror, was a main objective for the Anglo-Canadian forces of Montgomery's Twenty-First Army Group. It was an essential road hub, strategically astride the river Orne and Canal de Caen à la Mer. The Germans defended this stronghold with all their might, and it took six hard weeks of fighting and heavy shelling to capture the capital of Normandy. All of this contributed towards establishing a sound foothold on the Continent.

The capture of Caen and the securing of its environs during the first three weeks of July provided a starting line for the breakout from Normandy, the crossing of which gathered pace in the last week of July and marked the start of Phase II. The advance was rapid and saw the Anglo-Canadian forces move north-east through France, Belgium and into the Netherlands. The end of this phase was marked by Operation *Market Garden*, the unsuccessful operation to create a 64-mile salient into enemy-held territory with a bridgehead over the river Rhine, thereby creating an Allied invasion route into northern Germany. Again, this story has been well told by several historians. By and large it was carried out with air resources from the United Kingdom and 2nd TAF had a limited, supporting role. The operation though, is significant in the story of the tactical air force in that it committed much needed transport support aircraft to the airlift. Supply by air had become particularly important for the support of Twenty-First Army Group and 2nd TAF by this time and the service was effectively denied to them for the duration of *Market Garden* which lasted from 17 to 25 September. The further north the Allies moved, the longer the lines of communication became, and logistics was a real headache. The difficulties came to a head in August 1944 and several emergency measures, including emergency supply by air, were required to sustain the advance north of

Brussels. The diversion of air transport resources to Arnhem for Operation *Market Garden* could not have come at a worse time.

An important part of the story that emerges at this point is how the Allies planned to use supply by sea as they moved northwards. There were several hard-fought, smaller-scale battles, spearheaded by the First Canadian Army, to capture and utilise the minor Channel ports during September 1944 and this went some way to alleviating the supply difficulties. These ports provided further options for the import of war *materiel*, but they had to be captured from the enemy and repaired before they could be pressed back into service. This repatriation took most of September 1944 to achieve.

Notwithstanding the value of the minor ports, the capture of the 'major' deep water port at Antwerp soon became vital to meet the ever-increasing supply and demand of British and Canadian combat forces. Although the city and its port fell to the British 11th Armoured Division on 4 September 1944, its pathway to the North Sea, some 80 miles away via the river Scheldt, remained under the control of German forces, which occupied two fortified islands on the north and south banks of the estuary (Walcheren and Breken). Such was the significance of Antwerp that General Dwight D. Eisenhower in a message to Montgomery on 10 October 1944, declared that 'unless we have Antwerp producing by the middle of November our entire operations will come to a standstill'.[6] The operation to oust the enemy and to clear the Scheldt lasted until 28 November when the first Allied ship arrived at Antwerp – nearly three months after it was first captured. Until the port became fully operational, resupply to Twenty-First Army Group had to be met largely by road convoys, rail transport and emergency supply by air. Much of the overall blame for this can be attributed to the chaotic development of Allied strategy, primarily the uncertainty of possible outcomes from the broad-front/narrow-thrust argument pursued by senior commanders.

Essentially, this involved two points of view. Montgomery's, almost dogmatic view, was that a single thrust into the Ruhr and Berlin was the best strategy and would consolidate Allied forces to the north and then a rapid and powerful drive through the German defences and on to Berlin; Montgomery was adamant that this was the best way to defeat Nazi Germany. On the other hand, Lieutenant General Omar Bradley, commander of the Twelfth United States Army Group, also favoured a narrow-thrust approach, but further south towards Metz and the Saar. Eisenhower though, the Supreme Allied Commander, disagreed with both narrow-thrust approaches and favoured advancing into Germany on a broad front. Montgomery's preoccupation with winning this argument, as historian Richard Lamb states, were 'the two worst military decisions of his [Montgomery's] career'.[7] The first, as previously recounted, was the disastrous *Market Garden* operation. The second, as described by historian John Terraine, was his 'extraordinary neglect of Antwerp, the great port whose capture and clearance promised immense alleviation of the logistical difficulties which beset the Allies'.[8] It was not surprising that, amidst this strategic turbulence, many were struggling to understand where the battle was going next and when. Logistics by this time was at breaking point.

In Phase III, essentially the autumn and early winter period, the pace of advance slowed and by early December 1944 most of 2nd TAF's units had begun

INTRODUCTION

to consolidate their positions in anticipation of a typical continental winter with its inevitable constraints on air operations. Broadly speaking, the Allied front line had extended to a point between Nijmegen and Arnhem in the Netherlands.

The winter was indeed a cold and snowy one, a factor which the Germans took advantage of with their counter-offensive in the Ardennes on 16 December 1944, more commonly known as the Battle of the Bulge. The enemy was also aware by this time that the Port of Antwerp was critical to the Allies and their general intent was to push towards the city, dividing American and British forces, and to cut off the Allied supply source.[9] The offensive was beaten back by early February 1945, but it proved to be a very trying winter, both meteorologically and operationally.

The beginning of 1945 was not quite as expected with the Germans having one last throw of the dice on New Year's Day with what they called Operation *Bodenplatte*. To cripple what, up until then, had been a continuing overwhelming air superiority by the Allies, the German Luftwaffe launched a substantial, surprise attack on Allied airfields in Belgium, the Netherlands and France. Although *Bodenplatte* did incur serious damage, it was nowhere near as effective as the Germans hoped. They were never able to recover from their losses in the operation and it proved to be the beginning of the end for the Luftwaffe.

Phase IV, the concluding part of the campaign, lasted from mid-January until the German surrender in early May. This saw the Allies preparing for the final assault on the German frontier and into the Reich. As part of the preparations for the crossing of the Rhine, the British launched Operation *Veritable* at the beginning of February 1945, thus achieving an advance through the Reichswald forest and the Rhine plain. This was part of an Allied pincer movement, which also involved the Ninth United States Army in the southern part of the attack – Operation *Grenade*. By early March 1945, these operations enabled the Allies to clear the area between the rivers Maas and Rhine, and driving the German forces east of the Rhine.[10]

This secured the ground for a concentration of forces prior to the crossing of the river Rhine itself on 23/24 March 1945 with operations *Plunder* and *Varsity*. Montgomery's forces reached the Baltic at Wismar and Lübeck on 2 May 1945 and were able to seal off the Danish peninsula. The Germans finally capitulated at the beginning of May 1945 with the unconditional instrument of surrender being signed at Montgomery's tactical headquarters on Lüneburg Heath at 18.30 hours on 4 May 1945; the ceasefire order was issued to take effect at 08.00 hours on Saturday, 5 May 1945.[11] There was still much to be done. Although the war in the Far East went on until the middle of August 1945, the war in Europe was at an end. With the war over in Europe and with the RAF needing to maintain a presence in Germany, 2nd TAF, which had by then occupied a whole series of new airfields in Germany, became part of the British Air Forces of Occupation on 15 July 1945.[12]

That was the big picture of what happened in the relatively short period of just under a year from the landings on the Normandy coast in June 1944, to the defeat of Nazi Germany in May 1945. For 2nd TAF it had been a momentous period. The aircrews had played a significant part in the success of the campaign, but they would not even have been airborne without the indefatigable commitment of their ground support organisation. What follows is their story.

Part 1

THE PATH TO NORMANDY

Chapter 1

A New Air Force

On D-Day itself, 2nd TAF had only just celebrated its first birthday. This new air force hailed from the sands of North Africa where its forerunner, the Desert Air Force, had been highly successful in its key role as an integrated part of the ground campaign to defeat Erwin Rommel's Africa Korps. In effect, it was the first tactical air force, albeit the name as such was never officially adopted. Winning its spurs as a valued partner in the North African campaign had not been easy and much had been done to move on from the position that the RAF had found itself in at the outbreak of war. By the time Britain had made the momentous decision to declare war on Nazi Germany in September 1939, the whole idea of close cooperation between the RAF and the army had lost its way. Before joining 2nd TAF on their journey to Normandy and beyond, it is useful to understand some of this background.

Army Cooperation

The decline in the operational relationship with the army can be traced back to the early 1920s. The RAF had emerged from the First World War some seven months before the Armistice in November 1918 as a new, independent air force, which was quite separate from the army. The War Cabinet at the time also gave the new RAF a wider mandate, a key part of which was the development of a more strategic employment of air power. Coming from a merger of the Royal Naval Air Service and the army's Royal Flying Corps, the embryonic RAF was set to have a bright future. It had of course been shaped by its forebears, especially the Royal Flying Corps. As part of the army, the corps had a tight-knit relationship with land forces, albeit much of this was focused on the trench warfare, which dominated conditions of the Western Front. The Royal Flying Corps was viewed by many at the time as 'the finest tactical air force in the world'.[1]

Despite this pedigree, the inter-war period saw a notable shift in the RAF's operational relationship with the army. By the 1930s, horses, wagons and the early tanks had been largely replaced by an ever-expanding range of soft-skinned and more sophisticated armoured vehicles – all of which had enabled the army to become considerably more mobile and flexible. The RAF though, had started to stretch its wings in a different direction. In addition to existing Empire interests in India and Egypt, Britain also gained a responsibility for territories formerly occupied by the Imperial German and Ottoman dynasties under a League of Nations initiative which included Palestine, Jordan and Mesopotamia (Iraq). It was thus that the RAF began to secure a key role in what became known as imperial policing and the new service began to drift away from the tight bonds with the army that the RFC had forged and started along a new line of travel which saw the strategic application of air power having great merit in the future.[2]

RAF Organisation

This new way of thinking began to influence the way the RAF was organised. Its home command structure in the period up until 1935 was largely geographical in nature and simply divided into home and overseas areas. The home element was classed as the Air Defence of Great Britain. The overseas element was sub-divided into six components comprising: RAF Middle East; British Forces in Iraq; RAF India; RAF Mediterranean; Aden Command; and RAF Far East.[3] The diverse range of aircraft types and supporting activities introduced through the pre-Second World War expansion programme led to a major reorganisation in the RAF command structure in 1936 with, initially, the introduction of four new commands comprising Bomber, Coastal, Fighter and Training; three further commands were introduced in 1938 to include Maintenance, Balloon and Reserve.[4] This reorganisation established a clear focus for activities on a functional rather than a geographical basis.[5] Illogical as it might seem, the structure in the years leading up to a new world war, did not include any organisational provision for organised interaction with the army.[6]

It was the German invasion of France in May 1940 that really highlighted the shortcomings in army cooperation. The day after Britain and France declared war on Nazi Germany on 3 September 1939, the British Expeditionary Force was sent to France, along with air support consisting of Advanced Air Striking Force and Air Component together with assistance from Bomber Command. The arrangements, however, did not prove satisfactory due to several factors. The Advanced Air Striking Force and the Air Component had been formed especially for the campaign in France and ceased to exist following the withdrawal from the Continent in May and June 1940. In the United Kingdom, this left just Fighter, Bomber and Coastal commands operating almost independently from the army. It was not quite a complete disconnect with the army as the RAF did form Army Co-operation Command in December 1940 and this began to develop tactics for a future invasion of Europe. The new RAF command, however, was disbanded in June 1943 when tactical air power was reorganised in the lead up to Operation *Overlord*.

Lessons from North Africa

Despite this complex evolution in how British air power was organised, there were highly successful developments in ground air cooperation during the North African campaign of 1941–1942, with the RAF's Western Desert Air Force supporting the British Eighth Army and the Northwestern African Air Forces supporting the First Army. This demonstrated that a composite force of different types of aircraft under a single air commander, with highly mobile supporting echelons, could provide highly effective support of ground forces. Both air forces merged to become the Desert Air Force, effectively becoming the first tactical air force, although this term was not actually used.[7]

The potential of this concept for future operations in Europe was soon recognised and, following a staff and signals exercise in early 1943, Exercise *Spartan* was held from 1 to 12 March 1943. This was a major home forces' exercise for a future cross-Channel invasion but had a particular emphasis on exercising the RAF's new approach to providing air support for the army. At the heart of this was a composite group of various aircraft types, which would be under the control of a single air commander. The outcome of this would be the formation of 2nd TAF.[8]

Time to Reorganise – 2nd TAF is Born

By 1943, the RAF's nature of operations had changed quite markedly. Following the conclusion of the battles of France and Britain, the RAF's posture had shifted from a predominantly defensive, to an increasingly offensive role. By the beginning of 1943, the aircraft of Fighter Command were flying more and more fighter sweeps over enemy-occupied territory. Along with their fellow Bomber and Coastal commands, each were still fulfilling a role with quite different strategic objectives. With the planning for an invasion well underway, it was clear that the RAF needed to reorganise, especially now that it was working alongside the United States in a concerted effort to defeat the Axis powers.

With the future of Fighter Command in the balance because of the move towards more offensive operations, it was a convenient caretaker formation in which to start making changes for the immediate future. Changes began in June 1943, when the RAF's Army Cooperation Command was disbanded and its units, along with the light and medium day bombers of Bomber Command's No.2 Group, were transferred to Fighter Command. Two new composite groups of fighter-bomber and reconnaissance aircraft squadrons were also formed in Bomber Command, which were to eventually form the fighting heart of 2nd TAF: No.83 (Composite) Group in April and the No.84 (Composite) Group in July.[9] All three groups, became the new 2nd TAF in November 1943.

In the spring of 1944, a further group, No.85 (Base) was added to the order of battle of 2nd TAF, initially as an air defence organisation (with day and night fighters), but then with a much wider responsibility for most of the RAF's support activities in an invasion bridgehead. For the campaign in north-west Europe, the plan was that No.83 Group would operate in support of the British Second Army and No.84 Group in support of the First Canadian Army. Three specialist reconnaissance wings were also added to the order of battle:

A NEW AIR FORCE

No.34 (Reconnaissance) Wing under HQ 2nd TAF, No.35 (Reconnaissance) Wing under No.84 Group and No.39 (Reconnaissance) Wing Royal Canadian Air Force under No.83 Group. Both composite groups were also allocated air observation post squadrons to provide an artillery spotting capability and an air spotting pool, with a mixture of Fleet Air Arm and RAF squadrons, added to No.85 Group.

Many of the lessons learned from the North African campaign, especially the success of the close ground/air cooperation between the Desert Air Force and the British Eighth Army, were reflected in how 2nd TAF was set up and run. Key to this, were the senior RAF commanders. Although not an air commander for *Overlord*, the placing of Air Chief Marshal Sir Arthur Tedder as the deputy Supreme Allied Commander was an excellent choice given that he had been Commander-in-Chief (C-in-C) of RAF Middle East (which included North Africa) for two years. Tedder had recognised the importance of establishing good working relations with the army commanders and this experience reaped continual benefits in his role as Eisenhower's (the future Supreme Commander for *Overlord*) deputy. The shining star though, was to be the new Air Officer Commanding (AOC) 2nd TAF, Air Marshal Sir Arthur Coningham. Hailing from Brisbane in Australia, Coningham was popularly known as Mary, a corruption of Māori, a play on his early life in New Zealand where his family had moved to when he was still quite young. Coningham served with distinction as a pilot with the Royal Flying Corps during the First World War. He went on to serve with the RAF and by 1937 had risen to the rank of group captain.

At the start of the Second World War, he was an air commodore in command of No.4 Group Bomber Command. In July 1941, he went to Egypt at Tedder's behest as AOC No.204 Group. He went on to serve as a highly successful commander of the Desert Air Force. Of note was his effective use of fighter-bomber aircraft, the development of an efficient ground support system and ground controllers who could call in air attacks using radio. His experience left him with a firm conviction that tactical air power must be closely coordinated with the ground forces and that the priorities for its success (in order) must be to gain air superiority; to interdict enemy reinforcements of men and *materiel*; to isolate the battlefield and then to combine air attacks with ground assaults on the front lines. He went on to direct tactical air force operations in the Allied invasion of Sicily and Italy as commander of the Northwest African Tactical Air Force. There were few, if any, who would have been a better choice for the command of 2nd TAF.

Coningham's subordinate commanders in 2nd TAF also had a sound pedigree, especially those of the composite groups where extreme mobility would be a fact of life and close ground/air cooperation essential for support of the ground battle. Air Vice Marshal Harry Broadhurst was appointed AOC No.83 Group. Broadhurst had succeeded Coningham as the commander of the Desert Air Force, so he was well versed in the intricacies of ground/air cooperation. Another veteran of the desert campaign, the South African Air Vice Marshal Leslie Brown served as AOC 202 Group and was appointed AOC No.84 Group.

FORWARD AIR BASES IN EUROPE FROM D-DAY TO THE BALTIC

The command of No.2 Group rested with another highly distinguished officer, Air Vice Marshal Basil Embry who had been senior Air Staff officer at HQ Desert Air Force in late 1941. Responsibility for No.85 Group was initially with Air Vice Marshal John Cole-Hamilton until July 1944 and then Air Vice Marshal Charles Steele. Coningham's Air Officer Administration, Air Vice Marshal Thomas Elmhirst, was yet another officer who had had sand between his toes and had served in this role at HQ Desert Air Force and HQ Northwest African Tactical Air Force during 1942 and 1943. The new 2nd TAF also benefitted from several of its wing and squadron commanders having served in North Africa.[10]

The surrogate Fighter Command reverted to its pre-war identity of Air Defence of Great Britain and, along with 2nd TAF and the United States Ninth Air Force, came under the overall control of a new umbrella formation on 15 November 1943 – the Allied Expeditionary Air Force, under the overall command of Air Chief Marshal Sir Trafford Leigh-Mallory as its Air C-in-C.[11] Leigh-Mallory recognised that his span of command was extensive and that the air operations in immediate and direct support of the land battle (primarily 2nd TAF and the United States Ninth Air Force) should be specially coordinated and directed. This led to the creation

Air Chief Marshal Sir Arthur Coningham (centre) with two of his 2nd TAF commanders – Air Vice Marshal Harry Broadhurst (to his right) and believed to be Vice Marshal Basil Embry (to his left). This photograph was probably taken towards the end of the campaign in 1945. *(Author's collection)*

A NEW AIR FORCE

of a small operational organisation known as the Advanced Allied Expeditionary Air Force. Although already appointed as commander 2nd TAF, Air Marshal Coningham was also appointed as the AOC of this advanced element in a dual role until the Advanced Allied Expeditionary Air Force was disbanded on 5 August 1944 when he returned to the sole command of 2nd TAF. This appointment was particularly important for the early part of the campaign as it provided Montgomery, in his role as C-in-C Twenty-First Army Group and C-in-C Land Forces with just one air commander to deal with during the initial phases of the operation.[12]

The make of 2nd TAF was not just a British affair; the Royal Canadian Air Force formed a sizeable part of the order of battle: there were three Canadian wings in No.83 Group (Nos. 39, 126 and 127) and several Canadian support units including an air stores park, a repair and salvage unit, two mobile field photographic sections, a mobile field hospital and several mobile dental units. Other nations contributed too; there were Australian, Belgian, Dutch, French and New Zealand flying squadrons. Poland also fielded No.131 Wing, along with an air stores park, a repair and salvage unit, and a motor transport light repair unit in No.84 Group. The Czechs also provided a mobile dental unit that was attached to No.134 Airfield to treat Czech personnel.[13]

As the new air force formed, a number of old acquaintances were reforged, many from the days of the Desert Air Force in North Africa and elsewhere. One interesting and unusual example concerns Reverend T. Gordon Perkins, who joined 2nd TAF as one of its Methodist chaplains. He first joined the RAF as an apprentice in 1927. He served ten years as an aero engine fitter, and at one time to Air Marshal Sir Arthur Coningham. Fitter Perkins was released from the RAF to take Holy Orders and thereafter became Padre Perkins. His first post as RAF Chaplain was at Floriana, Malta, in 1940 and during the hundreds of raids on the island his church was hit during an air raid, but it never closed. He is believed to be the only RAF chaplain to rise from the ranks.

2nd TAF padre, The Reverend (Squadron Leader) Gordon Perkins, (centre) views a Merlin engine of a Spitfire Mk.IX with aircraft fitters, D. Branch (left) and R. Jones (right). *(Copyright IWM)*

FORWARD AIR BASES IN EUROPE FROM D-DAY TO THE BALTIC

New Air Force – New Airfields

There were insufficient existing airfields in the United Kingdom for the growing numbers of aircraft being allocated to 2nd TAF so twenty-three advanced landing grounds were constructed in Hampshire, Sussex and Kent, each capable of handling the rapid take-off of heavily loaded fighter bombers. Each of these airfields consisted of two metal tracked runways, one which was 4,800 feet long and the other 4,200 feet, plus 2.5 miles of perimeter track to enable aircraft to taxi between parking areas and the runways. Additionally, there was a track for motor transport vehicles, thirty-six dispersals for eighty aircraft, up to eight blister hangars for maintenance, bomb dumps and petroleum storage installations, which could hold up to 24,000 gallons of fuel. It was a remarkable construction programme, with each airfield being built in just 10 months by 2 flights from an airfield construction squadron using 156 men.

As these airfields were to be temporary bases for *Overlord*, there were very few permanent buildings and personnel operating from the sites were largely accommodated under canvas.[14] The airfields where 2nd TAF's flying squadrons were based before D-Day received a new identity, irrespective of whether they were a main station or a satellite location. The first seven such places were identified as Nos. 121 to 127. The last of these, for example was the former RAF Kenley. Additionally, pairs of airfields were linked to form a wing. This arrangement did not last long and the numbered airfields each became a wing. No.127 Airfield at Kenley, for example, became No.127 Wing. The number of flying squadrons in each wing varied from three to only one depending on the size of the location. All three of the groups consisted of a rear and main headquarters. The composite groups consisted of a reconnaissance and three fighter wings, together with the required supporting unit, and would generally operate from two airfields.

Group and wing support units were formed in spring 1944 and were responsible for maintaining the pool of aircraft, each modified to the latest operational standard, and ready to be issued to the flying squadrons of their parent group. They remained in the United Kingdom throughout the campaign. Much of the preparatory work involved modifications and adjustments, such as the harmonisation of armament, radio set up and test flights. The units also had a conversion/training flight, which provided refresher, conversion and continuation training for aircrew joining 2nd TAF units to ensure they were up to date on aircraft types and tactics. The unit was also 'home' to aircrew resting between operational tours and these were often used to carry out flight testing of aircraft and as delivery crew for aircraft that had been prepared for issue to squadrons.

The units in Nos. 83 and 84 groups were quite sizeable and had on charge some ninety Spitfires, Mustangs, Typhoons, Austers and (later in the campaign) Tempests. Three reserve aircraft were maintained for each squadron within each group. The units also had several Avro Ansons, which were used for passenger carrying and as a 'taxi' service to transport aircrew between locations. Three group support units and one wing support unit were formed and used throughout the campaign (one each for No.34 (Reconnaissance) Wing and Nos. 2, 83 and 84 groups.[15]

A NEW AIR FORCE

A close up showing the four cannons of a Hawker Typhoon Mk.IB of No.56 Squadron being serviced at RAF Matlaske, Norfolk in April 1943. (*Crown Copyright – Air Historical Branch MoD*)

By the time of the invasion, 2nd TAF's order of battle had become a complex affair. Excluding the reconnaissance wings already embedded within HQ 2nd TAF and the composite groups, there were now thirty wings (or airfields as they were known before May 1944), providing an over-arching command structure for the plethora of flying squadrons. Of these, four were Canadian, two Polish, one Czech and one Norwegian. Within No.85 Group, the units and squadrons committed to defence were brigaded within three base defence sectors.

At the outset, 2nd TAF operated a wide range of aircraft: No.2 Group flying Mosquito, Boston and Mitchells; No.83 Group flying Typhoon, Spitfire, Hurricane Mustang and Austers; No.84 Group flying Spitfire, Mustang and Austers with the headquarters element operating Spitfires as part of No.34 Wing.[16] Whilst many of the squadrons retained their own aircraft and aircrew, the ground crews were often assigned to the airfield or wing. This did not prove a popular move as it broke the ties with a particular squadron and the esprit de corps which that connection so often fostered. On its formation, 2nd TAF was allocated fifty-six squadrons across its three groups.[17]

By the end of 1943, the RAF's new tactical air force was up and running. For many though, it was a very different day to day existence. In his biography of 2nd TAF's commander, Sir Arthur Coningham, Vincent Orange comments that one of his first tasks (delegated to his Air Officer Administration, Air Vice Marshal Thomas Elmhirst) was to make the point to all his squadrons 'that they were about to go on campaign'. Orange goes on to remark that this meant 'separating thousands of men from snug permanent bases in the middle of a bitterly cold winter, giving them tents and transport and making them set up temporary camps on the edge of airfields'.[18]

The initial basing of some of 2nd TAF's groups also helped with fostering a closer relationship between the army and the RAF. The headquarters element of No.84 Group, for example, began to form in June 1943 at Cowley Barracks, Oxford. Whilst viewed by the group as 'scarcely an attractive residence, nor ... in pleasant surroundings', it did have benefits as the barracks were also the HQ British Second Army. The group soon found that 'the mingling of blue and khaki was the realisation of the interdependence of the tank and aircraft'.[19]

For many who were used to the relative comforts of living on an RAF airfield, this was a real culture shock. Although initially unpopular, this exposure of RAF men to living in field conditions and fieldcraft was to be a wise decision. By the time 2nd TAF deployed to the Continent the next year its personnel had become used to the idea of living in the field and invariably on the move. It was the new style air force that would make such a major contribution to delivering air power in the final, full year of the war. Planning though, was to prove key and much needed to be done before a single foot was set ashore on the Normandy beaches.

Chapter 2

Planning for D-Day

Field Marshal Erwin Rommel has been attributed as saying 'before the fighting proper, the battle is fought and decided by the quartermasters'. He was not alone in appreciating that logistics, the trade of the quartermasters, would invariably make or break a commander's fortunes on the field of battle. The Allies too recognised that in any venture to liberate Europe from Nazi occupation, logistics would be crucial. Any invasion though, would be complicated by the fact that it would have to be a predominantly amphibious operation against a well defended coastline. When the British Expeditionary Force set foot on French soil in September 1939, their arrival had been unopposed – troops, vehicles and equipment had been unloaded with ease through several of the French ports, almost under peacetime conditions.

At that time the Germans were far from the French border. By the time planning for D-Day had started in earnest, things were very different. Following their occupation of France in May 1939, German forces had incorporated the country into what became known as *Festung Europa* or Fortress Europe. Much of this centred on the development of what was known as the Atlantic Wall. Work on this had been extensive and comprised a system of coastal defences and fortifications, built along the coast of continental Europe and Scandinavia. The fortifications included coastal guns, batteries, mortars and artillery, manned by thousands of German troops. Getting ashore would be difficult enough, let alone securing ground to establish a bridgehead in which a support infrastructure could be established to support a following campaign.

From an air power perspective, aircraft operating from airfields in the United Kingdom could only participate in the battle for a short period after any landings on the Continent and would soon need to be based in Europe, along with their specialist support. Careful planning and attention to detail were clearly key. By the beginning of 1944, the earliest opportunity during the war that the Allies had to mount an invasion of Europe, valuable experience had been gained of amphibious operations, albeit on a smaller scale.

Planning for D-Day

The feasibility of an invasion of Northern Europe had been considered as early as 1941. The results of this work concluded that any main landing would have to be made between the rivers Somme and Seine in the Pas-de-Calais area, with an early capture of the port of Le Havre.[1] Work on planning for what would eventually be known as Operation *Overlord* began in earnest in early April 1942 when President Roosevelt's emissary and personal advisor, Harry Hopkins, visited the United Kingdom. The outcome of various discussions resulted in what became known as the first *Marshall Plan*, a key part of which was an agreement that France should be invaded at the earliest opportunity to relieve the Soviet Union, which, at that time, was still trying to repel German forces, which had invaded their country in June 1941 (during Operation *Barbarossa*). The air component of this outline plan called for 5,800 aircraft, of which 2,550 were to be provided by the British RAF.

It was the Casablanca Conference in January 1943, which considered the Allied European strategy for the next phase of the war. The nomination for the position of the Supreme Allied Commander though, was not made at this time for various reasons, but it was agreed that the British general, Frederick Morgan should be appointed as Chief of Staff to the Supreme Allied Commander (Designate) to begin detailed planning, a post which he took up at the beginning of April 1943 at Norfolk House, London.[2] It was at this stage that the overall operation was given the code name of *Overlord* but elaborated in more detail under the codename Operation *Neptune*, which was specifically for the 'launching of an assault from the United Kingdom across the English Channel, designed to secure a lodgement area on the Continent, from which wider offensive operations could be developed'.[3]

By the end of July 1943, General Morgan's planning team had developed an initial plan. Whilst the earlier view that the preferred invasion site should be the Pas-de-Calais area, this had become heavily defended and the Allies could not count on using ports in this area as they would most likely be heavily damaged and blocked by the enemy. Other analysis showed that a landing in the Caen-Cotentin region (Normandy) was a more viable option and this was therefore selected. Having been approved by Churchill and the British Chiefs of Staff, the outline plan for *Overlord* was one of the key topics at the Quebec Conference in August 1943; the plan was subsequently endorsed by US President Roosevelt and the US Chiefs of Staff. From here on, Operation *Overlord* was seen as the major Allied ground and air effort in Europe for 1944 with a provisional date of 1 May 1944.[4]

In September 1943, several American key appointments were made for the campaign, including Major General Omar Bradley as the commander of all US ground forces. This was followed on 6 December 1943 by the appointment of the American General Dwight D. Eisenhower as the Supreme Allied Commander. The decision regarding who should be the British ground forces commander was more complex and centred on just two candidates – General Sir Harold Alexander (then the commander of Allied ground forces in Italy) and General (later Field Marshal) Sir Bernard Montgomery (commander of the British Eighth Army then in Italy). After much discussion regarding suitability, Montgomery was appointed the British ground force commander on 24 December 1943. By April 1944, much fine tuning of the plan had taken place.

At a national level, *Overlord* was an Allied approach with the various forces working together to achieve the overall aim. The approach to much of the

PLANNING FOR D-DAY

administrative support, however, was more parochial. With perhaps the exception of reciprocal maintenance agreements between the United States Ninth Air Force and 2nd TAF, both nations evolved and maintained their own logistics support organisations and procedures for their national forces. To a large extent this was driven by the differing force composition and the geographical differences of the axes of advance of the British and American armies.[5]

The Normandy Lodgement Area

The assault on the Normandy coast was planned for a five divisional front on the east side of the Cherbourg peninsula, immediately north of the Carentan estuary and the river Orne (see Map 1 below). Although many of the D-Day narratives refer to this area exclusively as the bridgehead, from the moment of landing through to the eventual breakout, this is not strictly correct. Militarily, a bridgehead is a strategically significant area of ground at the end of a bridge or on the other side of a water crossing, usually defended by enemy forces.

Normally lasting for just a few days, bridgehead areas are either used as a 'springboard' from which to repel an enemy immediately or to be expanded into a more sizeable lodgement area from which a breakout can be prepared for. When developed, as would be the case for Normandy, such areas become substantial defended areas with the rear parts out of direct line of enemy fire.

The British assault area was divided into three beach sectors over which the Second Army would land: on the eastern edge was GOLD Beach on which 50th

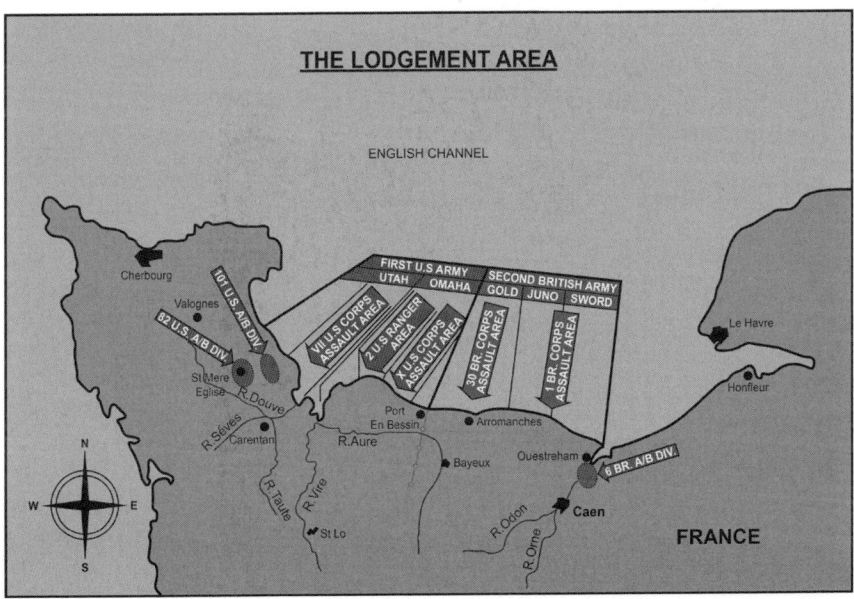

Map 1. The Normandy Lodgement Area.

FORWARD AIR BASES IN EUROPE FROM D-DAY TO THE BALTIC

(Northumberland) Division was to assault as the advance formation of No.30 Corps; in the centre was JUNO beach onto which 3rd Canadian Division would land and on the western end SWORD beach, which 3rd (United Kingdom) Division – who were known as the 3rd Infantry Division during the Second World War – were to attack. From Port-en-Bessin-Huppain westwards to the Cherbourg peninsula was the American sector, with two beaches codenamed UTAH and OMAHA over which the First United States Army would land.[6]

The Air Plan

The resources of 2nd TAF were part of a much larger Allied air effort, which had been brought together under the umbrella of the Allied Expeditionary Air Force. From the RAF, this also required support from RAF Bomber and Coastal commands. To cover the operations of all air forces which were assigned to Operation *Neptune*, an overall air plan was developed which covered: command and control of the various air forces; the principal air tasks and their development through the preliminary and preparatory phases, the assault and follow-up plus air operations after the assault and securing of the lodgement area. The Air C-in-C, Air Chief Marshal Sir Trafford Leigh-Mallory, set out six principal air tasks for the campaign:

- To attain and maintain an air situation whereby the Luftwaffe was rendered incapable of effective interference with Allied operations.
- To provide continuous reconnaissance of the enemy's dispositions and movements.
- To disrupt enemy communications and channels of reinforcement and supply.
- To support the landing and subsequent advances of the Allied armies.
- To deliver offensive strikes against enemy naval forces.
- To provide air lifts for airborne forces.[7]

The second of the tasks, air reconnaissance, saw 2nd TAF's No.34 Wing becoming very heavily committed from February 1944 onwards as arrangements for D-Day gathered pace. To build up a comprehensive intelligence picture, a vast range of targets were photographed including coastal defences, beaches and ports as well as the seabed off Normandy. Vast mosaics of Normandy were photographed as too were areas of bomb damage, railways, marshalling yards, bridges, airfields, V-1 sites, defence lines, river lines and radar installations. The range of the sorties also increased and saw the wing flying as far as Luxembourg, and Dijon and Poitiers in France.[8]

Forward Air Bases

Once the aircraft of 2nd TAF could move to the Continent, it was essential that forward air bases were established as quickly as possible, especially when trying to keep pace with the advancing ground troops. Whilst the area of Normandy was close to ideal for the assault landings, the Normandy countryside was not replete with aircraft landing

PLANNING FOR D-DAY

grounds. Apart from the airport at Carpiquet, near Caen, there were no other such facilities in the lodgement area that could be pressed into Allied service. Consequently, temporary airstrips would need to be constructed from scratch in the Normandy countryside and these would need to be up and running as soon as possible.

Identifying suitable sites was complicated by the obvious fact that on-the-ground surveys could not be carried out and airborne photo reconnaissance was the only viable way to glean such information. The task was allocated to the Mosquito photographic reconnaissance aircraft of 2nd TAF's No.140 Squadron and was carried out in late winter 1943/early spring 1944. It required ninety-one small areas of Normandy to be covered using survey cameras to identify suitable airfield sites for both 2nd TAF and the United States Army Air Force. The work was hazardous to say the least as it required the reconnaissance aircraft to fly over the target areas at about 9,000 feet. To achieve this, the Mosquitos were flown across the English Channel at 23,000 feet and dived down from that height onto the target. The Mosquito aircraft in the photographic reconnaissance role was unarmed and highly vulnerable to the many Luftwaffe Fw 190 and Me 109 aircraft based in the area.

Despite the high risk, the work was completed in less than two months despite very poor weather and on most of the sorties several sites were covered before the pilot had to return to base. All of this required intense concentration and accurate

A Hawker Typhoon pilot proudly poses in front of his aircraft in 1943. The aircraft played an important part in the campaign carrying out fighter sweeps over occupied countries, shooting up airfields, trains and ships. (*Crown Copyright – Air Historical Branch MoD*)

navigation. On some occasions pilots took their aircraft down to 9,000 feet and covered two or three sites before climbing again to 23,000 feet, while still over France, and then dived again on another group of potential sites. The squadron's unofficial account of this time comments that one Mosquito crew held the record by covering fourteen sites on one sortie on 15 February.[9]

A particular challenge identified in this early planning was the requirement to construct several temporary airstrips in the Normandy area from D-Day onwards. The total time individual fighter aircraft could spend over Normandy, if based in the United Kingdom, was severely limited by the need to return for refuelling. Air superiority over the battlefield was to be provided by Spitfires and Hurricanes for protection against enemy aircraft; rocket-firing Typhoons for offensive action against enemy tanks and transport in the immediate battle area; Mosquito and Mustang aircraft were used for operational reconnaissance. One hundred miles from base was the estimated effective limit of operational use.

One of the many attractions of the Normandy area for a potential invasion site was the suitability of its terrain for the rapid construction of airfields to accommodate close air support aircraft. They would, however, need to be constructed quickly – these airstrips would be crucial to the air battle. Not only did they mean that aircraft could be based in France, thereby eliminating transit time from the United Kingdom, but they could be refuelled and rearmed into the bargain. The planning target for the establishment of these up to, and including, D+90 was:

D-Day	One emergency landing strip.
D+3-4	Two refuelling and rearming strips.
D+8	Five advanced landing grounds.
D+14	Ten airfields.
D+24	Fifteen airfields.
D+40	Twenty-five airfields.
D+90	Forty-five airfields.[10]

For security reasons, the airstrips were referred to by a code number instead of location, which, in the case of British airfields on the Continent was prefixed with the letter B. This was sequentially assigned as airfields were allocated.

The RAF's Administrative Plan

Once the top-level plan for *Overlord* had been agreed, the RAF then set about their more detailed planning. From the outset, it was agreed that the main base for the operation would be the United Kingdom. It was clear that during the assault phase there would be limited shipping space for supplies and non-operational personnel – this would not allow a support area or 'base group' to be established during the early combat operations. As such, a temporary support arrangement would be required until the more permanent facilities to be operated by No.85 Group could be set up. It was also clear that 'extreme mobility' would typify operations after a breakout from the Normandy bridgehead – the units supporting Nos. 2, 83 and 84 groups would need to keep pace with the advancing ground forces and establish new operating bases as circumstances permitted.

Although much of the RAF was still operating from fixed airfields in the United Kingdom and overseas, much work had been done during the inter-war years to prepare for the likelihood of mobile warfare. Whilst Nos. 83 and 84 (composite) groups were newly formed and their establishment already included the required mobile ground units, No.2 (Light Bomber) Group, had been an existing Bomber Command formation since 1936, with twelve flying squadrons.[11]

Having operated from purpose-built airfields in the United Kingdom, there had been no need for it to be mobile. Its assignment to 2nd TAF though, required it to be reorganised in autumn 1943 ready for its role in Operation *Overlord*.[12] The planners were forward thinking and really understood what would be required. In reconfiguring No.2 Group, they applied four key 'conditions of mobile warfare' which provide an insight into the concepts involved:

Mobility	The force must be able to move at short notice, although a lesser degree of mobility can be accepted for No.2 Group than for the composite groups.
Flexibility	No.2 Group must be sufficiently flexible in order that the whole or part of its effort can be concentrated on the front of a particular army.
Technical Control	Under the conditions of mobile warfare first-class technical supervision is essential.
Economy	In the re-organisation of No.2 Group, economy in personnel and equipment is required.[13]

The RAF could not be entirely self supporting, and agreements were made with the army, many of which had evolved during more general, pre-war planning work. At the heart of these was the basic principle that support services, which were common to both services should be provided by one service for the use of both: this would be the service that was best placed to do so (and economically) considering available and qualified manpower, equipment, experience and organisation.[14]

In practice, much of this support from the army involved movement of the RAF's fuel and munitions. Whilst the RAF (through the Air Ministry) was responsible for provisioning its aviation fuel, the in-theatre transport, part of the way to airfields was the responsibility of the Royal Army Service Corps. For much of the earlier part of the campaign, fuel had to be transported in the ubiquitous jerry can and was deposited by the army at an agreed point from where the RAF would collect and then deliver to their airfields. When fuel could be delivered in bulk, this was done using road tankers.

Later in the campaign it was expected that this could be achieved by pipeline, again provided by the Royal Army Service Corps in conjunction with the Royal

FORWARD AIR BASES IN EUROPE FROM D-DAY TO THE BALTIC

Engineers.[15] Bulk fuel storage tanks for airfields were designed to be easily erected, disassembled and transported but use was also made of flexible fuel tanks. These were produced in various sizes, with capacities ranging from 500 to 3,000; many of which could be transported on flat-bed lorries or rolled up when empty.[16]

A similar arrangement was made for the supply of RAF munitions with the army responsible for moving required stocks from what they termed as a line of communication terminal maintenance area and then to a forward maintenance area located in smaller dumps for collection by the RAF. Much of the movement of munitions and packed fuel stocks in the forward areas was to be carried out by RAF aviation fuel and ammunition parks.[17]

That was the broad outline for how 2nd TAF would support its flying squadrons on the Continent. Following this preliminary work, the planners were able to firm up the formal RAF Administrative Plan which was issued by HQ Allied Expeditionary Air Force on 19 February 1944.[18] There was still much to do, and the next chapter explores the plan in more detail, highlighting the various capabilities which were developed to support 2nd TAF on its journey from the shores of the United Kingdom to what was at that time, an uncertain destination on the Continent.

RAF personnel stacking ammunition boxes, somewhere in Normandy, 1944. (*Crown Copyright – Air Historical Branch MoD*)

Chapter 3

The Support Plan

Overall, there were three key elements to the support of 2nd TAF. Following the landings an initial or temporary maintenance arrangement that could operate in the inevitable chaos and confusion of the very early days of the landings would be required. Once sufficient men and *materiel* had been landed and the safety and security of the lodgement area had been improved, a more robust 'Base' maintenance arrangement could be established. When the breakout from the Normandy bridgehead was made, mobile maintenance arrangements would then commence to provide support on the move for 2nd TAF. These stages are important in understanding how the complex structure of 2nd TAF functioned and is worth further explanation.

Temporary Maintenance

At the tip of the invasion spearhead were the assault troops and their key task, after neutralising enemy opposition, was to establish a bridgehead inland from the beaches. Close behind them, the support units had the vital task of establishing a temporary maintenance capability to provide essential support. Once sufficient ground had been secured and the combat troops could move further inland, a more robust lodgement area would then be developed.

The RAF needed to build-up their resources quickly so that they could establish their airfields quickly and ensure they could keep as many of their aircraft as possible in fighting condition – there could be no hitch in the chain of supply and maintenance.[1] The planners anticipated that temporary maintenance arrangements would probably continue until D+30 at the earliest. By this point the more sizeable lodgement area would have been established, enabling a more permanent rear maintenance area to be set up.

The RAF's frontline players for temporary support were its beach squadrons. These had been formed in 1943 and were responsible for disembarking personnel, vehicles, and supplies, then marshalling them into temporary concentration areas and supply dumps. They also looked after a number of balloon flights which would be deployed throughout the bridgehead when it was established. Their work was critical to the RAF's involvement in the operation with much of it involving the manhandling of supplies from landing craft to beach supply dumps and the marshalling of men and vehicles prior to them moving off the beach area. The motor transport sections were equipped to repair what were referred to as drowned vehicles – those that had landed in deeper water than intended and had become literally flooded, cutting out the engines.²

Landing men and *materiel* over the beaches was only ever intended as a short-term operation until cargo ships could be brought into one of the French ports. Whilst the choice of the Normandy coast for the landings made strategic sense, it did present a problem in that the nearest major, deep-water ports capable of handling large, ocean-going vessels were situated at Cherbourg to the north-west at the tip of the Cotentin Peninsula and Le Havre to the north-east. Both ports were heavily defended and there was little doubt that they would have been difficult and costly targets to capture.

It was against this challenging backdrop that two temporary ports, or Mulberry harbours, emerged. Construction began in the summer of 1943 at various sites on the River Thames and the River Clyde, in many cases using existing dry dock facilities. Two harbours, each the approximate size of the port of Dover, were eventually constructed: one at OMAHA Beach (Mulberry A) and the other on GOLD Beach at Arromanches (Mulberry B) – the latter becoming affectionately known as 'Port Winston'. Each of the quays was to be connected to the Normandy shoreline by floating roadways which had been designed to enable a rapid an offload as possible.

The planners reckoned that each of these harbours would be able to handle some 7,000 tons of cargo per day of operation.³ Despite the enormous effort and *materiel* which went into these structures, they were intended to operate in the region of just ninety days. The RAF would contribute to the operation of these using its embarkation units, which would arrive much closer to the opening date of the British Mulberry harbour at Arromanches. These units had been in existence for

Side view of the Mulberry Harbour B, Arromanches. (*Crown Copyright – Air Historical Branch MoD*)

THE SUPPORT PLAN

many years and were used for the loading and unloading of stores, as well as the embarkation and disembarkation of personnel, mainly at the seaports in the United Kingdom and overseas at increasingly more locations as the war progressed.[4]

In the longer term, the planners recognised that further ports and beaches would need to be developed in succession until Antwerp or Rotterdam could be reached. It was intended that Le Havre would be the first base port and then the advance would be parallel with the coast to shorten the line of communication which would be based on successive ports or beaches as they were captured.

Once Antwerp was in Allied hands, the intention was that it would become the main base for a subsequent advance into Germany across the Meuse north of Liege.[5] That was the plan but, as will be seen later in Chapter Six, the delay in capturing the deep-water port at Antwerp was to be the proverbial straw that nearly broke the camel's back of campaign logistics.

Base Maintenance

Once a lodgement area had been established a more permanent rear maintenance area could then be developed. The plan was for this concentrated maintenance area to be centred around the town of Bayeux, some 4 miles inland from the landing beaches. Eventually, this would become an enormous retail park serving the needs of the army and the RAF and capable of receiving the stores and supplies already accumulated in the temporary supply dumps which would be set up in the temporary Beach Maintenance Area.

In time, these stocks would be expanded from the much larger volumes of *materiel* and vehicles that would come into Normandy through the Mulberry harbour. For the RAF, most of this was sent to France through an RAF forward equipment unit at Bicester in the United Kingdom. The Rear Maintenance Area would remain in Normandy for many months after D-Day and became home to several of 2nd TAF's support units, most of which were part of No.85 Group.

Inside a No.401 Air Stores Park equipment storage tent, Normandy, 1944. *(Author's collection)*

FORWARD AIR BASES IN EUROPE FROM D-DAY TO THE BALTIC

With much *materiel* having to move by sea to and from the Continent, resupply from the United Kingdom was a lengthy process. Wherever possible equipment would be repaired, and a Forward Repair Unit was established which would provide a conduit between the RAF's repair and salvage units and motor transport light repair units which would operate on the Continent and the repair organisation back at the home base in the United Kingdom. A similar unit, a Base Signals and Radar Unit, was formed to provide an in-theatre repair and overhaul capability for the main ground wireless and radar equipment which could not be done by the mobile equivalents in 2nd TAF's composite groups.

With so many RAF personnel destined for Normandy and for the following campaign, it was essential that suitable support was provided for the people which made up 2nd TAF. Whilst the training and preparation of the force reflected the need to 'rough it' and to instil field living as a way of life, its people still needed to be administered and cared for to ensure that they remained fit for duty in body, mind, and spirit. Most of the support units were self-contained, and their officers and NCOs remained responsible for the well-being of the men under their command.

There was, however, still a need to maintain a TAF level coordination of personnel support. At the heart of this was a Base Personnel Centre within No.85 Group. This unit was responsible for administering RAF personnel arriving in and departing from 2nd TAF units on the Continent. To interface with this centre, each of the groups had their own personnel transit centres.

For medical and dental care, several types of specialist units were formed. In the Base Area, No.85 Group was to host No.8 RAF General Hospital. For each of the groups within 2nd TAF, five mobile field hospitals were attached, each acting as small but complete units which could provide all but the most complicated of treatment. As such, they were able to provide medical and surgical services to RAF personnel and either return them to the RAF general hospital or repatriate them to the United Kingdom. The mobile hospitals were highly flexible in their design and organisation and could, when required, detach smaller groups such as advanced surgical teams, to help with casualty evacuation.

Closely allied to the medical units were those dedicated to providing dental care. As far as possible, personnel deploying on Operation *Overlord* were to be as dentally fit as possible to minimise the need for emergency treatment in the field. A number of self-contained mobile dental units and dental laboratories were formed for the operation, each of which were based on a Fordson WOT 1 vehicle chassis with their electrics wired to run off a 220- or 110-volt mains supply or a 24-volt auxiliary supply for which batteries and generator were carried. Eventually, some thirty-two mobile dental units and eight mobile dental laboratories would accompany 2nd TAF on the campaign.

Most of the dental units and laboratories were attached to the wings of Nos. 83 and 84 groups but some were attached to the mobile field hospitals. Each of the dental unit vehicles was equipped with a field dental chair and a treadle drill. They were also equipped to deal with maxilla-facial injuries and carried the required medical supplies for this type of treatment to last for a year. Each vehicle also carried a sleeping tent and a camouflage net.

THE SUPPORT PLAN

The last, but highly important element of 2nd TAF's medical capability was casualty air evacuation. In the United Kingdom a sophisticated system was established to handle incoming casualties evacuated by air with aircraft coming into Transport Command's No.46 Group stations at RAF stations Down Ampney, Blakehill Farm, Broadwell and Watchfield. The lion's share of the task fell to transport Dakota aircraft, most of which were modified to include stretcher racks or special webbing supports, both types which could be easily and quickly stowed away to enable the aircraft to be used in a more general transport role. The RAF also had several obsolete Harrow bomber aircraft, which had been stripped out and renamed Sparrows. Additionally, Anson and Oxford aircraft played their part in the air evacuation effort. In Normandy, and for the rest of the campaign, two casualty air evacuation units would be deployed and would go on to provide a vital and lifesaving service.

Once established, the Rear Maintenance Area would become the overall responsibility of HQ Twenty-First Army Group but with active involvement of Second Army and 2nd TAF units. The role of No.85 Group covered a broad span of responsibilities beyond purely administrative functions. Added to this, there was a panoply of other units providing operational support, air and ground defence, medical, dental and general personnel services.

It also was home to several other medical and administrative units to support the large numbers of 2nd TAF personnel that were not just operating on the Continent, but also returning home for various reasons or were newly posted to the theatre of operations. No.85 Group's AOC was also responsible for the co-ordinated defence of the ports and installations in selected areas on the Continent, for all forms of defence against air attack in the British Zone and for the supply chain (or line of communication as it was known) to and from Normandy.

Mobile Maintenance

Once the base area was established, the RAF would then need to use a highly mobile forward maintenance organisation, which could support 2nd TAF as they accompanied Montgomery's advancing ground forces, through France, the Low Countries and into Germany. This is where the light bomber and composite groups of 2nd TAF parted company from the embracing arms of the Base Maintenance Area which had provided support on the doorstep whilst they were operating from the landing grounds in Normandy.

Once the advance from Normandy started, 2nd TAF units would need to move forward to new airfields, thereby shortening aircraft transit times to and from the forward edge of the battle area. This would also reduce aviation fuel consumption and the progressive wear and tear of the aircraft and their engines through reduced flying hours. Away from Normandy, it was likely that the RAF could use former enemy airfields. It would, however, not be straightforward, as such locations would likely be well defended and have sustained physical damage in the battles to capture them, let alone being sabotaged and/or booby trapped by the vacating enemy. This would need the attention of the RAF's bomb disposal units to make them safe and then make good by various elements of the army's and RAF's airfield construction units.

As the various units and flying squadrons moved away from the bridgehead, they needed the support organisation to keep pace with them. Like the concept of the servicing commando units, this is where a further range of highly mobile and self-contained specialist units came into play. All of these would need to operate independently for indefinite periods in support of their assigned group's forward airfields. It was essential that all their personnel, irrespective of their trade were familiar with life under canvas, and if required could defend their base from enemy attack.[6]

As with the temporary airfields in the Normandy lodgement area, the plan was to move in the RAF servicing commando units to site at the earliest, and safest opportunity, and to provide turn-round support for aircraft, usually for about one week. They would then be replaced by the advance refuelling and rearming parties of the wing headquarters, which would move-in to the new operating bases as soon as possible.

To bolster the limited aircraft maintenance work carried out by the wing headquarters, several repair and salvage units were attached to each of the composite groups, each of which was usually responsible for up to six flying squadrons. The units were established based on one per six flying squadrons and located as close as possible to their operating airfields. They could carry out more complex work, but only on tasks that would take no more than seven days to complete. This policy enabled a relatively quick turnover and avoided the accumulation of longer-term work.

2nd TAF squadron groundcrew working on a Spitfire propellor on a portable workbench, somewhere in Normandy, 1944. (*Crown Copyright – Air Historical Branch MoD*)

THE SUPPORT PLAN

Additionally, they were responsible for the collection and disposal of salvaged *materiel* within specified areas. In the early days of the landings when the RAF servicing commando units were the prime means of supporting aircraft, there was little opportunity for much repair or salvage. These units were, however, landed as soon as possible in order that they could help keep the landing strips free of damaged aircraft. As such, they were intended to be small and highly mobile, supporting two airfields of three squadrons each.

It was intended that the airfields these units were supporting were in the battle zone where most of the aircraft casualties were likely to occur. They were not required to maintain more than two basic types of aircraft. The collection of crashed aircraft was carried out by the salvage sections after their armourers had made such aircraft safe by removing ammunition and munitions. They travelled to Normandy with, or soon after, the airfield headquarters. Once set up, they were then able to carry out more comprehensive repairs. Their role was two-fold: firstly, to provide close technical support for the airfields they were assigned to, undertaking work beyond the capacity of the forward airfields, which could be completed within ten to fourteen days; secondly, they were responsible for the collection and disposal of salvage within a specific area.

Repairs which were estimated to take longer than seven days to complete were outside of their capability and such aircraft were then returned to the United Kingdom, when possible, until No.85 Group's Forward Repair Unit was set up in the Rear Maintenance Area. In the early days of the operation, they might be required to re-use parts from damaged aircraft to service another – a practice rather gruesomely known as cannibalisation. It was intended that damaged aircraft or equipment would be returned by salvage trailer from the theatre of operation to the United Kingdom using a dedicated sea passage by a military ferry service. It was initially intended that the service would operate from beaches, but it eventually operated from the captured Continental port of Le Tréport (near Dieppe) from the beginning of September 1944.[7]

The vital function which enabled all this to happen was of course transport. Apart from the vehicles which were held by the various units, transport was vital; supply and transport columns provided a central pool of load-carrying vehicles (as a service) and when the forward airfields were up and running, to transport their requirements for fuel and munitions from army drop-off points. Each group within 2nd TAF had their own column, each comprising some 300, 3-ton load carrying vehicles, which would enable the forward airfields to be pre-stocked at the same time as the operational units were moving in to occupy them. Possibly of greater significance was that these columns also enabled the tactical groups to be fully mobile, a factor that would prove to be critical during the breakout from Normandy and the subsequent advance.

Amidst all this support work there was always the need for spare parts and other equipment. This was taken care of by Air Stores Parks. These had been one of the earliest mobile units that the RAF had developed during the inter-war years, the concept emerging from analysis carried out in 1927 to consider requirements for a future RAF expeditionary force. The first park had been

FORWARD AIR BASES IN EUROPE FROM D-DAY TO THE BALTIC

formed in the Middle East during late 1935 and they were used with great success in several operations before *Overlord*, especially in North Africa and Italy. For *Overlord*, it was intended that the parks were landed at the same time as the airfield headquarters, and designed to meet the needs of two of these headquarters, along with one repair and salvage unit. These were intended to be small and highly mobile and were at the heart of spares support for the flying squadrons and other units allocated to them.

Each was responsible for supporting three squadrons (for no more than two basic aircraft types) on each of two airfields. The parks were required to maintain one month's requirements of equipment and spares (except for motor transport) for their allocated units. Much thought had gone into the design of the parks with the range and level of stockholdings being derived after months of research involving visits to operational units, discussions with technical and equipment staff, analysis of consumption data and identification of high turnover items for aircraft types, vehicles and other major equipment types. Each park carried a month's worth of stock to support specific aircraft types, along with the bulk of spares required by the motor transport light repair units and mobile signals servicing units.

As far as re-supply was concerned, the parks were topped-up by the Forward Equipment Unit when it became established in the Base Maintenance Area. For urgently required spares that were grounding an aircraft (known as aircraft on ground requirement), an encoded signal was sent by their respective mobile

Personnel of HQ No.418 Air Stores Park, Belgium, September 1944. *(Author's collection)*

THE SUPPORT PLAN

signals unit to the United Kingdom, where it was then sent by teleprinter to all the major RAF maintenance units. When the item was located it was then sent out to the Continent as urgent air freight. By 1944 most of the vehicles were 3 tonners although there were a few 25CWT prime movers and trailers. The parks were manned by approximately 150 personnel of various trades, with approximately 120 trucks and utility vehicles which were specially modified with internal racking to carry spares and equipment for a particular type of aircraft.

Two of the more challenging aspects of resupplying the flying squadrons were the physical and safety issues involved with aviation fuel and munitions. In the early *Overlord* planning, it had been assumed that responsibility for reserve stocks of these vital commodities for the RAF would be entirely in the hands of the army and that they would be held in the army's base depots, an agreement that had been made between the Air Ministry and the War Office. Experience in North Africa, Sicily and Italy, however, had shown that it was in the RAF's interests to hold its own reserve stocks.

For *Overlord*, the RAF's reserve stocks were therefore held by No.85 Group in the Rear Maintenance Area.[8] The army welcomed the relief of the complete responsibility, but the physical movement of fuel and munitions for the RAF was a combined responsibility: the army delivered packed fuel and oils, ammunition, stores and supplies to RAF aviation fuel and ammunition parks, each of which

Living and working in the field. A stores issue point of No.401 Air Stores Park in Normandy, 1944. The relative lack of camouflage on this site would suggest the photograph was taken in late July 1944. *(Author's collection)*

was normally within 40 miles of RAF units. The parks held ten days' worth of fuel and munitions, a quantity which was believed to be adequate for normal operational rates of effort. An additional park was attached to No.85 Group, but this held one month's reserve stocks for all of 2nd TAF. The RAF used their own supply and transport columns to move the various loads to the airfields.[9] The movement of bulk fuel was carried all the way to airfields by the army as this was usually by road tanker (known as bowsers) and could not be off-loaded at temporary transfer points.

The glue that held all this together was motor transport – it was not just the aircraft which required repair and maintenance. The heavy and critical demands placed on motor transport led to the need for an on-hand repair capability, catered for in the form of motor transport light repair units. These units could not just carry out running repairs but were also able to carry out major inspections. Complete vehicle overhauls and repairs which would take longer than three days to carry out were taken care of by the Forward Repair Unit in the Rear Maintenance Area.[10] Each unit held a small pool of replacement vehicles, along with seven days' worth of 'quick turnover' spares. Like the repair and salvage units, they were attached to each of the composite groups.

As with their naval and army colleagues, communication, along with radar, was essential for the RAF and there were many mobile signals units and accompanying servicing units attached to many of the units within 2nd TAF for air-to-ground and point-to-point wireless telegraphy and radio telephony communications.

RAF Motor Transport Repair Section at work. (*Crown Copyright – Air Historical Branch MoD*)

THE SUPPORT PLAN

Air Transport

This aspect of air power was to play a significant part in the campaign, but the RAF's air transport capability had taken much longer to evolve than its offensive and training functions. The RAF formed a dedicated Transport Command in March 1943, but it took until the beginning of 1944 for it to start developing a more effective transport capability.[11] The real game changer for the RAF came with the purchase of large numbers of the Douglas C-47 Dakota from the United States of America under a lend-lease agreement. Unlike many of the RAF's earlier aircraft used for transport duties, the C-47 Dakota was produced with larger cargo doors and strengthened floors; this, coupled with its ability to operate from rough terrain airstrips, made it an ideal aircraft for general purpose transport.[12]

This vital addition to the RAF's aircraft fleet made an enormous difference. Of significance though, is that the planning for *Overlord* doesn't seem to have taken on board just how vital it was to have dedicated aircraft assigned to a tactical air force. It could be argued that this was perhaps a question of resource availability, given that, as the operational plan for the invasion began to develop, there was a more pressing and immediate requirement for the airlift requirements of the initial airborne assault. For this requirement, the RAF formed No.38 Group, transferring it to the Allied Expeditionary Air Force in November 1943.

To strengthen this capability, it was agreed that Transport Command's No.46 Group, with its predominantly Dakota-equipped squadrons, would operate under the control of No.38 Group as part of the British lift for the airborne assault.[13] By the beginning of 1944, RAF air transport was on a much stronger footing – just in time for what lay ahead with the imminent campaign in north-west Europe.

By the end of May 1944, the Supreme HQ Allied Expeditionary Force had finalised the agreed procedures for supply by air, a broad term which was defined as 'the transportation by air of all types of stores/supplies, reinforcements/replacements, etc., and includes both scheduled and emergency supply'. The scheduled category included commitments, which could 'normally be anticipated and planned for, prior to the commencement of operations' whereas the emergency category was for 'unforeseen and/or unexpected operations requiring the urgent movement of supplies or personnel and cannot be planned for in advance'.[14]

The overall control and tasking of all scheduled and emergency airlifts was to be carried out by a Combined Air Transport Operations' Room at the headquarters of the C-in-C Allied Expeditionary Air Force at Stanmore, just outside of London, with an Air Freight Control Centre at Poulton, close to the main No.46 Group airfields in Wiltshire (Broadwell, Down Ampney and Blakehill Farm). Poulton's role was to receive freight from both the army and RAF, prepare it for air transport and then send it to the nominated departure airfield.[15]

All boded well for *Overlord*, except an emerging development in modern warfare – airborne operations – would add to the number of conflicting priorities for a finite number of aircraft. The concept, and the enormous resources required,

FORWARD AIR BASES IN EUROPE FROM D-DAY TO THE BALTIC

is well illustrated in the 1977 film *A Bridge Too Far*, which tells the story of the ill-fated Operation *Market Garden* in September 1944. Notwithstanding views regarding its accuracy, the film shows how large numbers of transport aircraft were required to deliver paratroopers, along with air-towed gliders carrying the air landed component of the airborne force, plus their equipment and light vehicles. A British airborne division had been formed alongside of the RAF's Army Cooperation Command in 1941, primarily to investigate how this capability could be developed. The RAF was a key player in this initiative and had formed No.38 Wing within the command specifically for work with airborne forces.

During the second half of 1943 the RAF and army planners on the *Overlord* staff, amidst the vast array of topics they needed to address, started to consider the role which airborne operations and air transport generally would play in the invasion of the Continent. Of the many planning assumptions that they were having to entertain, the one which influenced much of it was the widely held view that any invasion would most likely meet stiff resistance, rather than a partial or complete collapse of the enemy. The result of this view was that the priority for transport aircraft use would be supporting an airborne operation part of the initial assault phase of *Overlord*. In coming to this position, both the army and RAF planners believed that the difficulties of landing supplies by air without proper airfields in an already congested beachhead, the use of transport aircraft could only be justified for supply by air for 'in the event of grave emergencies such as the incidence of a spell of bad weather in the early stages'.[16]

To meet the increasing role of airborne operations in *Overlord*, the existing No.38 Wing was upgraded to group status, and shortly after, No.46 Group was formed in Transport Command. The primary role of both of these groups would be in the airborne role during the assault phase initially, and then normal transport roles which would include more general support to enable 2nd TAF to keep up with the battle, to bring in reinforcements and urgent supplies. Additionally, it would also help with casualty evacuation, evacuating selected prisoners of war, captured equipment and priority freight.

Of the two transport groups, No.46 Group, was the more significant as far as supply by air was concerned. Stores and supplies required by 2nd TAF were ordered from the RAF's equipment depots and then sent to the RAF's Forward Equipment Unit for Operation *Overlord* at RAF Bicester, near Oxford, where they were packed for air transport and then sent to Poulton. They were assembled into aircraft loads and then transported to the nominated airfield from where they were flown to the Continent.[17]

Bids for stores and supplies requiring airlift (usually dictated by the urgency of need) were submitted by 2nd TAF through the Allied Expeditionary Force Combined Air Transport Operations Room based at RAF Bentley Priory in the United Kingdom, which had been established for the 'purposes of controlling the employment of Allied troop carrier and transport aircraft on air supply missions, other than those for airborne forces'. Although the air transport needs of the army were not a functional concern of 2nd TAF, it had been agreed that naval and/or army group demands would only be accepted through HQ 2nd TAF or, in the case of the Americans, HQ United States Ninth Air Force.[18]

Airfield Construction

The beating heart of the tactical air force would be its forward air bases and the work to achieve this would be a combined effort of specialist civil engineers from the army and the RAF. The latter had formed an Airfield Construction Service in March 1941, specifically to carry out emergency repairs to their airfields which had been damaged by enemy action. For the Normandy campaign, they formed special field force wings (hereafter referred to with the suffix (Airfield Construction) added to avoid confusion with ground defence organisations).

Although part of the Allied Expeditionary Air Force, they worked with and came under the operational control of the army's airfield construction groups of the Royal Engineers.[19] At least for the first five days after the initial landings, it was planned that these groups (with their RAF wings) would work under the chief engineer of the respective assaulting army corps. Sites for the various airfields in the lodgement area were all pre-selected using maps and the aerial photographs taken by No.34 Wing.

One of these new wings would be a highly mobile 'spearhead' formation, whilst the other four would be less mobile, heavy formations that would work in the rear area. The mobile element was provided by No.5357 Wing and followed close behind Montgomery's Twenty-First Army Group, under the deputy chief engineer who was responsible for building new airfields and repairing those captured during the advance. Throughout the campaign, the general way in which this wing worked was that a reconnaissance party from the wing headquarters would go forward with the advancing troops to select sites for landing strips or survey captured enemy airfields and to assess how quickly they could be made ready for Allied aircraft.

Once the site had been selected, a squadron or flight would immediately come in and prepare a grass landing strip so that fighters and fighter-bombers could operate.[20] The wing consisted of a headquarters section and two squadrons, each of which consisted of six field flights, a field plant flight, an electrical and mechanical flight for repairing or installing power generation plant and a motor transport flight.

The remaining four wings were designated 'heavy' wings as they were much larger and less mobile. They worked in the area of operations of the Royal Engineers and were controlled operationally by the director of works, line of communications. This organisation was responsible and equipped for the more permanent construction work on the Continent, primarily the construction of larger airfields to accommodate heavy traffic. They were often involved in building new or repairing existing accommodation on sites which had suffered from the heavy Allied air attacks.[21] The heavy wings comprised a headquarters section, four construction squadrons (each of seven flights) and a combined plant and motor transport squadron.

All the airfield construction work required myriad specialist machinery or plant as it is known in the trade. Although the machinery was necessarily robust by design it was essential that they were repaired and maintained, and a Plant Repair Unit was established in France for this purpose. Two wings were also retained in the United Kingdom to carry on with airfield construction work and to provide a repair response force which might be required should the Luftwaffe attempt to attack Allied airfields supporting the D-Day operation.

Operating the Airfields

Once the airstrips were ready for use, each of them needed an interim operating staff, which could move in quickly, refuel and rearm the aircraft and carry out basic turn round servicing until the squadron's home-based ground crews could deploy from the United Kingdom and set up their own airfield headquarters. These tactical units would take control of the site for as long as was required and then move on to another landing ground and repeat the process. It was for this temporary requirement that the RAF had formed servicing commando units.

The first four units (Nos. 3201 to 3204) were formed at the beginning of 1942. A further five were formed by August 1942 and, along with the first four, all played a highly successful role in the invasion of North Africa, Sicily and mainland Italy, as well as in Burma supporting Operation *Thursday* with Brigadier Orde Wingate's Chindits along the Irrawaddy River.[22] Each unit was generally made up of 2 or 3 technical officers, and between 130 and 160 men of varying ranks, who had their own vehicles with some 16 3-ton trucks, a jeep and a motorcycle. They usually lived in tents, which enabled them to move at very short notice.

Personnel were trained to service several different aircraft types up to daily inspection standard, as well as being able to carry out light repair work that would not last longer than a couple of days or a days' worth of motor transport work. They also carried a stock of fourteen days' essential spares for the aircraft types that they supported; these were replenished in the form of complete packs, directly from the United Kingdom. Whilst they were manned by highly qualified tradesmen, they had all been taught combined operations' techniques and their field training enabled them to operate independently.[23]

It was planned to use four units on the Continent, two of these working as pairs in both Nos. 83 and 84 groups. On the advanced landing grounds in France, each of the units had attached to it a repair and salvage element, a propeller fitting party (with twelve fully assembled propellers) and a wing flying control section with fire tenders and ambulance. The chief technical officer of the wing which was to take over the advanced landing ground was attached to the servicing commando party to act as the chief technical officer of the new-found airfield. Once the airfield headquarters moved in, the intention was that the Servicing Commando Unit would move on to a new tasking.

One of the RAF official histories that covers the campaign comments that 'owing to the nature of the operation none of the servicing commandos was employed as

THE SUPPORT PLAN

extensively as had been planned, but it was demonstrated that one commando could meet a peak load of 100 fighter sorties per day'.[24] In the end, though, they were only used up until the breakout from the bridgehead when the airfield headquarters and the flying squadron maintenance personnel were able to provide forward parties for the occupation of new airfields during the advance from Normandy.

Air and Ground Defence

The use of air power during the campaign in north-west Europe was a multi-faceted affair. In addition to the predominantly close air support role that characterised 2nd TAF, there was also an air defence role that would prove to be critical in establishing a secure bridgehead in the Normandy lodgement area.

One of the many risks involved with establishing the bridgehead was the vulnerability of the area to enemy air attack during the first few days of the assault. By early 1944, Allied strategic bombing and counter-air operations had severely degraded the German Luftwaffe's daylight capability in Northern France. Despite this, there was still concern that the enemy might attempt air offensive operations against the Allied bridgehead at night. Senior commanders were particularly keen to deploy ground-based radar to the operational theatre at the earliest opportunity during the landings to give air defence and control above the Normandy battlespace, especially during the cover of darkness.

In mid-1943, the AOC of RAF Fighter Command tasked Group Captain R.G. Hart to examine the role of radar in the planned invasion; this task was subsequently taken up by HQ Allied Expeditionary Air Force which evaluated the British and American radars to determine who could best meet the requirement. The outcome was that the RAF was better placed to provide ground control intercept and early warning of both day and night fighters, using its mobile radar capability.[25] It was thus that the RAF became committed to providing three base defence sectors: No.21 to be located in the American zone inland from OMAHA Beach until their control facilities and night fighter squadrons could be made available; No.24 covering the British and Canadian zones, located just inland from GOLD Beach and No.25 which was initially to be deployed to cover the Brittany peninsula protecting the key ports of Brest, Lorient and St Nazaire.[26]

Although commonly referred to as base defence sectors, these were the operational areas of responsibility of base defence wings. Each of these was a sizeable, fully mobile grouping comprising: a wing headquarters, an operations room, five ground control intercept convoys, one mobile radio unit, an army air formation signals unit, several mobile signals units and a mobile signals servicing unit.

At the heart of the rather generically named base defence sector was the provision of radar warning, especially Ground Control Intercept. This had been a crucial factor in winning the Battle of Britain in 1940 where the reporting of incoming raids, predominantly through the Chain Home radar network during daylight hours, along with input from the Royal Observer Corps, enabled the RAF's control centres to scramble fighter aircraft and direct them to the incoming enemy aircraft. The advent of air interception radar sets installed in night fighter aircraft was a further step forward, but these lacked the range to be used independently. A ground-based intercept station had much greater range and its equipment enabled them to plot the actual courses of both the enemy and the intercepting fighter aircraft. Once close enough, the fighter would use its air intercept radar to pinpoint the target.[27] For the British and Canadian sectors, air raid reporting and fighter control would be the responsibility of No.85 Group, but with direct operational responsibility to headquarters Allied Expeditionary Air Force. The base defence sector capability was provided in two parts – afloat and ashore.

Firstly, fighter direction tenders would be situated just offshore. As the Normandy beaches were well beyond the range of radar stations on the south coast of England, these vessels provided radar, communications and intelligence gathering services, enabling them to intercept enemy communications, and detect and plot enemy aircraft activity. This data was then passed to ships headquarters, which operated as command-and-control centres near the landing beaches. The tank landing ship design proved ideal for the purpose and successful trials of seaborne radar were carried out using No.301 in May 1943. Three further vessels were converted and tested under operational conditions off the beaches of Sicily and Anzio in mainland Italy. For *Overlord* there was great competition for landing ship allocation, but agreement was reached for three more ships to be allocated from American shipyard production (and later converted into tenders).

The second element of the base defence sector capability was a special group of vehicle-mounted radars and communications equipment (very similar to those on the fighter direction tenders) that would go ashore and operate from pre-determined operating sites. The Telecommunications Research Establishment at Malvern was commissioned (as late as March 1944), to design and modify a range of prime movers and trailers using existing radar apparatus and communications equipment. These vehicles became the fleet of what were known as ground control intercept convoys.[28] Once ashore, the first task of the convoys, after setting up, was to establish communication with its parent fighter direction tender and, in partnership, gradually take on the ground control role. As the operation progressed, it was intended that these convoys would gradually take on the complete intercept control task, enabling the fighter direction tenders to return to the United Kingdom for re-deployment.

With each of the base defence sectors, a British Army air formation signals unit was attached to establish a main trunk telephone network for the deployed RAF units in Normandy and to run an overland delivery service using jeeps and motorcycles.[29] Whilst the various elements of the Air Ministry Type 25 stations were all cutting-edge technology at the time, it was still large and bulky equipment. All were lorry or trailer mounted, with the aerials/detector units being foldable where possible.

The final aspect of the defence picture was, certainly in the earlier part of the campaign, more directly tied to the protection of individual airfields. The highly successful blitzkrieg tactics developed and used by the Germans to secure many

THE SUPPORT PLAN

A mobile radar unit Type II Detector designed to overcome German jamming. This equipment operated in the 500 to 600 Mc/s range and had a range of up to about 125 miles. *(Copyright Through Their Eyes)*

of their conquests in 1939 and 1940, had shown that the characteristics of warfare were very different from those seen during the First World War. Of particular concern to the RAF was the security of its airfields – without these, its ability to operate would be severely limited.

The need to provide both ground and low-level air defence was critical, but it had become quite clear that this capability could not be provided by the army. It was thus that on 1 February 1942 the RAF Regiment was formed. The early years of what is technically classed as a corps within the RAF, saw them serve with great distinction within the United Kingdom, North Africa, the Middle East, the Central Mediterranean and South East Asia. The campaign in north-west Europe was to be another proud chapter in its history.[30]

By late March/early April 1944, the RAF Regiment had provided three distinct types of fighting units within 2nd TAF: rifle squadrons for ground defence duties, light anti-aircraft squadrons for low-level air defence and armoured car squadrons for reconnaissance work. For command and control, the squadrons were placed under command of an RAF Regiment mobile wing headquarters, each of which was configured to control a combination of any squadron type rather than by specific function. The involvement of the RAF Regiment varied, not just over the duration of the campaign, but also by which 2nd TAF group they were assigned to.

At the beginning of the campaign, fourteen of the RAF Regiment mobile wing headquarters, most of the light anti-aircraft squadrons, and some rifle and armoured car squadrons, were allotted to Nos. 83 and 84 groups. Five wing headquarters and the rest of the rifle and armoured car squadrons were divided between Nos. 2 and 85 groups. Whilst the light anti-aircraft squadrons played a key role in the low-level air defence of the various airfields, the men of the rifle and armoured car squadrons were to be employed in a wider range of duties. In Nos. 2 and 85 groups, they were to be mainly involved in supporting the air technical intelligence teams, which moved in to captured former Luftwaffe airfields.

As the advance progressed regiment personnel found themselves helping to move urgently needed supplies of aviation fuel, along with reinforcing the British and Canadian armies' infantry and armoured units when they became overstretched in holding the line of the river Maas, and the Wilhelminakanaal and Leopold Canal in September and October 1944. Other operational demands such as the surprise enemy offensive in the Ardennes and the final assault on Germany itself saw the RAF Regiment putting its 'shoulder to the wheel' in a similar fashion.[31] Its versatility would prove of great value throughout the campaign and was to earn many of its ranks various awards for gallantry and meritorious service.

Camouflage and Deception

Since time immemorial, armies have endeavoured to conceal their whereabouts albeit the wearing of brightly coloured uniforms on the battlefield, especially during the eighteenth and early nineteenth centuries might suggest otherwise. The whole concept had started to develop as an art during the First World War although the predominantly trench based nature of the Western Front called for more physical protection of troops. The war at sea though, with ships much more visible on the open ocean, had led to much experimentation with the highly bizarre 'dazzle' schemes seen on many of the warships of the time.

The game changer was the aeroplane and, once used in an aerial observation role, a much greater need started to develop for the concealment of ground forces. The development of the tank, along with a wide range of other armoured and 'soft skinned' vehicles, enabled greater movement of troops and this enabled much greater mobility in the evolving nature of warfare in the twentieth century. This all led to armies having a much larger visible footprint, extending far beyond large concentrations of troops.

The Second World War brought a whole new chapter in the development of camouflage, along with an accompanying magicians' sleight of hand in the art of deception. The Air Ministry formed a secret department to coordinate means by which enemy bomber aircraft could be fooled using decoys and deception. The department was run by Colonel Sir John Turner, a former army royal engineer, then the director of works and buildings at the Air Ministry in London. His skills as a qualified pilot and airfield construction methods made him an ideal candidate for the role. Known as Colonel Turner's Department, its headquarters was located at the Sound City Film Studios in Shepperton, Surrey.

The new organisation made much use of film industry men who were used to working in studios alongside the clever use of scenery and lighting to make the film sets look highly realistic. Turner's men were therefore ideally placed to manufacture dummy aircraft and equipment as well as developing the surprisingly successful Q Sites. These were dummy airfields, usually set out on large open spaces such as fields and heaths. They were put into use at night and used a clever range of lights and pyrotechnics to simulate an active airfield with runway flare-paths and obstruction lights.[32]

It was against this backdrop that RAF planners developed a policy and plan for the establishment of RAF concealment and decoy units. Four of these were formed,

THE SUPPORT PLAN

Natural concealment. Vehicles belonging to No.401 Air Stores Park under cover of trees, Normandy, June 1944. The lorry on the far left shows how such vehicles were modified to carry stores and supplies. *(Author's collection)*

two each attached to Nos. 83 and 84 groups. Each unit consisted of an officer and forty-four other ranks and were established with three 3-ton Bedford trucks, two jeeps and seven motorcycle combinations. As such they were self-contained, and each could be split into six crews if required which could operate independently.

Essentially, each unit was specially trained for three key tasks: night lighting in protective and deceptive decoys; special deceptive schemes for the army as they did not have any night decoy units and assistance to airfields when required for special schemes such as camouflage netting and erecting dummy aircraft. These units were in addition to the airfield-based concealment teams (one corporal and five airmen) that looked after similar duties specifically for their location. Although the mobile units were under the administrative control of the group to which they were assigned, they were operationally tasked by HQ 2nd TAF and could be called upon to undertake requirements for specific airfields, wings, other RAF formations or army units.[33]

Training

The final, and indeed crucial aspect of the overall plan was training. Hand in glove with acclimatising to harsher living conditions, was a training regime, which encompassed a much wider range of battle and field craft skills. Soon after their formation in June 1943, units of No.84 Group had taken to the road and participated in a string of exercises which lasted until October of that year. With codenames such as *Punch*, *Judy* and *Columbine*, many felt that these were not entirely inappropriate terms for those who were struggling with field telephones, 3-ton trucks and tent guy ropes for the first time!

Some RAF units which had a much closer operational command relationship with the army experienced a particularly extensive training regime right up until the day they embarked for France. The month of April 1944 was one of the most intensive training periods for the RAF's No.5357 (Airfield Construction) Wing. From the beginning of that month the wing had been placed under the operational control of the Second Army's chief engineer for technical training, although it remained under No.85 Group's administrative control. With time fast running out before D-Day, all such training had to be prioritised, a practice which was usually the responsibility of unit commanding officers (CO). The airfield construction wing's training priority list was typical for such units and comprised (in order):

> Movement which included packing-up of equipment, loading of plant, standard motor transport signals, wet-shod drill, driving proficiency, care of vehicles, convoy drill and waterproofing.
>
> Training of reconnaissance parties in site selection, rapid survey of selected areas, transmission of messages, preparation of Works Tables and mines and booby traps drill.
>
> Physical fitness and endurance.
>
> Airfield works, particularly the operation and co-ordination of plant.
>
> Other training such as aircraft recognition, tactical movement, anti-gas, fire, sanitation and hygiene.

A typical week's training programme for early April included numerous sessions covering rifle drill, firing practice with the Sten Gun on the 30-yard range, organised games, physical training and tactical exercises. In addition to this unit-based training, personnel went further afield for longer, specialist courses such as an eight-day convoy course at Derwent Camp at Keswick in the Like District, a six-day course on wet-shod driving at Dundonald Camp at Troon in Scotland and a thirty-day course on plant operation at Great Barrington in Oxfordshire.[34]

The men of the RAF's servicing commandos and beach squadrons, along with some units of the RAF Regiment had an even more rigorous training regime with demanding courses at the Dundonald training centre. The culmination of many of the training courses involved going to sea in one of the tank landing craft, vessels and coming ashore for practice beach landings. The training was of course more rigorous for the RAF units that would come ashore during the assault phase of Operation *Overlord*. For those who were to set foot in Normandy much later in the campaign, they were still schooled in the finer art of living under canvas and on the move.

Part 2

THE JOURNEY

Chapter 4

A Foothold on the Continent

One of the many aspects of Operation *Overlord* which receives little, detailed comment in the literature, is how the vast Allied invasion force was brought together in the relatively small area of southern England.

Mounting the Operation in the United Kingdom

Large numbers of camps, depots and new roads had to be built to accommodate troops, vehicles and equipment. For most of the ground support units that would eventually become part of 2nd TAF, the RAF was able to accommodate most of them on many of its existing stations throughout the United Kingdom. Known as the unit's tactical location, this sensible use of space eased the demand for new real estate that was required for the build-up of the Allied invasion force.

The use of existing facilities was essential as nearly 1.5 million servicemen from North America, along with millions of tons and supplies, had to be found a new home. Hundreds, if not thousands, of hours were spent visiting and surveying new sites, arranging construction and then putting in place the support needed to sustain personnel during the build-up period. Given that nothing on this scale had previously been mounted from the United Kingdom, much thought went in to considering the problems which were likely to arise from the inevitable congestion that would occur on the roads, especially in the concentration areas. The planners reckoned this would be at its worst some two weeks before D-Day until the end of the first stage of the transition to the Continent. Priority on the roads needed to be given to moving units progressively closer to their embarkation points.

To help minimise other traffic, the RAF endeavoured to develop a greater level of self-sufficiency during this time so the new advanced landing grounds of 2nd TAF in southern England were pre-stocked with a range of essential stocks of equipment and supplies. This, it was planned, would ensure the 'efficient operation of units during the period of intensive air operations based in the United Kingdom, and to make it possible at the conclusion of that period to cross to the Continent with their correct establishment of stores'.[1]

A FOOTHOLD ON THE CONTINENT

As outlined in the previous chapter, what was needed to support 2nd TAF had been carefully thought out. The 'where', in terms of an interim base until departure from the United Kingdom, had been addressed. As the spring of 1944 began to unfold, and the date of invasion drew ever closer, attention was turning to one of the great organisational achievements of Operation *Overlord* – setting in motion all that was needed to enable the 'when'.

The real headache for the planners was how to control the movement of the components of the invasion force which required shipping space, to their designated points of embarkation. It was recognised early on that the 'choke' points in this process would be the relatively small number of ports capable of handling the range of craft assigned to D-Day. To ease this pressure, several hard surfaces were also constructed on beaches to enable the direct loading of vehicles from what was commonly referred to as 'sand to ship'.[2]

The key to the movement and loading conundrum was the careful scheduling of units, vehicles and equipment, which were required for embarkation. The entire force had to land in the right order and on the right day and time. Amidst this intricate web, which point of embarkation and at what time, were details that required meticulous attention to detail to ensure that specific units were prepared for the off and despatched along pre-arranged routes to their awaiting shipping. Clearly, trying to control and route convoys from literally thousands of locations throughout the country was a near impossible task and a series of holding areas, as close as possible to the coast, were established as staging points before units were called-forward to points of embarkation. This was similar to a modern-day ferry port operation, albeit on a much greater scale, but with its loading area vehicle park being a number of miles away! Strict movement and traffic control was essential in all of this and was enforced largely by military police, in close cooperation with the local civilian police force.

For the units of 2nd TAF, this supervision was carried out by RAF Movement Control, with overall tri-service coordination of movement resting with the combined headquarters at Portsmouth in Hampshire. The movement of RAF units was an involved process. Starting from their tactical locations, units were called-forward to a concentration area where they would spend in the order of forty-eight hours, usually about five days before the planned landing date in France; the RAF's area was at RAF Old Sarum, outside Salisbury. Those RAF units due to land on D-Day or D+1 proceeded through one of the other military concentration areas with a target arrival date there of about D–8. The next stage was to a marshalling area where units were assembled into a load for eventual embarkation on a specific type of ship or craft. It was a very precise process with units moving into the marshalling area in suitably sized convoys. The convoy commander of each was required to despatch an officer to the marshalling area's regulating post one hour before its scheduled arrival time to report full details of the convoy in advance of its arrival.

Once in the area, the marshalling began with an officer or non-commissioned officer appointed in charge of each party. An OC troop was appointed for each ship or craft, and he remained in command until disembarkation in France. Formations would spend about eighteen to thirty-six hours in the marshalling areas. The final stage of the process was a journey to the embarkation area where vehicles and personnel were called forward for loading on to ships or craft. These were in very close proximity to the marshalling areas and, for the purposes of *Overlord*, there were five main embarkation areas sited on the south coast. For example, Area A was centred on the city of Portsmouth with two embarkation areas, each of which was located either side of the coastal entrance to the harbour itself. To feed-in to these, there were four marshalling sub-areas, stretching in a broad arc around the city from Hamble to the north-west across to Emsworth on the eastern side of the city. The marshalling sub-areas were well chosen, all aligned with railway lines with each area having a designated de-training station.

Road movement was carefully regulated, with the main routes designated as either one or two-way roads across the area. To provide room for flexibility, a waterproofing requirement was extended to all those vehicles that would be disembarking on the Continent until D+42. Consequently, all vehicles had to be waterproofed for wading up to a depth of 3 feet and 9 inches. This was a complicated and lengthy process that had to cater for many vehicle types. The process was carried out in three stages, each of which was completed in the concentration, marshalling and embarkation areas respectively. On completion of the waterproofing, vehicles were driven through a water-filled wading pit to test the thoroughness of the work. At the completion of each stage, vehicles were annotated on the offside wing with a small, coloured paint mark (blue, yellow, and red respectively for each of the stages). This was a simple and effective system, and no vehicle was permitted to be loaded on a ship or vessel unless it bore all three marks.[3]

The story of the tension-filled days which preceded the Supreme Allied Commander's momentous decision, 'OK, let's go!', has been well described in many of the excellent accounts of *Overlord*. It was a historic decision and one that committed 3 million men and 2,727 ships to the operation, which turned the tide of the Second World War. Although much of the planning had taken place near London, by the time that D-Day was launched, the Allied commanders needed to be much closer to the assault troops and their ports of departure. Consequently, the Supreme HQ Allied Expeditionary Force was moved to Southwick House, a former Georgian mansion, just to the north of Portsmouth in Hampshire. It was in the operations room, in sight of the enormous wall map that had been specially commissioned for *Overlord*, that the decision to launch D-Day was taken.[4]

As part of the preparatory operations to the invasion, which had started as early as 1 April 1944, the Allied Expeditionary Air Force, along with the RAF's Bomber and Coastal commands, in concert with the United States Eighth Air Force had flown some 200,639 sorties, dropping 195,380 tons of bombs. The aircraft of 2nd TAF alone flew 28,587 sorties during this period, dropping just under 7,000 tons of bombs and losing 133 aircraft. Although the Allied air forces lost 1,987 aircraft in combat, 2,655 enemy aircraft had been destroyed. The range of missions was extensive and included: dislocation of the enemy lines of communication; disruption of enemy radar and communications; attacks on military facilities; harassing of coastwise [*sic*] shipping and sea mining; attacks on airfields; air reconnaissance; protecting the assembling invasion forces and *Crossbow* operation – attacks against the V-1 flying bomb launching sites in the Pas-des-Calais and Cherbourg areas.[5]

The disruption of enemy radar was a particularly important, if not vital, mission with the approach of D-Day. These installations gave complete cover to the whole of the western European seaboard and would make it impossible for aircraft or shipping to approach the Continent without being detected. The aircraft of No.84 Group, along with others, were involved in attacks on at least twelve such installations during May 1944. These were particularly hazardous operations as the sites were invariably well defended. One such example was the attack on 24 May on the radar reporting station at Cap de la Hague/Jobourg, carried out by a combined total of eight Typhoons from Nos. 198 and 609 squadrons (No.84 Group). The after-action report by one of the pilots gives a taste of just how hazardous such missions could be:

> 40 x 60 lbs R/P [rocket projectiles] and canon fired. Numerous strikes on hoarding. One of the missing aircraft seen to crash at base of hoarding. Two concrete pillboxes strafed with unobserved results. F/Sgt Vallely and F/O Freeman collided on the run-in. F/Sgt Vallely crashed in flames over the target. F/O Freeman seen crashing in vicinity of the target.

What marks this account out from many such others is that it was later corroborated by a prisoner of war who was captured months later. The attack had left such an impression on him that he insisted on recounting it to his Allied interrogators:

> Three Typhoons came in from the valley flying very low. The second aircraft got a direct hit from a 37 mm flak which practically shot off the tail. The pilot, however, managed to keep some sort of control and continued straight at the target. He dived below the level of the target structure, fired rockets into it, and then tried at the last moment to clear. The third aircraft, in trying to avoid the damaged Typhoon, touched the latter's fuselage with a wing tip. Both aircraft locked together and crashed some 100 yards beyond. The radar installation was never again serviceable. Of the cables leading up to the target, 23 out of 28 major leads were severed.[6]

Such experiences were typical of the missions flown in the run-up to D-Day and were just a foretaste. The missions to neutralize enemy radar installations were extensive. In the period up until D-Day, 1,668 sorties were flown by the Allied Expeditionary Air Force. Of these, some 694 sorties were flown by Typhoons, which fired 4,517 rocket projectiles. Typhoons and Spitfires also made 759 dive-bombing sorties, dropping 1,258 500lb bombs.[7] It would test both the air and groundcrews of 2nd TAF to the limit. In the never-ending quest to maintain air superiority, it was vital that as many aircraft were kept operationally available. Lost

FORWARD AIR BASES IN EUROPE FROM D-DAY TO THE BALTIC

aircraft and crews of course had to be replaced, but battle damage repair consumed time and resources.

In the week leading up to D-Day, the front-line strength of 2nd TAF had reached some 1,348 serviceable aircraft in 80 flying squadrons. Of these, thirty-three were fighter, eighteen fighter-bomber, twelve light bomber, five tactical reconnaissance, five photographic reconnaissance and seven artillery observation. Additional RAF, Fleet Air Arm and United States Navy squadrons came under 2nd TAF control to act as an air spotting pool for both Royal Navy and United States Navy gunfire support.

By the afternoon of 5 June 1944, all aircraft involved with the invasion were painted with the distinctive black and white invasion stripes on wings and fuselages, a distinguishing feature which enabled Allied aircraft to be quickly and easily recognised. This latter exercise was a massive undertaking. Some 10,000 aircraft and gliders needed to be marked on D-1 requiring 100,000 gallons of distemper paint. Within the United Kingdom such quantities were not immediately available; extensive work was done to assemble the required amount with supplies to civilian customers being stopped. The paint was one thing, but the job also needed 2,000 brushes to apply the paint scheme, much of which was done by hand.[8] All was now set for D-Day itself on 6 June 1944.

On the day of invasion and operating from their airfields in the United Kingdom, 2nd TAF began its part in supporting the assault in Normandy, participating in the five principal tasks, which had been allotted to the air forces: protecting the cross-Channel

A Typhoon of No.183 Squadron display its four 20mm wing-mounted cannon for the photographer. The black and white invasion stripes are clearly visible on the underside of the wings. (*Crown Copyright – Air Historical Branch MoD*)

movement of the assault forces; neutralising the coast and beach defences; protecting the landing beaches and shipping concentrations from enemy attack, dislocating enemy communications and control during the assault and airborne operations.

Protection for the invasion armada was provided by Mosquito night fighters which maintained standing patrols over the English Channel and France. During the landings, defence was provided in-depth by fighter aircraft whose main task was to head-off any enemy aircraft heading for the Normandy area. Some eighteen squadrons of RAF Typhoons alone were committed to support landings in the British sector of GOLD, JUNO, and SWORD beaches. The rate of effort was intensive. The fighter squadrons flew 1,226 patrol sorties over the beachhead and some 90 escort/convoy protection sorties. They reportedly encountered little resistance. The fighter-bomber squadrons flew 400 close air support and armed reconnaissance sorties in support of the landings and lost 8 Typhoon aircraft. The reconnaissance squadrons flew eighty-seven tactical and twenty-three photographic reconnaissance missions. Some 435 naval spotting sorties were flown over the British and American landing areas with seven aircraft lost to enemy action.

From 04.30 hours on D-Day and throughout daylight hours during the assault phase, the air forces maintained a continuous low level fighter cover, at nine squadron strength, over the entire assault area. During daylight, low-level cover up to about 5,000 feet was a British responsibility, predominantly by six Spitfire squadrons of 2nd TAF. For higher levels, up to 20,000 feet, the Americans provided three squadrons of the Republic P-47 Thunderbolt fighter of the United States Ninth Air Force. During the hours of darkness, air cover was provided by night fighters equipped with airborne interception radar.

Journey to Normandy

The task of coordinating the naval aspects of the operation was complex to say the least. Hundreds of vessels had to be loaded, then set sail to various holding locations, before heading across the English Channel to France. Whilst many of the personnel heading to Normandy had by now started to understand what they were taking part in; the finer detail was yet to be briefed and for most of the troops this was done at sea. Accounts of many of the units involved comment on a mixed range of emotions as it became clearer what lay ahead.

The war diary of No.2834 Squadron RAF Regiment provides a good example of a typical voyage and an idea of the apprehension felt by most if not all of those who were about to embark on the much-awaited liberation of France and the Low Countries. The squadron's embarkation had commenced on the hards at Felixstowe with personnel and equipment being loaded on two Tank Landing Ships, on 1 June 1944. This RAF Regiment squadron was to have an important part to play in defending what was planned to be the first operational airfield in Normandy. The unit, like many, remained on board for several days but finally received sailing orders for Sunday, 4 June – this was postponed following the deferment of D-Day itself and their convoy set off at 08.00 hours on Monday, 5 June.

FORWARD AIR BASES IN EUROPE FROM D-DAY TO THE BALTIC

The unit's war diary recorded:

> Convoy sailed. All Naval craft in the river saluted as each ship of the convoy passed, the ships company's [sic] being mustered on deck and standing to attention. The troops stood to attention in each LST, and the captain returned salutes. The Admiral came slowly up the convoy in his barge and wished each ship good luck as he passed. The senior service certainly gave us a terrific send off from Felixstowe.

Later that morning, all the squadron's personnel were briefed on both ships:

> General Montgomery's personal message to all was read out. Their enthusiasm was unbounded. It must be remembered that they got practically the whole of the Grade II and Grade I briefings in one and the picture of the operation was practically complete and most convincing. And they knew something that Hitler did not – yet!

Like many of the units involved, the squadron had experienced numerous problems with its preparation and was still trying to resolve several issues. It was inevitable, given the sheer scale of the operation and the vast number of arrangements that had to be in place for hundreds of units and thousands of men.

The men of No.2834 Squadron were under no illusions as to what the true priorities were as their diarist recorded on 5 June:

> After the 'O' Group and the final memorising of the terrain from the maps and fervent prayers from all that the maps would prove to represent the ground, the tension of the last few weeks appeared to slip away. The final administration problems, the doubtful barrel [Bofors gun] it had not been possible to exchange, the extra map boards which did not arrive, now seemed small in comparison with the great events about to take place. And the next 36 hours or thereabouts were the Navy's headache, except for the provision of spotters and AA [anti-aircraft] gunners for their 20 mm cannon. This was easy for us.[9]

Fighter Control During the Assault

Firstly, the various units providing control of aircraft in the battle area, for both offensive and defensive operations, needed to be in the right place at the right time. Key to this were the early positioning of the fighter direction tenders offshore and the landing of the units of the base defence sectors with their vital ground to air radar and communication capability.

Until the mobile radar units could be put ashore, the fighter direction tenders were a critical part in controlling the Allies' use of air power during the landings.

There were three of these tenders: No.13, which was initially held in reserve, was positioned approximately 40 miles offshore in the main shipping lane approach to the beaches; No.216 situated just off OMAHA and UTAH beaches covering the American sector and No.2717 situated just off JUNO Beach, between SWORD and GOLD beaches, covering the British and American sectors.

Overall, these tenders initially operated as satellites to a 'master' tender (No.217). These first units were reinforced by further stations, along with additional radar capability which would enable a comprehensive radar cover to be gradually built-up in the bridgehead. Indeed, by two weeks after D-Day, it was intended that some nineteen radar units would have been deployed.

With their crews all fully briefed, the two fighter direction ships that would provide the critical radar and communications coverage for the Anglo-Canadian and American sectors were in position just 5 miles offshore, well before daybreak and observing strict radio and radar silence. All was to change when 'H-Hour' came. Leading Aircraftman Karl Work, a Canadian volunteer serving on Fighter Direction Tender No.217, recorded in his diary:

> All 3 FDTs in position by 0430 hours. At 0730 hours full radio and radar silence was broken. Traffic of aircraft and vessels was unbelievable. We were shadowed by a Navy ship and an ASR (Air Sea Rescue). Stationed 5 miles offshore. Bay full of ships. Advised that we were off Arromanches, Normandy, France.

There was little time for Karl to write-up his diary as the events unfolded, but the next few days remained memorable. On 7 June he observed: 'A flak ship tied alongside for our protection. Night-time looked like the 24th of May (Victoria Day in Canada) with tracers and flares lighting up the sky from gunners of ships around us'.

The day after, it was still apparent that enemy resistance was active 'First sight of Jerry over our beach. Reports said our radar beacons were OK. Ordered to shut down our Mk IV beacon as it was believed that Jerry might home in on it'[10] Karl's ship remained stationed just off the British/Canadian beaches until 15 June when it moved to the American sector to replace tender No.216 which had incurred some damage.

By that time, full radar cover had been established in the British and Canadian sectors by the mobile radar convoy (No.15083 Ground Control Intercept), which landed during the afternoon of D-Day. Throughout the time the fighter direction tenders remained on duty, only enemy 'tip-and-run' attacks by Junkers (Ju) 88, Messerschmitt (Me) 109 and Focke-Wulf (Fw) 190 aircraft were experienced.

The RAF Goes Ashore

Just half an hour after sunrise on 6 June 1944, the assault phase of operations *Overlord* and *Neptune*, was launched. The amphibious landings were preceded by extensive aerial and naval bombardment and an airborne assault which preceded the landing of 24,000 American, British and Canadian airborne troops shortly after midnight.

Allied infantry and armoured divisions began landing on the coast of France at 06.30 hours. Many of the units who were at sea and due to land after the initial assault at H-Hour very quickly became aware of what was happening as the diarist of No.2834 Squadron RAF Regiment described:

> The first evidence that the 'party was on' became apparent. Fighter patrols, squadrons proceeding on and returning from sorties, Spitfires and Mustangs, Lightnings, Marauders and Mitchells, mostly seen through gaps in high broken cloud. As we approached the French coast large numbers of LCTs H-hour craft, were passed returning to England.

The public at home first learned of the invasion on the wireless. At 09.30 hours on 6 June 1944, the BBC broadcast Supreme HQ Allied Expeditionary Force's Communique No.1, beginning the announcement with 'Allied naval forces, supported by strong air forces, began landing Allied armies this morning on the coast of northern France'. Of the large numbers of RAF units still in the United Kingdom and waiting to embark for the Continent, many were only just becoming aware of the significance of the operation they were about to take part in.

At the same time as the landings began in Normandy, the CO of B Echelon of Ground Control Intercept Convoy No.15083, a radar unit part of No.24 Base Defence Sector, had just set off from the unit's temporary holding base in Wartling, East Sussex to begin the gradual move of his unit closer to their eventual embarkation point at Gosport in Hampshire. They would not set sail until early July and the enormity of the occasion was beginning to dawn on them.

The unit's war diary entry for the day records that 'all through the early hours great air activity had been noticed and it was suspected that Glider aircraft had been going over the camp in great numbers, but it was not until the 10.00 hours stop [at] Wisborough Green that the full importance of the day was known. D-Day had arrived and was being announced over a wireless set from a nearby house'. As the radio announcement was being made, the first RAF personnel of 2nd TAF were going ashore in Normandy.

The majority of the war diaries for 2nd TAF units heading to Normandy on that morning are unanimous in their recording of how well organised the embarkation process actually was, a remarkable feat in itself given the vast numbers of men, machines and *materiel* flowing into a limited number of ports. Many of the diaries record the collective thoughts of the units (through the edited efforts of the diarist!) regarding the sea journey and their apprehension of what lay ahead. Some are quite matter of fact and stoical in their narrative, such as a comment made by one of the mobile radar units in No.83 Group who commented: 'This last party [on one of the tank landing ships] had some distraction on the way over, including some indecently intimate views of passing torpedoes'.[11]

A FOOTHOLD ON THE CONTINENT

Apart from the miserable weather, many of those alighting from the vast number of vessels that made it to the beach, had been at sea for some time. The conditions that day did little to give any respite to the seasickness that many experienced. Strong winds and rough seas were problematical for the landing craft, bringing the tide in more quickly than expected, and made the Atlantic Wall beach obstacles more difficult to navigate.

These obstacles were to provide a formidable challenge. Ever since Hitler had appointed Generalfeldmarschall Erwin Rommel as Inspector of Coastal Defence in November 1943 an incredible amount of work had been expended on strengthening the Atlantic Wall. Indeed, Rommel believed that 'an attempt must be made, using every possible expedient, to beat off the enemy landing on the coast and to fight the battle in the more or less strongly fortified coastal strip'.[12] It was this intensive defensive focus that made getting ashore so challenging on D-Day. In addition to the shore-side bunkers and gun emplacements, which could rain-down fire on the assaulting troops, the slope of the beach, out to about 400 yards from the high-water mark, was criss-crossed with perilous lines of cleverly designed obstacles.

At the farthest point from the shore were lines of Belgian gates – 10-foot-wide by 10-foot-high lattice-faced angle iron barricades that would tear the bottom out of landing craft at high tide and block them at low tide. Towards the shore were then lines of log posts and log ramps (a tripod type construction), many of these with mines attached. Closest to the shore were structures known as 'hedgehogs', some 5 feet hight and made of three crossed steel beams.[13] The number of these defences was extensive. On JUNO Beach alone, where No.2 RAF Beach Squadron was to land, there were 915 obstacles on MIKE sector (2,200 yards wide) and 2,701 on NAN sector (5,500 yards wide). If that was not enough, the Germans had also created extensive minefields, the effectiveness of which had been made apparent to Rommel during his time in the desert as commander of the Africa Korps.

All in all, this presented the Allies with a formidable 'welcome to France'. The troops were to find that, as forewarned by Eisenhower in his pre-invasion note to the participants, the 'enemy is well trained, well equipped and battle hardened. He will fight savagely'.[14] It is little wonder that many who landed that day felt that they had sailed into the mouth of hell itself.

As the ramps of the landing craft came down and the predominantly khaki clad troops waded ashore, RAF blue battledress could also be seen amidst the ranks. This, however, would prove problematical later in the campaign when faded and dusty blue battledress often became confused with the field grey colour of the German uniforms, with potentially serious consequences. The operations record book of various units describes how some RAF personnel tried to swap their blue uniforms for the more familiar khaki worn by the army. The diarist of No.21 Base Defence Sector recorded how, on 7 June, one of its officers who was trying to carry out a reconnaissance of a road leading out of the hamlet of Les Moulins, found the road coming under cross machine gun fire 'and that he had been fired at a number of times, on one occasion having his steel helmet knocked off'. Anecdotally, it was believed that 'this fire is considered to have come from the Americans, who were trigger conscious and repeatedly mistook the RAF Blue for the enemy'.[15]

FORWARD AIR BASES IN EUROPE FROM D-DAY TO THE BALTIC

The experience though was reported by the personnel of No.21 Base Defence Sector on 9 June and recorded in their operations record book: 'The Americans continually sniped at the RAF Blue, so Denims were given to as many of the troops as possible to avoid this'.[16] Whilst many of the well-known images of the landings on D-Day show the infantry, armour and combat engineers wading ashore, over 1,800 RAF personnel and 456 vehicles also landed before the day was out. By 9 June, the RAF had over 3,500 personnel and 815 vehicles in Normandy, mainly working on airfield construction, aircraft servicing and forward controlling of tactical aircraft.[17] The RAF units that landed as part of the assault phase were exposed to very similar, if not identical risks and conditions as the combat troops. A number were killed and wounded in action. Most of the groundcrew casualties were sustained in the early days of the campaign but losses continued to be experienced right up until the end of the war.[18]

On D-Day itself there were five types of units which needed to come ashore and to become operational as soon as possible. The first of these, the RAF beach squadrons, were a vital enabler and would provide the means of receiving and processing the RAF's vehicles, men and supplies as they came ashore from the various vessels. Working as part of the army beach groups, these units had the challenging task of controlling the landings in the British and Canadian sectors on SWORD, JUNO and GOLD beaches. Secondly, the Ground Control Intercept Convoys needed to be disembarked so that they could set up at a deployed operating site and provide the vital ground-based intercept capability. This would enable them to take over this service from the fighter direction tenders.

The third element that needed to land were the RAF's part of the airfield construction effort, in the form of No.5357 Wing. This wing, in conjunction with the airfield construction units of the army's Royal Engineers, was to play a vital part in building the many temporary airfields in Normandy required by the RAF's Administrative Plan. Hot on their heels would be the fourth component, the RAF servicing commandos who would then pre-stock the airfields with fuel and ammunition and remain on-site to refuel and rearm the aircraft until an airfield headquarters unit could move in and take over. All this needed to be under the protective umbrella of the fifth key component, the anti-aircraft defence provided by the RAF Regiment.

On SWORD beach the first elements of No.1 Beach Squadron (No.101 Beach Flight), came ashore on Queen Roger Sector, between Ouistreham and Lion-sur-Mer at 09.25 hours. Although this was nearly three hours after the landings first commenced, there was still strong enemy opposition with heavy shell, mortar, and small arms fire; the arrival of the flight's commander, Squadron Leader J.N. Dobbin MC, a little later at 11.15 hours. was equally hazardous when his landing craft was hit by enemy fire just below the water line, as it touched down on the beach.

Further west along the coast on JUNO Beach, between Courseulles and Saint-Aubin-sur-Mer, No.2 Beach Squadron also made a troublesome landfall. The first components of its No.104 Beach Flight landed on NAN Beach at 08.45 hours. The ship carrying Sergeant Sherlow and Leading Aircraftman Hey hit one of the

A FOOTHOLD ON THE CONTINENT

Members of an RAF beach squadron unload fuel jerry cans by hand. (*Crown Copyright – Air Historical Branch MoD*)

submerged Belgian Gate obstacles, with the resulting explosion damaging one of the gangways – presumably there was a mine attached to this structure. Fortunately, there were no casualties.

The first elements of No.103 Beach Flight landed during the afternoon, setting foot on MIKE Beach at 15.00 hours, having been held offshore for some four and a half hours. One of the first members of the squadron to land was Ted Inge who was the 'X' NCO responsible for setting up an explosives dump a mile or so inland from the landing beach. Ted had joined the squadron from No.3 Embarkation Unit on Merseyside and his account of coming ashore says much about of the squadron's experience:

> I was the only RAF type on my LSI. All the remainder were Canadian assault troops and the only person I knew was a Major who apparently had been at Anzio. He was to do for the army what I was to do for the RAF i.e., set up an explosives dump. The landing was not too bad. I had experienced worse on practice landings. When I got ashore the Canadians were still milling around in Courseulles. It was no place for us with just two Smith & Wesson .38 revolvers between us. So, I brewed up and the major left me to recce, only to return hours later pushing a cycle with the news that he was setting off for his site. I decided that I would stay the night in the grounds of some chateau and push on in the morning light. The rest of my squadron were to have a terrible time being kept offshore for three

or four days. Priority being given to fighting troops. I have no idea what time I actually landed but I was scheduled for D-Day plus two hours and have always thought that I must have been one of the first of RAF ground staff to land in France. However, it would seem that in all probability that honour could go to the boys in No.1 Beach Squadron. We collected two Croix de Guerre and I was lucky in the draw for Oak Leaves.[19]

On GOLD Beach, No.4 RAF Beach Squadron came ashore, with its Nos. 107 and 108 beach flights landing on KING RED and JIG GREEN sectors. The flight commander of No.107 Flight landed at 08.50 hours on KING RED Beach from an Assault Landing Craft, with his landing officer and NCO close behind with their jeep from a Tank Landing Craft. Their comrades in No.108 Flight had made their landing at little earlier around 08.00 although Flight Lieutenant Bruce and Flight Sergeant House took an unexpected swim ashore after the vessel they were travelling in was sunk offshore.

This beach was also the landing site for Ground Control Intercept Convoy No.15083, which was to form part of the base defence sector radar coverage for the British and Canadian sectors. Its convoy of some twenty-seven vehicles landed during the afternoon, reporting to the beach master around 15.30 hours. Even then, enemy opposition was still active and one of their vehicles was hit during an attack by a strafing enemy aircraft. They needed to move off the beach quickly but found

The first RAF beach squadron headquarters to be established on SWORD Beach, 6 June 1944. (*Neil Huband Collection*)

this difficult due to a long convoy of Royal Army Medical Corps vehicles and ambulances bringing the first casualties back from the forward edge of the battle area.

Moving through the villages of Ver-sur-Mer and Meuvaines, they eventually arrived at their first designated operating site. Apparently, it was an ideal site except for two points. Firstly, there were several Allied tanks on the site ready for an expected German counterattack. Secondly, and one that appears largely cosmetic, was that grass was very long – given the number of power and communication cables used to link the various vehicles this was a considerable hindrance. Even amidst the destruction and carnage that the invasion had brought to the Normandy countryside, the local population was keen to help wherever they could.

It is little surprise that the farmer in this area was soon persuaded to cut the grass, thereby enabling the complex mass of sophisticated radar equipment to be set up. It was long, hard work but by night-time they had one of their operations rooms up and running and at 22.30 hours took control of their first Bristol Beaufighter night fighter operating from the United Kingdom.[20]

Amidst these early landings, the men and equipment of the RAF balloon squadrons were also making their debut, with Nos. 980, 974 and 976 squadrons making their landfall on all three of the British and Canadian beaches. Getting to the shore on JUNO proved particularly hazardous for No.974 Squadron and a number were wounded when at least two vessels they had been embarked on were hit by a drifting mine and an enemy bomb. A similar experience was had by No.976 Squadron with one of their Infantry Landing Crafts being hit by shell fire at the moment of beaching putting the port landing gangway out of action. The helmsman swung the craft's stern round to port to give greater cover for the disembarking troops. The subsequent landing was described as 'very wet, the water being more than waist high'. It was to be a familiar story for many who landed that day. The thick, wool serge battle dress uniform of the British and Canadians was not comfortable at best when dry, but when wet it became heavy and uncomfortable. Coupled with the heavy load of personal kit and weaponry each man was carrying, going ashore was physically draining to say the least.

It was particularly hazardous for these units as their highly conspicuous barrage balloons had been transported across the Channel tethered to various craft and landed already inflated at what was known as the landing height of 100 feet cable length. When positioned on land they were then extended to an operational height of 2,000 feet. Although nominally part of 2nd TAF, each of the balloon squadrons came under the control of the army's anti-aircraft defence commander. Each balloon was manned by a crew of two and while at sea were given a 1/25,000 scale map showing the barrage area in which they would install their balloon, usually some 7,000 yards long by 1,000 yards deep. On SWORD Beach the initial phase was to install nine balloons in the centre of the sector, with subsequent waves placed inland to the east and west. That was the plan but getting to the barrage area was difficult as the experience of the squadron CO, Squadron Leader B.W.B. Chapman shows. After landing he made his way to the anti-aircraft report centre and found, the landing plans being generally harassed and delayed by shell and mortar fire and sniping from the two flanks Lion sur Mer and Ouistreham, particularly mortar fire from the latter. As it was just high tide the area between the water's edge and the sand dunes at the back of beach was extremely narrow, a mere 30' or so. Behind this was barbed wire and mined areas. Into this small beach strip already littered with knocked out tanks, bull dozers, vehicles, etc., more and more equipment was being pushed and owing to the lack of space for lateral movement it was not possible to get it all out through the hastily formed beach exits. The assault waves had obviously suffered considerable casualties and excellent work was being done in moving the wounded, but the dead could not yet be cleared. The 17 balloons due in at H+240 arrived on time but in view of the comparatively short length of beach as yet cleared of obstacles, mines, etc., and the congestion of vehicles deployment further inland was made extremely difficult. While the crews were sorting themselves out, enemy mortar fire tended to increase and was now added to by fairly continuous shellfire.[21]

Barrage balloons had become a familiar sight in the United Kingdom. These balloons flew at 2,000 feet by night and just below cloud base by day and were intended to deter enemy aircraft from getting close enough to target the area from overhead, by bombing or strafing fire but were ineffective in the case of high-flying bomber aircraft. Their deployment on the D-Day beaches, though, soon led to growing concern.

The CO of No.976 Balloon Squadron recorded in his unit's war diary that 'Many Unit commanders hastily formed the opinion that the balloons were being used by the enemy for aiming and many requests were received for them to be removed'. It is unlikely this was the case as the enemy knew the area intimately. Before long though, many of the balloons had been cut adrift.

As agreed during the planning for *Overlord*, the RAF was required to deploy a base defence sector for the Americans to provide vital ground-to-air radar coverage in their sector of the lodgement area. The devil in the detail though, was that the men and equipment of this unit had to come ashore on OMAHA Beach as part of the American assault force. It is one of the lesser-known stories of the RAF on D-Day.

Generally agreed as the most heavily defended of all the assault beaches, what became known as bloody OMAHA took the greatest number of US casualties on D-Day.[22] It was not just a story of American casualties though, for it was here that 2nd TAF lost six of its men killed in action that day. If battle honours could have been awarded to RAF ground units, one, without any doubt, should have gone to the men of No.21 Base Defence Sector who landed here to provide the ground control intercept service for the American sector.

Whilst the fighter direction tender for the American sector had been in place offshore since 04.00 hours, the mobile No.21 Base Defence Sector was not due

RAF barrage balloons flying above GOLD Beach, June 1944. (*Crown Copyright – Air Historical Branch MoD*)

to land until mid-morning after the first assault waves had landed. Its first attempt at landing was made at 11.30 hours but as it approached the beach it was clear that OMAHA was still under heavy machine gun and artillery fire, and it was ordered to withdraw by one of the American patrol boats controlling landing craft movement. The order to go ashore finally came late afternoon, but as the landing ship approached the shoreline it became clear that the flotilla it was part of, was heading for Dog Red sector, rather than the planned landing point at Easy Red. It remains unclear why this was so but the actual landfall point turned out to be the most heavily defended part of OMAHA Beach.

Several of the men who landed on D-Day received awards for their bravery and devotion to duty whilst under fire. Of note was the uncommon award to RAF personnel of four Military Crosses and two Military Medals. The citation for these awards was published in *The London Gazette* in November 1944. The content of these says much of the calibre and courage of the men. Of the Military Crosses bestowed, awards were made to the unit's chaplain and medical officer. The Reverend Geoffrey Harding, wearing the rank of a squadron leader, 'worked for 36 hours, most of the time under direct fire, giving help to the wounded and burying the dead. He set an inspiring example and was responsible for saving many lives'.

There was no end to his coolness and disregard for his own safety that day as in the evening 'he walked along a road, which was under fire, into a village in enemy hands. He entered a house in which were many snipers and obtained water which he took back to the wounded'. The unit's medical officer, Flight Lieutenant Noel Rycroft, was recorded as being 'the only medical officer on one of the beaches of Normandy on D-Day' but owing to the 'intense bombardment, it was not possible for him or any member of his unit to move off the beach for six hours'. In the carnage of OMAHA, Noel Rycroft worked for forty-eight hours 'tending casualties among the personnel of his unit and also aided some seventy-five American wounded. He was himself slightly wounded but his efforts on behalf of others were untiring'.

Of the Military Medals awarded, the citation for Leading Aircraftman John Reid (a medical orderly working with the unit medical officer) states that: 'Whilst the beaches were under intense fire for many hours, he attended to some 100 wounded. This involved moving many times across the whole beach'.[23]

The story of the RAF at OMAHA went untold for many years after the war. This omission in the public understanding of the D-Day story was particularly evident at the sixtieth anniversary ceremony at the Normandy American Cemetery in 2004 (attended by presidents Bush and Chirac). Veteran Leslie Dobinson, a former leading aircraftman wireless mechanic with No.309 Mobile Signals Servicing Unit who landed at OMAHA on 6 June 1944, attended as a guest – the only British Normandy veteran to be so invited. He related how, in the VIP enclosure, he had the opportunity to mix with American veterans and several three- and four-star generals. Leslie was astonished to find that 'none of these VIPs had any idea that British forces personnel had participated in the D-day landings on OMAHA Beach, in support of the Americans'.[24] A long overdue memorial to the men of No.15082 Ground Control Intercept and mobile signals units was eventually erected in the vicinity of Dog White and Dog Red sectors of OMAHA Beach at Vierville-sur-Mer in June 2012.

With so much going on across the expanse of sand on GOLD, JUNO and SWORD beaches, command and control was clearly a must and by the evening of that first day an advance party of HQ No.83 Group was ashore and starting the difficult job of coordinating the RAF's work amidst the chaos and uncertainty that was commonplace across all of the landing areas. This was their task until HQ 2nd TAF arrived in Normandy. It was a two-way relationship – having a coordinating

A FOOTHOLD ON THE CONTINENT

hub enabled the RAF units in the beachhead to channel their problems and needs, as well as a conduit for communication with the army ashore and HQ 2nd TAF back in the United Kingdom. One of the functions performed by the advanced headquarters, which was crucial to the build-up, was prioritisation of units into the bridgehead. With such a vast volume of men, machines and equipment literally flooding-in, congestion was, and remained for many weeks, a constant problem. It was vital that only RAF units that were essential to current operations were allowed ashore.

The RAF was acutely conscious that unless they could locate as many of the short-range aircraft squadrons as possible in Normandy in these early days, much flying time would be wasted transiting to and from the United Kingdom. Indeed, it was estimated that unless these squadrons could be moved to the Continent within seven weeks, 'the rate of effort that could be maintained would not be enough to maintain air superiority, to harass enemy communications and delay the build-up of enemy ground forces which could otherwise concentrate in superior numbers against the bridgehead.' Notwithstanding, the overall achievement in the early days of the invasion was impressive. On D+1 (7 June) the bridgehead was approximately 22 miles long and 10 miles deep. Three days later two refuelling and rearming strips were in constant use. From then on, with the outstanding efforts of the army's airfield construction units, the RAF was able to establish new airfields at the incredible rate of one every two days.

Life for all in the bridgehead remained challenging in those early days. The gruelling rate of effort during the day and the difficulty of getting a good night's sleep sapped the strength of even the toughest. At night the noise of battle continued – prowling enemy aircraft and the rumble of nearby guns both did their part in disrupting much needed rest.

RAF airmen watch as a bulldozer towing a scraper levels ground as work commences on the construction of the first Allied airstrip in Normandy, 8 June 1944. (*Crown Copyright – Air Historical Branch MoD*)

Chapter 5

Developing the Bridgehead

The key to achieving Coningham's priority of basing his squadrons in Normandy as quickly as possible was the rapid construction of airfields. In the early part of the campaign, the RAF was entirely reliant on the five Royal Engineers' airfield construction groups of Twenty-First Army Group to do this work – the RAFs own such capability was not planned to arrive on the Continent until the end of June/early July. The requirement for the first week after the initial landings (D+3-4) was to construct one Emergency Landing Strip on D-Day itself, followed by two further refuelling and rearming strips by 10 June at the latest.

In the early days of the campaign, the method of construction for the airstrips, especially those in Normandy, was described as of 'hasty airfield construction'. The most basic of these were just graded earth strips which were specially compacted to withstand only short periods of intensive use, predominantly by fighter aircraft. For sites where more intensive operations were to be conducted and for a longer duration, a more robust operating surface could be laid with a range of ingenious surfacing:

> Square Mesh Track. This was generally used at sites operating fighter aircraft and made up of heavy-duty wire joined in three-inch squares. It was a lightweight option, relatively easy to work with and could be laid like a carpet in under seven days. Whilst this was a quick and easy solution, the open mesh structure allowed dust clouds to be generated from the dry and exposed soil beneath.

> Pre-Bituminised Surfacing. Consisting of an asphalt-impregnated jute material, it came in 300-foot rolls and was between 36 to 43 inches wide and laid from long, continuous rolls with the strips sealed in overlapping layers. Developed by the Canadians from a British origin, this was used as an aid to rapid airfield surfacing.

> Pressed (or pierced) Steel Planking. Unlike the lighter-weight square mesh track, this material was much heavier and could provide an all-weather surface, suitable for use by light bomber aircraft. Each plank was ten feet long and 15 inches wide and could be joined together and laid perpendicular to the line of flight. Its weight made airfield construction much more time consuming and, made from steel, was also a war production material that was much in demand.

DEVELOPING THE BRIDGEHEAD

It was originally planned that the mesh track and bituminised surfacing would be used independently but, in practice, a combination of the two proved to be more durable. The mesh was also used in conjunction with steel planking in non-critical areas or, where supplies of the planking were limited. Runway length on each of the airfield types varied. The emergency landing strips were just 600 yards long, refuelling and rearming strips, along with the advanced landing grounds were 1,200 yards for fighter operations and 1,650 yards for fighter bombers.

As intended, the first airstrip to be made ready on the Continent was the Emergency Landing Strip, designated as Airfield B.1, at Asnelles-sur-Mer, just inland from GOLD Beach. Cleared and made ready by the army's No.16 Airfield Construction Group, the advance party of which landed on D-Day. The site, as its designation implies, was effectively just a touchdown strip for aircraft that were in trouble and unable to reach another airfield. At only 600 yards long, it was built to the bare minimum standard with a surface of just compacted earth. This was sufficient for an emergency landing but not for take-offs. The site was constructed under very challenging conditions on D-Day itself and was ready for use on D+1. Within a stone's throw of the airfield, an advanced surgical team of the RAF's No.50 Mobile Field Hospital, which had landed on D-Day, was in place to provide full surgical aid to both RAF and other service units in the area ahead of the main field hospital which was not due to arrive until 14 June. Thankfully, the work of this surgical team was less than expected, largely because of the high degree of Allied air superiority which was able to minimise the extent of enemy air attacks.

The intended first operational airfield in Normandy was to be at Advanced Landing Ground B.2, at Bazenville, situated between the villages of Crépon, Bazenville and Villiers-le-Sec, just 4 miles from the sands of GOLD Beach. Hot on the heels of Asnelles, work was started on the site by No.16 Airfield Construction Group just after midnight on D-Day. It was initially operational as a refuelling and rearming strip and then upgraded to advanced landing ground status. The runway here was 1,700m long with a surface of square mesh track. Due to be completed on 9 June, its starring role as the first operational airfield was snatched from its grasp by a B-24 Liberator that crash landed on the airfield on the morning of the 9 June causing significant damage to the square mesh track matting.

Following repairs, the landing ground was finally operational on 13 June and became home to the Spitfires of No.127 Wing Royal Canadian Air Force, led by the famous fighter pilot Wing Commander 'Johnnie' Johnson, from 16 June 1944. Refuelling and rearming were carried out here by No.3207 Servicing Commando, which had landed in the early hours of D-Day and had picked their way through a minefield to reach the site at Bazenville.

Ground-based defence (perimeter and anti-aircraft) at Bazenville was to be provided by the light anti-aircraft guns of No.2834 Squadron, RAF Regiment. This unit was scheduled to land at H+12 with orders to have 'guns in action last light D-day'. This would have given them just under five hours for deployment after landing on JIG GREEN Sector of GOLD Beach. Both Tank Landing Ships (Nos. 214 and 321) carrying the squadron dropped anchor just off their appointed sector on GOLD Beach at 18.00 hours.

FORWARD AIR BASES IN EUROPE FROM D-DAY TO THE BALTIC

Hawker Typhoon pilots of No.181 Squadron leave the briefing tent at Airfield B.2 Bazenville, for a midday sortie over the Normandy battlefield. (*Crown Copyright – Air Historical Branch MoD*)

To get the squadron and its vehicles ashore though, required the use of a 'Rhino' ferry, essentially a form of barge made from several connected pontoons and equipped with outboard engines. The low draft of these barges was well-suited for shallow beaches, but they were in very short supply as the fleet available had suffered a high rate of loss. By 20.00 hours it had become clear that the squadron could not be unloaded that night so the ships had to lay offshore and attempt to land their load the next day. It was to prove a hazardous and fateful night for the squadron though as the Luftwaffe's bombers and fighter bombers became active soon after dusk and the ship's 20mm cannon were continuously in action.

During all this, Tank Landing Ship No.214 carrying the squadron headquarters and B Flight was hit twice during the action and suffered considerable damage. Sadly, the squadron suffered its first casualties, both in ship No.214: Leading Aircraftmen Finch being killed, and Salmon being seriously wounded both at the same time from a stick of anti-personnel bombs. The next morning, D+1 was to prove equally difficult and both ships had continued difficulty with unloading. In the event, the captain of ship No.214 obtained clearance at 11.30 hours whilst the captain of ship No.321 decided to wait for what was known as a Rhino ferry. All this, plus the lengthy process of unloading and marshalling the squadron's vehicles

DEVELOPING THE BRIDGEHEAD

and men delayed the unit taking up its position in defence at the site of Bazenville airstrip until 23.30 and, as proudly recorded in its war diary, it was to become 'the first RAF Regiment guns in action in France'.[1]

Once dug in, the Bofors light anti-aircraft guns of the RAF Regiment were to be in regular action for several nights after the initial landings to greet the Luftwaffe's night-time raiders. The night of 10 June, for example, saw an enemy raid where a stick of anti-personnel bombs was dropped on one of the airfield sites, with four of the unit wounded, three of which were serious and required evacuation to the United Kingdom. The raid also brought home the importance of digging-in personnel, guns and equipment. The airmen escaped unhurt as they were sleeping in their slit trenches. Not so fortunate for the Bofors gun the men were manning which had been moved to the site the previous afternoon; they had not had time to dig it in. All the tyres on the gun, plus its towing truck were punctured, along with the sump, plus windows and screens shattered. Whilst a monotonous and often arduous job, digging slit trenches to gain some protection from enemy fire and shrapnel was to become a vital task throughout the campaign and provided remarkably good protection from the shrapnel and debris created by the enemy's air dropped anti-personnel bombs. Excavating such trenches proved to be relatively easy in the dry, friable Norman soil.

Keeping the men not on duty occupied during daylight hours, once essential daily maintenance and housekeeping had been carried out, was always a challenge and it is interesting to note that as early as 20 June the RAF Regiment squadron commander obtained permission for up to thirty men to go swimming at Arromanches (normally out of bounds to troops unless on duty) in the afternoons, in designated safe areas. Such visits were greatly appreciated by the men, 'in spite of the heavy traffic and dust, a 2-hour drive each way for a distance of only 10 miles'.

Such difficulties in movement were caused largely by the rigidly controlled one-way system on roads which were enforced by military police in the lodgement area. This was essential in order that the almost continual flow of vehicles coming ashore could be moved inland as quickly as possible and traffic jams minimised.

As things began to settle down and the airstrip at Bazenville became more established, local civilians began to venture out more and naturally were more than curious about this new airfield which had apparently sprung out of nowhere on their farmland. The No.2834 squadron diarist recorded how 'French civilians [were] becoming a nuisance on the airfield which appears to be becoming a Sunday promenade. Orders given that they are to be politely but firmly kept a respectful distance from all gun sites and detachment lines'.

Although Bazenville was only intended to be a temporary airfield, it had an extensive range of facilities, including aircraft dispersals around its perimeter, a fuel and ammunition dump and tented accommodation for nearly 1,000 men in orchards to the south-east of the site. The site, also served as the No.83 Group Control Centre (believed to be in Bazenville Church), from 7 June until 10 August 1944. The site was never far from the action – on its opening, it was just 5 miles

FORWARD AIR BASES IN EUROPE FROM D-DAY TO THE BALTIC

away from the front line and even during the first month of operation, the front line had only moved 11 miles away. The landing ground was used until 28 August 1944 when the real estate was returned to its respective owners.

Despite the wartime conditions the Allies did try to respect the livelihoods and property of the civilian population. When many of the temporary airfields were vacated, the commandeered real estate was invariably returned to the various landowners. Where arable farmland had been used with crops ready for harvest (especially during late July and August 1944), service personnel often helped farmers with gathering in the all-important harvest. Like many of the temporary airfield sites, nothing remains today but an imaginative and impressive memorial to Airfield B.2, and those who served there, has been erected outside of Bazenville church in the form of a Spitfire wing shape.

The airfield that was to become the first operational airfield in Normandy, albeit by just a matter of days, was Advanced Landing Ground B.3 at Sainte-Croix-sur-Mer, just to the north-east of Bazenville, inland from GOLD Beach. Constructed by the Royal Engineers' airfield construction group, work began just after D-Day. The group built a runway and dispersal areas, while communications facilities were provided by equipment installed in vehicles. It was initially up and running as a refuelling and rearming Strip by D+4 and then upgraded to an Advanced Landing Ground later.

Douglas Dakota Mk.IIIs of No.46 Group at Airfield B.2 Bazenville, Normandy, loading casualties for evacuation to the United Kingdom. Identifiable aircraft include KG432 'H' of No.512 Squadron RAF (centre), and KG320 'B1' of No.575 Squadron RAF (extreme right). *(Copyright IWM)*

DEVELOPING THE BRIDGEHEAD

Refuelling and rearming at this site were carried out by Nos.3205 and 3210 Servicing Commandos. Both units landed on D+1 but the war diary of No.3205 provides a more detailed commentary on their experience. Like the majority of the other RAF units, No.3205 was routed through the RAF's concentration area at RAF Old Sarum on the outskirts of Salisbury and then on to their allocated marshalling area at Fareham on 5 June where everyone was issued with rations for the voyage plus the three days following their landing in France. They also received French currency in exchange for an advance of 1 pound Sterling. Having embarked in four separate craft from Gosport, the unit landed around Ver-sur-Mer on GOLD Beach throughout the day on D+1.

Even though it was the day after the initial assault landings, it was not without its problems as two airmen were wounded when a landmine exploded on the beach in the vicinity of their vehicle and two Bedford trucks became flooded by the rising tide. Valuable technical equipment was lost but the occupants were able to swim ashore safely. By D+2 the unit and its vehicles had all been accounted for and had established a temporary headquarters near the village of Ver-sur-Mer about 1 mile from the airstrip, which was nearing completion.

Like many of their colleagues in RAF blue, life on the move in Normandy during those early days was still hazardous and stops such as this invariably involved digging slit trenches and mounting guards at carefully chosen defensive points. In addition to their specialist duties, days in Normandy were invariably long and tiring. On both 8 and 9 June, No.3205 Servicing Commandos worked hard to unload technical equipment, as well as transporting a range of stores from the MIKE and NAN sectors on JUNO Beach to the airstrip, including petrol and munitions.

In concert with their comrades nearby at Airfield B.2, A Flight of No.2809 Light Anti-Aircraft Squadron, RAF Regiment moved in to provide defence at Sainte-Croix on 8 June. Like many RAF units that landed in those early days, this squadron, and its mobile wing headquarters (No.1304), had trouble in coming ashore. They had boarded tank landing ships Nos. 180 and 215 at Southampton on 2 June, eventually anchoring just off Courseulles-sur-Mer on JUNO Beach mid-morning on D-Day. The first Rhino ferry load of their vehicles and equipment had endeavoured to go ashore in the early afternoon of 6 June but difficult landing conditions and damage from a mine delayed the units landing until early afternoon of 7 June – just over thirty hours behind schedule. As the sun set on 9 June, the RAF servicing commandos, and their RAF Regiment guardians were looking forward to a good night's sleep and were as good as ready to receive their first customers the following day.

Come the morning of 10 June, prosaically described as the day of days by the No.3210 Servicing Commando diarist, events did not quite unfold as expected. Barely half an hour after sunrise an unexpected arrival touched down on the airstrip. At 06.20 hours a Hawker Typhoon of No.245 Squadron piloted by Flying Officer Bill Smith had to make an emergency landing after his aircraft had been hit by enemy anti-aircraft fire.[2] The pilot was somewhat surprised that his welcoming committee included members of the press (presumably war correspondents) who had assembled to greet the planned landing of the AOC No.83 Group, Air Vice Marshal Harry Broadhurst who actually landed two and a half hours later.[3]

FORWARD AIR BASES IN EUROPE FROM D-DAY TO THE BALTIC

Pilots of No.168 Squadron relax under an apple tree at Airfield B.8 Sommervieu, Normandy, during a break from operations. Their North American Mustang Mk.Is can be seen at dispersal points in the background. (*Crown Copyright – Air Historical Branch MoD*)

It is not entirely clear from the unit war diaries but it would appear that Smith's Typhoon took off again at 09.00 hours after battle damage repairs had been carried out. It proved to be a busy day thereafter with the servicing commandos refuelling Spitfires of Nos. 349, 401 and 442 squadrons as well as supporting some forty sorties flown into and out of the landing ground. On 10 June 1944, which was a day of firsts, with three Dakotas landing on the strip at 17.00 hours conveying RAF and army staff officers – the first transport to land in France since D-Day. Further firsts occurred on 11 June when Nos. 132 and 453 squadrons were the first RAF squadrons to stay overnight on site in France, and then on 13 June 1944 when Spitfire Mark IXs of No.341 Squadron landed for refuelling and rearming – this was the first Free French squadron to land on French soil following the invasion.

After going operational, things settled down to the routine of servicing aircraft until the night of 12 June when, the diarist of No.3210 Servicing Commando, 'things got pretty "HOT". Cpl Fennall was hit with a small piece of shrapnel'. The ever-present threat of danger was, however, often offset by more lighter moments. The RAF attached much importance to providing some of the comforts of home, both physically and spiritually, even during the very fluid movements and basing of its units in the first few weeks after D-Day. Along with issues of pay to the men, the war diaries record the distribution of cigarette rations – despite the health issues which are now acknowledged, a smoke break was often a welcome diversion for men whose exposure to danger was in a very different and more immediate context.

DEVELOPING THE BRIDGEHEAD

Whilst NAAFI (Navy, Army and Air Force Institutes) comforts were made available, the RAF also saw to it that a most popular liquid refreshment was made available and flew in supplies of beer contained in underwing drop tanks of fighter aircraft such as the Spitfire. Normally used for carrying extra fuel, this means of conveyance could be a mixed blessing. Again, the diarist of No.3210 Servicing Commando relates with his usual flair that on 13 June 'a drop tank full of beer arrived, but unfortunately it was tainted with petrol'. A wasted load? Apparently not, as the diary goes on to comment that 'it was not possible to smoke and drink at the same time'!

As so often experienced by those caught up in war, spiritual matters were also uppermost in the minds of many, and RAF padres travelled many miles from unit to unit to conduct services in the field. On the evening of 27 June, the diarist of No.3210 Servicing Commando recorded that 'the deputy padre of 2nd TAF conducted a very good open-air service, followed by Holy Communion. This was greatly appreciated by the men.'

The work of both servicing commando units at Sainte-Croix-sur-Mer was critical to the support of 2nd TAF operations. Indeed, during the 5 days they were on site they supported 322 sorties in and out of the site, involving 6 different aircraft types from 15 different British, Canadian and US flying squadrons. Their support of the famous Typhoon aircraft involved rearming them with the rocket projectiles that were used with much devastating effect throughout the campaign. As originally intended, the servicing commandos stayed just long enough to enable the respective wing headquarters organisation to move in for longer-term support. On the morning of 15 June, both Nos. 3205 and 3210 servicing commandos moved on to Airfield B.4 at Beny-sur-Mer, having handed over their responsibilities to the airfield headquarters element of the Canadian No.144 Wing. The airfield was used until 4 September 1944. Just outside the village of Sainte-Croix-sur-Mer stands a small memorial to the airfield and the men who fought there.

No.3205 group of the Servicing Commando went on to provide start-up refuelling and rearming support at Airfields B.4 Beny-sur-Mer and B.10 Plumetot when they became operational and then moved to Sainte-Croix-sur-Tonne carrying out various aircraft maintenance and salvage work until they returned to the United Kingdom at the end of July 1944. Their work remained hazardous: in mid-June during a five-day spell in an orchard at Villiers-le-Sec for rest and reequipping with Typhoon spares, two airmen were wounded by fragments after the explosion of an enemy high explosive anti-personnel bomb. One of the men ended up being evacuated to the United Kingdom by sea the next day whilst the other was able to return to light duties.

After their accompanying role at Beny-sur-Mer, No.3210 Servicing Commando trod a different route, moving on to Airfield B.9 Lantheuil on 20 June and then B.7 Martragny at the end of the month assisting No.405 Repair and Salvage Unit. During the early part of July, the unit carried out work for No.85 Group's heavy glider repair unit on gliders in the Benouville district. Even at this stage of the campaign in the lodgement area such work out in the open was still hazardous. The unit diarist described how 'work proceeded quite well despite occasional shelling and attacks by enemy aircraft'.

FORWARD AIR BASES IN EUROPE FROM D-DAY TO THE BALTIC

RAF servicing commandoes refuelling a spitfire using 5-gallon jerry cans. (*Crown Copyright – Air Historical Branch MoD*)

After a few days, though, work had to stop when the enemy shelled the position when they saw that a completed glider was being moved to a more sheltered position. The rest of the month found them involved in repairing various battle-damaged aircraft before the unit also returned to the United Kingdom at the end of July 1944. The work of both servicing commando units was acknowledged in a congratulatory message from the AOC of No.85 Group:

> I wish to thank you and all ranks ... for the fine efforts you have all put up in support of the invasion of Europe. Both I and my staff [*sic*] are grateful for your loyal and successful work, and we regret much that you should have to leave us. We know that you have often wished for more work than has been given you. This reflects great credit on your enthusiasm, spirit de corps and efficiency. The best of luck for the future.

The point the AOC made about the unit wanting to have done more is an interesting issue which emerges from Phase I of the campaign. The unit diarist of No.3210 Servicing Commando had commented at the end of June that 'it must be recorded that they could have coped with at least three times as much work' and were 'disappointed that more work could not be found for them'. He concluded the entry for June 1944 with the observation that it had been 'an historic month, but WE CAN DO MORE [original caps]'.

DEVELOPING THE BRIDGEHEAD

Of the two post-war histories of the servicing commandos, the work by Peter Kellett and Jeff Davies includes an enlightening chapter which comments on this issue. Of their many insightful observations, they held a general view that the RAF and Combined Operations had a short-term view of how the commando units were tasked, with less thought being given to their longer term or wider campaign employment.[4]

This was indeed the case for the campaign in north-west Europe. It could be argued though, that by this stage of the war many lessons had been learned regarding mobile operations in expeditionary warfare. As commented on in the previous chapter, much had been done to design-in mobility to the support units of 2nd TAF. In respect of the forward air bases, the high level of mobility and independence of the airfield headquarters units meant that they were able to move in to newly found airfields quickly, thereby significantly reducing the length of time the servicing commandos were required on site. There can be no doubt that the servicing commandos were highly valued and enabled the advanced landing grounds to be up and running rapidly – in many cases, barely hours after the airfield construction engineers of the army and RAF had laid the last strip of runway surfacing.

The RAF Regiment light anti-aircraft squadrons were also a vital part of the story in these very early days. Nos. 2809, 2819 and 2834 squadrons had all landed on D+1 and were quickly up and running, providing vital low-level air defence at the airfield construction sites. A further two squadrons, Nos. 2817 and 2876 soon joined the RAF Regiment presence in the bridgehead. The convoy of three tank landing crafts carrying No.2817 Squadron was attacked by two enemy E-boats just off Le Havre between 03.00 and 04.00 hours on 8 June. Despite the efforts of Allied naval forces to keep the coastal approaches clear, these fast attack boats were able to get through and achieve several menacing hit and run raids.

The E-Boats were masters of attack, first dropping illuminating flares around their 'prey' and then shelling two ships which were carrying the squadron's personnel. The ship carrying their vehicles and guns was sunk. Tragically, three airmen of No.2817 Squadron – Sergeant James Parker, Corporal Lionel Batchelor and Leading Aircraftman Norman Dring were killed with a further three seriously wounded. Some fifty survivors were picked up by one of the ships which had escaped the attack unscathed.

By this time the convoy had broken up and the remaining vessels were off course near Le Havre at dawn. What remained of the convoy managed to land at Grange-sur-Mer during the morning and had largely managed to assemble as a squadron by late afternoon. No.2817 Squadron located to Airfield B.5 at Le Fresne-Camilly and No.2876 to Airfield B.6 Coulombs.

The men of the various RAF Regiment squadrons were to prove valuable in not just their primary roles throughout the forthcoming campaign. Those who were not manning the light anti-aircraft guns were also pressed into service with several other essential jobs to help get these early airfields up-and-running.

On 15 June, for example, fifty airmen of No.2817 Squadron at Le Fresne-Camilly, helped to unload 72,000 gallons of aviation petrol and fourteen lorry loads of ammunition, along with providing guards. By 18 June 1944, the RAF Regiment

FORWARD AIR BASES IN EUROPE FROM D-DAY TO THE BALTIC

Armourers fit rocket-projectiles to the under-wing racks of a No.247 Squadron Hawker Typhoon Mk.IB at Airfield B.6 Coulombs, Normandy on 16 June 1944. (*Crown Copyright – Air Historical Branch MoD*)

had two mobile wing headquarters and ten light anti-aircraft squadrons deployed across ten airfields in Normandy.[5]

It was thus that in just over the first week of the landings, the British had met the planners' target for D+4 and had established one emergency landing strip and two advanced landing grounds in Normandy. Up until approximately the middle of June, most 2nd TAF aircraft were returning to their bases in England for the night. From this point on though, it was judged safe enough for aircraft to stay overnight without risk of enemy air or ground attack and it became possible to start moving the squadrons in 2nd TAF from their advance landing grounds in southern England to Normandy.

Consequently, on 15 June, No.144 Wing (Nos. 441, 442 and 443 squadrons) landed their Spitfires at Airfield B.3 Sainte-Croix-sur-Mer.[6] The high degree of air superiority, coupled with the high standard of rapid airfield construction enabled Coningham to take what he considered to be a justifiable risk in concentrating more aircraft on each airfield than was originally planned. From 16 June to the end of the month a further eight British Advanced Landing Grounds were operational in Normandy (Airfields B.4 to B.11) accommodating a total of nine wings with their supporting units.

By the end of June, excluding the emergency landing strips, ten airfields had been constructed in the beachhead area. This rose to seventeen by the end of July,

DEVELOPING THE BRIDGEHEAD

of which eight had tracked runways of square mesh track and one with Bituminised hessian runways. Thirteen airfields were being operated by 24 July.

The movement plans for this operation worked extremely well enabling the squadrons to continue operating during the daytime. Each of the wings was divided into three parties consisting of a main, airlift and rear party. The main party travelled by sea and was established at the new site in Normandy before the wing was moved. While the main party was in transit (around ten to twelve days including packing-up, concentration, marshalling, shipborne time, landing and onward transit), the wings and squadrons moved to one of three back-up stations in the United Kingdom and carried on operating from that location until the advance party in Normandy signalled to say that they were ready to receive the aircraft.

The operational squadrons then flew to Normandy, accompanied by the airlift party in Dakota aircraft; the airlift requirement for a typical wing of four squadrons was approximately ten to twelve complete aircraft loads. A small rear party followed by sea after the airlift party had flown to Normandy. The rapid transfer of squadrons during June and July from the United Kingdom to Normandy, and the delay in being able to breakout from the bridgehead led to much congestion. During this time, 2nd TAF's commander commented that there was 'only standing room on the Continent for the moment'.[7]

With the servicing commandos having moved on, a more robust maintenance arrangement was required to support the ever-expanding range and number of aircraft that were now based on the Continent. This became the responsibility of what were known as the slightly misleading name of airfield headquarters. These were large units which were set up on airfields, primarily for the servicing and maintenance 2nd TAF's flying squadrons within the main groups and No.85 Group. Each of the headquarters held stocks of spare parts that would last up to seven days and were equipped to carry out aircraft servicing up to, but not including, major inspection standard.

By and large, they were not intended to repair aircraft that required more than forty-eight hours to complete or vehicle repairs that would take longer than twenty-four. The first of these headquarters that went to Normandy were equipped to be fully mobile, but those that were scheduled to land later needed the help of the supply and transport columns if they needed to move as a complete unit. This arrangement ensured that the vehicles required for complete mobility were available for those units needing them. This had been a lesson learned from the campaign in France in 1939/1940 where motor transport availability had been a major issue and the British Air Forces in France had experienced a significant lack of mobility from the underestimation of vehicle requirements.[8]

With Nos. 3205 and 3210 servicing commandos having returned to the United Kingdom at the end of July 1944, their place was filled by Nos. 3206 and 3208 servicing commandos, which landed in France on 15 and 16 June respectively. The war diaries for both units shows that they continued to support numerous 2nd TAF airfield moves in France, Belgium and the Netherlands through until April 1945 when they both returned to the United Kingdom.

FORWARD AIR BASES IN EUROPE FROM D-DAY TO THE BALTIC

Other Battles to Fight – The Normandy Dust

One of the early technical problems that the RAF experienced in Normandy was the high level of aircraft unserviceability (especially the Typhoons) resulting from the dense clouds of dust stirred up by the powerful propellers of the fighters and fighter-bombers on the forward airstrips during taxiing, landing and take-off. Once the airfield construction groups had cleared surface vegetation, the exposed soil soon began to dry out when the June weather conditions started to improve. Rainfall during the invasion period was below normal for the time of year and some 75 per cent below what would have been expected in southern England and over most of the battle area in Normandy.

Some airfields were sprayed with water to minimize the dust hazard to visibility and engine wear. Obtaining suitable volumes of water though was not easy. Whilst sea water was used, it was difficult for water bowsers to get back to the coast due to the limited access points available and the volume of incoming traffic from the beach landings. Fresh water was the alternative but many of the airfields were not always close to the water towers in local towns and it often took some time to bring in the quantities they needed.

One further complication was that water was mostly drawn by electrically powered pumps from deep underground wells. The electrical supply for this was drawn from the power generating station in Caen. The fact that this remained in enemy hands until the end of July 1944 meant that the airfield operating organisations had to obtain petrol-powered pumps.[9] At some locations a mixture of oil and water was used and sprayed on to the operating surfaces.

Where possible, the warming-up time of aircraft engines was kept to a minimum to help further reduce the stirring-up of the fine dust. In time, the ground crews gradually got the problem under control, but it took liberal measures of ingenuity and careful management to do so. Where possible, later airfields were constructed without disturbing grass surfaces, whilst a rougher surface could be tolerated in the dispersal areas.

The source of the problem was the largely loessic, friable soils, which had a very high silica content, and which led to a build-up on the aircraft engine spark plugs. Much of this dust came about from being pounded day and night by vehicles, especially from tank tracks. It was worse on small roads where the surface was easily broken up and in many places was inches thick. It was particularly prone to being blown by the wind onto sites in fields and personnel found it virtually impossible to keep it out of tents and food stores.

Operationally, though, it was to aircraft that it became particularly troublesome and by mid-June 1944 this had become a serious problem for the RAF. The Spitfire benefitted from operations in North Africa and already had a filter system fitted. Trials on the Typhoon had been carried out with a small number of aircraft fitted with a tropical air intake. For various reasons, the aircraft was not used in the Mediterranean theatre and there was no need to modify further aircraft. Consequently, 2nd TAF Typhoons suffered greatly from the Normandy dust.

DEVELOPING THE BRIDGEHEAD

A Supermarine Spitfire IX fitted with a 45-gallon slipper fuel tank, raises the dust as it taxies past a Hawker Typhoon Mk.Ib of No.181 Squadron at Airfield B.2 Bazenville, Normandy on 17 June 1944. On the port wing can be seen a member of the groundcrew operating as a 'spotter' for the pilot to avoid holes and obstacles at the temporary airstrip. (*Crown Copyright – Air Historical Branch MoD*)

A short-term, emergency solution was found however, and a circular plate was fitted in front of the air intake, which was estimated to be 53 per cent efficient. Following further investigation, two further designs were produced, the first of these was produced by Napier (the aircraft's engine manufacturer) and was judged to be 88 per cent at take-off power. The second design was produced by the Royal Aircraft Establishment in conjunction with Vokes Engineering Limited at Henley Park near Guildford, which was judged to be 93 per cent efficient. There were advantages and disadvantages of both filters, but eventually 200 of Napier's design and 1,500 of the Royal Aircraft Establishment/Vokes filter were ordered, the first batch of which were delivered in early July and the remainder just a few weeks after. The new filters proved highly effective and, once fitted, the problem was virtually eliminated.

It was not just aircraft engines that suffered from the Normandy dust. The RAF's aircraft armourers soon found that aircraft cannons were suffering frequent stoppages due to dust ingress. The solution to that was more basic; joints were taped over, and the spent rounds ejector ports had tissue fixed over them sealed with a coat of dope varnish. Once airborne, the first round fired broke this seal.

FORWARD AIR BASES IN EUROPE FROM D-DAY TO THE BALTIC

Now You See Me, Now You Don't

Whilst the Allies had secured much needed air superiority over the bridgehead, there was always a risk of enemy air attack, especially during the early weeks following the invasion. Amidst the many support organisations working hard behind the scenes, 2nd TAF used the expertise and ingenuity of RAF camouflage and concealment units to hide its hardware in the field. This was relatively straightforward for vehicles, but the newly constructed airstrips were another matter altogether. Most of the strips constructed in the bridgehead area had been cleared by bulldozers, after trees and vegetation had been cut down.

The result, whilst providing a blank canvas for a new runway, stood out as a scar on the landscape, especially when viewed from the air. It was in the interests of the ground crews on these airstrips to do their bit to make it less obvious what the purpose of the sites were. Imagination, rather than technology, was often effective in tricking the eye as an account from a veteran of the Royal Canadian Air Force shows. Frank LeBlanc, then a flight sergeant airframe mechanic with No.421 (Red Indian) Squadron, was based at Airfield B.2 at Bazenville. This airstrip had been constructed on the site of a former orchard, with the tress having been cut down and the wire netting laid on the surface. Frank recalled that they 'even had imitation cows, black and white, made out of wheelbarrows that we would spread out here and there. That way, if the Germans flew over, they wouldn't see that it was a landing strip'.[10]

It was not just enemy air attack which proved troublesome; enemy shelling also proved to be costly, both in terms of human lives and aircraft. The war diary of No.1301 Mobile Wing RAF Regiment recorded how, on 17 July 1944, the day after they arrived on site at Airfield B.12 at Ellon:

> The airfield was shelled by the enemy. Shelling was in two phases from 03.30 to 03.40 hours and again from 04.30 hours to 04.45 hours. Approx. 80 x 80 mm shells were fired (anti-personnel). Two airmen were killed, one other died from wounds, and six airmen were injured. Twenty aircraft were damaged, and a petrol bowser set alight. The shelling was answered by our artillery.[11]

To protect and cover potential beach targets from enemy bombing attacks at night on GOLD and SWORD beaches up to the end of June 1944, five concealment and deception parties (identified as A to E) were tasked with putting in place a range of measures. Parties A to E were initially composed of both RAF and army Royal Engineers, but these became staffed by entirely RAF personnel by D+9/10. Party E was made up entirely of Royal Engineers. Parties A and B worked around Arromanches at the western end of GOLD Beach (No.30 Corps landing area) and set up a complete decoy beach to the west of the town, along with several decoy beach exits from the coastline. Parties C to E worked on SWORD Beach (1 Corps landing area) and provided similar deceptions to those on GOLD Beach.

A well camouflaged group of vehicles belonging to No.401 Air Stores Park, Normandy, June 1944. *(Author's collection)*

In addition to a decoy beach and beach exits, they also put in place decoy bridges over the river Orne and Canal de Caen à la Mer. Summary reports on each of the areas, apart from the work required at the eastern end of SWORD Beach, which remained in enemy hands for some time, show that the work was largely successful. Whilst enemy bombing was never intensive, the effort was well worth it and it was estimated that at least half of their attacks were carried out on the decoy sites.[12]

Field Living

Unlike their army comrades and the men of the RAF Regiment, living under field conditions was something many of the RAF were not accustomed to. Having said that, those who had served their time in North Africa and Italy earlier in the war had become used to this. Given the large numbers, which were now heading to Normandy there were still many who had served much of the war on the relative comfort of RAF bases where accommodation was invariably in buildings with heating and lighting. Coningham's reminder to his men, back when 2nd TAF was formed 'that they were about to go on campaign' became a reality for all those who went to Normandy and became part of the campaign thereafter.

FORWARD AIR BASES IN EUROPE FROM D-DAY TO THE BALTIC

Broadly speaking, the 160lb ridge tent was the mainstay for sleeping and office use. Once the breakout occurred and the advance began, much greater use was made of requisitioned buildings albeit these had to be carefully checked before occupation to ensure that booby traps, a commonplace legacy from the retreating Germans, had been removed. Sadly, and despite regular warnings, many casualties were sustained, often due to a combination of carelessness and curiosity. Much later in the campaign, a wide range of building types became regular haunts, ranging from luxury hotels and villas to disused cattle sheds and farm buildings.

By the winter of 1944, most RAF units had found themselves in this sort of accommodation, with even poor-quality buildings seen as preferable in the poor weather that year. It was a degree of comfort that was relatively short lived as once the move across the Rhine began in Phase IV (February 1945 onwards), most saw themselves return to the tented norm of greater mobility and field service conditions.

Field living did need to be managed carefully, with standards of health and hygiene monitored closely. It was nothing new and from time to time, generations of warriors before them had endured the infections and diseases, which can result from poor standards of hygiene in the field. It was not just a matter of inconvenience – outbreaks of disease and infections can have a debilitating effect on fighting efficiency. Perhaps the most devastating example is the Crimean War (1854–1856) where out of the 730,000 British, French and Russian combatants, 34,000 were killed in action, 26,000 died from wounds and 130,000 died from diseases such as cholera and typhus.[13]

With so many men pouring into and confined to Normandy for nearly two months since D-Day before the breakout, hygiene became a growing concern. The invasion and constant push to drive back the enemy had understandably placed a focus on maintaining the best possible operational efficiency. Medical staff soon noticed that health and hygiene standards were not being maintained and, in some cases, 'was of a very low, even dangerous standard'.

The official medical history commented that personnel 'were liable to relegate such matters as sanitation to the background as of little importance – forgetting the part hygiene itself played in keeping the men efficient'. Perhaps more worrying was the official historian's prosaic suggestion that units were of the view that 'we are very busy and are likely to move any moment, so what is the use in digging holes and constructing appliances which we may never use?'

Notwithstanding what had been drummed into the men during pre-invasion training, 2nd TAF's Air Officer in charge of administration became particularly concerned at how standards were being maintained. As early as 16 June – just ten days after they first set foot on French soil – he issued a general directive to TAF units in which he reminded units of the importance of protecting food against flies and dirt, leaving camp sites clean on vacation and the need for food handlers to maintain high standards of cleanliness. Unit officers were also required to inspect cookhouses and latrines once a week and to inspect the hands of all cooks and food handlers. It was a timely warning because by early July, several cases of enteritis had developed. These gradually increased towards the end of the month causing serious concern. The exact number of cases contracted is difficult to pin down but, during July, nearly seventy cases were severe enough to warrant admission to hospital, albeit for only around three to four days at a time. Nonetheless, at its height, the outbreak was estimated to have affected around 20 per cent of the force and most certainly lowered the output of work.

Hygiene became much improved and easier to maintain after the breakout from the lodgement area, mainly because airmen had become used to maintaining hygiene in the field, a factor greatly aided by a move into 'clean' country uncontaminated by large numbers of resident troops and with the onset of colder weather in the autumn and winter.[14] Interestingly, cases increased markedly when 'compo' rations ceased to be issued in the latter part of July and many units went on to field rations. Compo rations had been the mainstay during the early days of the invasion as they were easy to transport and could be issued to individuals with packs designed to cover a set period, which proved to be useful when communal feeding was not possible during periods of enemy activity.

Overall, the availability of food and drink does not seem to attract much comment in the records although the lack of variety in diet after many weeks on compo rations does seem to have taken the edge off this convenient means of feeding the troops. Not surprisingly though, there were two areas of complaint concerning the popular British beverage of tea plus biscuits, which were provided as a substitute for fresh bread. Tea was provided in the form of a compressed tablet of tea, milk and sugar and described as 'a brew foreign to the average English palate'. The biscuit substitute for bread was not popular and was summed up by one medical officer who remarked 'If I have another b..... biscuit, I'll bark'. The supply of water in the lodgement area was a notable success and the supply of safe water was an army responsibility.

By all accounts they did a tremendous job with most RAF units collecting their supplies in 350-gallon water carts, which were provided based on 1 cart per 350 men. Supplies of water were usually sufficient to enable men to do their own laundry with an increased ration of soap being made available to do this. The men were encouraged to wash their clothes as regularly as possible, but the official medical history notes that in the dust laden atmosphere of the Norman countryside, 'clothes often appeared no cleaner after washing than before'.

Whilst RAF personnel gradually became accustomed to the vagaries of life on campaign and the challenges of field living, such conditions also gave rise to a range of accidents in addition to battle casualties and medical conditions. Broadly speaking there were four main types that were experienced. Firstly, and most frequent, were injuries sustained from the mishandling of firearms. Unlike their army comrades, many RAF personnel were not used to handling weapons on a regular basis. There was, as the official medical history recounts, a tendency for men to '"fiddle" with arms, with the obvious result'. This was particularly common with captured German arms taken as war 'souvenirs'.

Secondly, burns from petrol fires were often sustained when trying to brew up some tea on the spur of the moment. Ordinary vehicle fuel was dangerous enough but with RAF personnel having access to 100 octane aviation fuel the outcome could be even more tragic.

FORWARD AIR BASES IN EUROPE FROM D-DAY TO THE BALTIC

The administration tent of HQ No.401 Air Stores Park, Normandy, 1944. *(Author's collection)*

A third category, albeit limited to a specific group of individuals, was motorcycle accidents involving despatch riders. The carriage of urgent messages by motorcycle was commonplace but did involve bikes being ridden at high speed, often on poor quality surfaces, congested with tanks and tracked vehicles. Coupled with the dust problem in Normandy, it was inevitable that this would happen.

Fourth, and particularly common in the Beach Maintenance Area, were fractures sustained by personnel on unloading duties. This was particularly seen when unloading supplies from boats in rough seas. It was not unknown for men to lose their balance or footing in such conditions and to fall back into holds or be crushed by runaway vehicles and heavy freight. There was little that could be done to avoid this and was an unfortunate fact of life for many.[15]

Supplies to Normandy

Hand in glove with the development of the forward airfields and the gradual basing of 2nd TAF's flying squadrons on the Continent was the need to keep them resupplied with the wide range of stores and supplies, which were required to support the ever-growing number of aircraft, men and equipment. Most units carried sufficient stocks to keep them going for several days after landing, but it

DEVELOPING THE BRIDGEHEAD

was not long before the Allied Expeditionary Air Force Forward Equipment Unit at RAF Bicester back in the United Kingdom started to send its first consignment to Normandy.

On 11 June an urgent requirement was despatched, comprising of thirty-six complete tool kits of various types for No.3207 RAF Servicing Commando to replace similar kits lost by enemy action. A few days later on 13 June, a daily freight service by fast sea coaster from Southampton began operating. Additionally, a low/high loader vehicle service (Queen Mary semi-trailer) began operating via RAF Gosport, near Portsmouth. The vehicles and trailers were invariably backloaded with crashed or seriously damaged aircraft for attention by various maintenance units of the RAF's repair organisation in the United Kingdom.[16]

Air transport was used for urgent requirements although the first such trip was not made until a week after D-Day, on 13 June, when emergency supplies were flown into Airfield B.2 at Bazenville by No.271 Squadron. The planned, regular air freight service to Airfield B.6 at Coulombs did not commence until 6 July. This destination was virtually at the heart of the RAF's sector of the Rear Maintenance Area, which was developing around Bayeux and became quite a busy air transport hub. The service consisted of three Dakota aircraft daily with each aircraft carrying 4,500lbs of freight.

These operated from No.46 Group airfields in the United Kingdom with each receiving their daily loads directly from the Forward Equipment Unit at RAF Bicester. Whilst this service worked well, it is surprising that the aircraft were not flown into and out of Bicester directly, thereby saving transport, time and

A *Queen Mary* trailer pictured just after the war. This view shows how large sections of aircraft could be transported with relative ease. *(Author's collection)*

labour. Nonetheless, a wide range of cargo was carried including medical supplies, armament, some munitions, aircraft spares, vehicles and personnel. Empty cargo space on return flights was used extensively for casualty evacuation. By the end of August 1944, No.46 Group had carried some 2,636 long tons of freight plus 8,815 passengers to the Continent and evacuated 22,814 casualties.[17]

One commodity that was particularly challenging to move and accumulate, especially during the period of temporary maintenance, was bulk aviation fuel. The high-performance aero engines that had been developed by this stage of the war were particularly fuel hungry. The Supermarine Spitfire, for example, consumed some 60 to 90 gallons per hour. It took twenty-five jerry cans to fill the 122-gallon internal fuel tanks from empty.

The planner's target, requiring an emergency landing strip to be up-and-running on D-Day, followed by two refuelling and rearming strips and five advanced landing grounds in little over a week, put pressure on the supply organisation for sufficient aviation fuel to be on hand quickly. In the early days of the landings, it was agreed that the army would transport fuel jerry cans to the airstrips, until the RAF could take over and pre-stock new operating sites as they were established. It was planned that fourteen days' reserve of fuel needed to be on hand by D+41.

The optimal solution for aviation fuel was the establishment of bulk stocks in tanks and bowser vehicles to make transfers and for refuelling. This would come, once fuel could be brought ashore from sea going tankers and piped to bulk storage tanks in the Rear Maintenance Area. With this stage of the landings under control, the idea was to then establish the more permanent base maintenance area into which the arriving stores and supplies could be accumulated.

The arrangements put in place for the supply of aviation fuel worked particularly well during this time and enabled the RAF to build up reserve stocks in Normandy much as planned. Initially, though, much of the initial stocks of aviation fuel came ashore by hand in the ubiquitous 5-gallon jerry can. Once the tactical situation permitted, the use of the small harbour at Port-en-Bessin close to Arromanches, enabled aviation fuel tankers to discharge their loads via onshore pipelines, to bulk storage tanks at Coulombs in the Rear Maintenance Area; the first such discharge took place on 2 July.[18] By 20 July, RAF holdings of aviation fuel in Normandy amounted to some 816,000 gallons; due to this favourable stock position, 2nd TAF saw no reason at that time to submit bids for the period D+74 to D+83. A similar position had been achieved for stocks of munitions.[19] What is not generally known is that the Allied *Pluto* pipelines (operational from late September 1944) were used only for ground use petroleum products and not aviation fuel. This was primarily due to the need to maintain much higher quality control standards for aero engine use. Even when it was cleared, the channel from Le Havre was shallow, but coastal tankers carrying fuel from the United Kingdom were able to navigate it and discharge in Rouen. Boulogne was captured on 22 September, and the port was opened for Allied use on 22 October.

The disembarkation and build-up of the RAF in the bridgehead was rapid. By the afternoon of 9 June, 3,537 of its men and 815 vehicles had been landed. By 13 June, the RAF had managed to stockpile enough aviation fuel, ammunition, and rocket projectiles to support three day's maximum effort of 200 sorties a day. By 20 June, these figures had increased to 1,300 men and 3,200 vehicles having been disembarked. On this date too, the RAF had amassed some 3,000 tons of fuel in dumps and at certain airfields, 2,500 gallons of oil and 500,000 rounds of ammunition.[20]

Mulberry Eases the Load

As described previously, the much-needed facilities of the Mulberry harbours needed to be put in place. On 7 June (D+1), the first of the caissons (codenamed *Phoenixes*) had been moved into position. These were large concrete chambers, which had been floated across and then sunk in position to form some 6 miles of breakwater. As the campaign unfolded men worked night and day to build the complex infrastructure, which then followed. By 13 June, enough of Mulberry B had been constructed to accommodate up to seventy-five Liberty ships and other, smaller vessels.

Whilst much of the operating workforce at Mulberry B were army personnel, the RAF provided similar specialists from its embarkation units. These units had been formed before the war as embarkation offices, embarkation staff or port detachments. All of these units had a very similar role, which included the loading and unloading of stores, as well as the embarkation and disembarkation of personnel. This took place mainly at the seaports in the United Kingdom but then overseas at increasingly more locations as the war progressed; this miscellany of units was renamed embarkation units during the autumn/winter of 1941/1942. Three new units were formed for *Overlord* in February and March 1944 and were intended to be allotted to the first two British-operated ports to be opened and the British Mulberry at Arromanches. The unit based at Arromanches also looked after the discharge and sorting of the large quantity of stores brought ashore by the ubiquitous DUKW amphibious vehicles, to the transit area behind the Mulberry harbour.

A fourth unit was allotted to the American Mulberry at OMAHA Beach but was moved to Cherbourg in early July after the American port was abandoned after the great storm on 19 June 1944. A fifth unit was formed in early June 1944 and moved to Dieppe in early September 1944.[21] The embarkation units were further reinforced by a number of men from the four RAF beach squadrons, which were disbanded in August 1944 by which time there was no requirement to land men and *materiel* on the open beaches. Within the first three weeks of Mulberry B being opened for use, RAF stores were already accounting for approximately 10 per cent of the tonnage coming through the port.

The technical achievement of the Mulberry harbours has not surprisingly attracted many accolades since the war. Some historians, however, and perhaps with the benefit of hindsight and analysis in isolation from the broader campaign, have questioned whether the effort and the significant material and labour costs were worth it.[22] Although the installation and operation of Mulberry B took place

FORWARD AIR BASES IN EUROPE FROM D-DAY TO THE BALTIC

Unloading supplies at a Spud pierhead on Mulberry B, Arromanches. (*Crown Copyright – Air Historical Branch MoD*)

largely during Phase I of the campaign, the vehicles, equipment and supplies enabled substantial reserves to be built-up for 2nd TAF, which lasted well into the advance from the bridgehead in August and September 1944. The unloading of British cargo and personnel through Mulberry B had largely come to a halt by the beginning of November 1944 and was not used substantially after 19 November. Dismantling of this marvel of civil engineering commenced on 2 December.

Debate continues regrading just how effective the harbour was. The target dates for achieving certain tonnages of stores discharge were somewhat optimistic and a post-war report on the part the 'synthetic' harbours played in *Overlord* does make the point that the actual figures did fall short of expectations.[23] Nevertheless, the harbour provided a vital facility for the unloading of ships until suitable ports could be captured. In the five months that the harbour was in use over 2 million men, half a million vehicles and over 4 million tons of supplies passed through it.

DEVELOPING THE BRIDGEHEAD

As will be appreciated from this and the previous chapter, landing men and *materiel* on the open beaches was labour intensive and hugely time consuming. For the larger vessels, this required offloading to smaller vessels, thus leading to double handling as, in turn, the vessels would have to be unloaded again onshore. Although the breakout from Normandy took much longer than planned, it needed the resources, especially combat supplies, to be brought ashore quickly and assembled in concentration areas ready for the off.

Whilst 2nd TAF was initially operating from airfields in the bridgehead it would need its support units and their resources on hand to develop the forward air bases in France and the Low Countries. Mulberry B enabled the larger vessels, especially those carrying the vehicles to be unloaded quickly and without double handling. This was all the more important given that the first major French port at Cherbourg was not captured until just after two weeks from when Mulberry B was up and running on 11 June 1944.

The Rear Maintenance Area Develops

As the bridgehead was consolidated, the Rear Maintenance Area was established in the area surrounding Bayeux. This was ideally placed in terms of road communication links and was just inland from the British Mulberry harbour at Arromanches.

The delay in the breakout from Normandy and the air superiority which had been achieved, enabled substantial volumes of stores and supplies to be accumulated throughout June and July; this proved to be particularly advantageous as it 'primed' the supply chain and enabled an almost continuous source of supply until the line of communication was stretched to its limit in Belgium and the Netherlands. During the build-up period of the campaign, support for 2nd TAF units was straightforward as the distance between the bridgehead airfields and the Rear Maintenance Area was relatively short.

One particularly important aspect of support provided in the Rear Maintenance Area was medical services. By D+8, the majority of the RAF's Nos. 50 and 52 (Royal Canadian Air Force) mobile field hospitals had arrived in Normandy and had established their operating locations to the east of Bayeux as part of No.83 Group. Like many units setting up in the Rear Maintenance Area during the early days following the landings, No.50 Mobile Hospital found that it was still uncomfortably close to the enemy's presence.

Having landed on 14 June, the hospital established its first operating location at Creully and just as they were moving into the site, they were visited by an army brigadier 'whose utility was held up by the hospital's lorries turning into the field'. He expressed surprise that a hospital was setting up so far forward as, apparently, the enemy was just 3,000 yards down the road! An urgent visit to HQ No.83 Group reassured the unit that there were just small pockets of resistance remaining and the nearest larger presence of the enemy was some 4 miles away. With much hard work erecting tents and equipment, the hospital was up and running, ready to receive patients by the morning of 15 June.

FORWARD AIR BASES IN EUROPE FROM D-DAY TO THE BALTIC

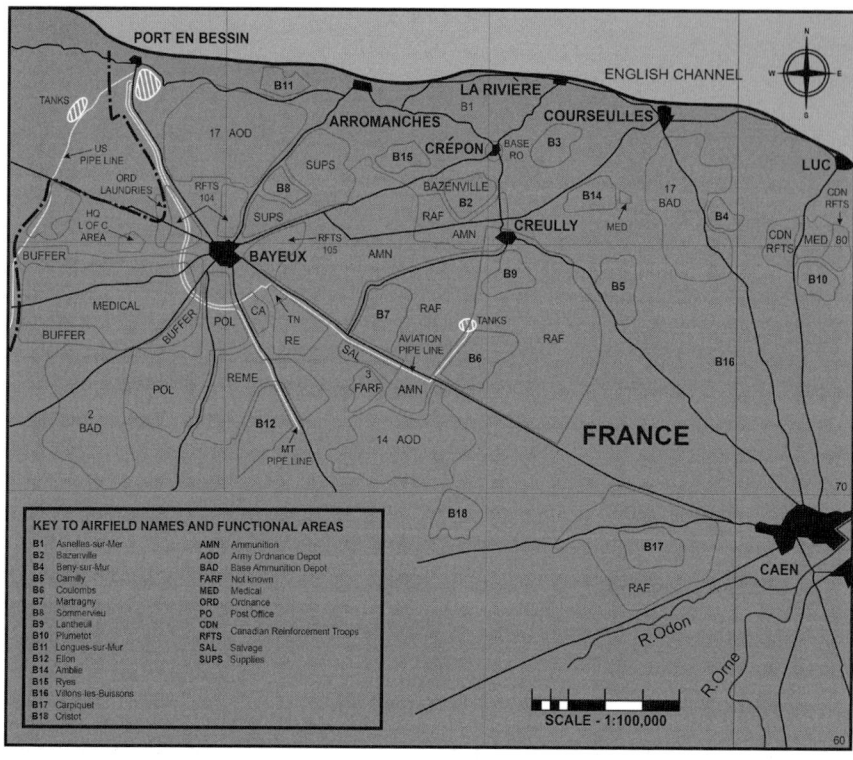

Map 2. Final Layout of the Rear Maintenance Area in Normandy.[24]

The RAF's No.50 Mobile Field Hospital also held the distinction of having the first British women to land in France as part of their nursing complement. Sisters (flying officers) Mollie Giles of Barry, South Wales and Sister Iris Ogilvie of Swansea, formerly of St Mary's Hospital, Paddington had landed with their male compatriots on 14 June and endured the same hardships since their arrival. The British press, however, took great delight in a stereotypical report (for the time) following the two ladies taking some well-earned time-off in Bayeux on 22 June 1944.

The Reuter's correspondents reported in the *News Chronicle* that:

> Two RAF nursing sisters – they were the first British women to land in France after the invasion – have made the occupation of Bayeux complete. They invaded it yesterday with a handful of francs and revelled in the town's supply of cosmetics, bought a few bottles of wine, dined at the best hotel, and bought a 'a few snips of things; ... Their charm added a welcome feminine touch to Bayeux, which is packed with grim and tough-looking soldiers.[25]

DEVELOPING THE BRIDGEHEAD

Similar articles appeared in the *Daily Sketch* and the *Belfast Telegraph* that same month, but the latter was somewhat more enlightening in terms of the hazards and hardship both women had faced.

In August and September 1944, three further such units would arrive in Normandy to bolster the RAF's mobile medical capability (Nos. 53, 54 and 55) and accompanied 2nd TAF as they advanced.[26] When the breakout from Normandy was made, the forward deployment of the mobile field hospitals away from Normandy and the extent over which the Allies held control, soon justified the establishment of the large and semi-static No.8 RAF General Hospital which was established in tented accommodation in the Bayeux area in mid-August, becoming fully operational by the end of that month.

Hand in glove with the field hospitals of course was the requirement to evacuate casualties requiring urgent treatment to the United Kingdom. In the initial campaign planning it had been estimated that no large-scale evacuation of casualties would be possible from the beachhead area until at least D+28, into the first week of July 1944. Army planning was therefore working on largely sea evacuation of casualties up to that date.

It was soon recognised, however, that the Dakotas that were soon airlifting in bombs, fuel and other urgently required supplies could be utilised for casualty evacuation on their return journey to the United Kingdom. Some 180 to 250 stretcher cases alone could be transported this way which was much faster than by sea. In the early days following the landings, this rather ad hoc casualty airlift used personnel from the RAF's No.50 Mobile Field Hospital's Advance Surgical Team and from the Canadian manned No.127 Wing in No.83 Group. Initially, this enabled two temporary mobile evacuation units to be formed.

A third unit was formed from personnel in the Canadian No.52 Mobile Field Hospital, but this remained static as it was conveniently situated within 2 miles of the airfields at Bazenville and St Croix. The Dakotas enabled a sizeable number of casualties to be evacuated each day, amounting to between 100 and 400 per day, depending on whether they were sitting, or stretcher borne cases. The casualty evacuation units were usually set up approximately 500 yards from the perimeter of the airfield to minimise problems from dust and the marquee type tents used were of course well camouflaged.

Despite the temporary nature of these early air evacuation operations, they soon evolved into a well-honed operation, albeit the use of personnel away from the mobile field hospital made it somewhat challenging in terms of manning. With much appreciated assistance from the RAF Police, who signposted the units and provided marshals to direct the ambulance convoys at confusing road junctions, arrival of the casualties was timed to about two hours before the inbound Dakota's estimated arrival time. It was not always plain sailing as aircraft could be delayed due to bad weather and ambulances because of congestion on the roads.

An indication of the typical complexity of the arrangements is graphically depicted in the content of a signal received at No.50 Mobile Field Hospital from the senior medical officer of the casualty evacuation section on 16 June:

FORWARD AIR BASES IN EUROPE FROM D-DAY TO THE BALTIC

> H.715 June 16. Send out D.R. [*despatch rider*] to recall your evacuation from B.4 and send them to B.5. T.950780 CAMILLY. If B.5 under shell fire bivouac at safe distance and move in the morning. If still under shell fire in the morning, move to B.6. T.890760 COULOMBS. 13 Dakotas E.T.A. 10.00 [hours]. Will land at CAMILLY if not under shell fire but if under shell fire at COULOMBS.[27]

In addition to attention from medical staff following arrival, patients were provided with very welcome hot tea and snacks, along with the ubiquitous supplies of cigarettes, chocolate and periodicals, which were flown over on the inbound aircraft. Broadly speaking, most of the casualties had been wounded just ten to fifteen hours prior to arrival and little beyond basic first aid and therapy was seen as necessary.

This initial arrangement was a great success and over 3,000 casualties were evacuated between D+7 and D+28, the latter date of which was the original earliest evacuation by air estimation. In practice, there were considerably more slots available on returning aircraft, but aircraft could often be landing at three or four airfields, and it was not possible to transport the casualties to all the available aircraft. The timing, destinations and numbers of inbound aircraft also proved to be difficult to manage – sometimes just three- or four-hours' notice was given, destination airfields changed at the last moment and greater numbers of aircraft than expected all played a part in making the air evacuation process challenging. Despite the success of the initial, temporary arrangement, it was not until November

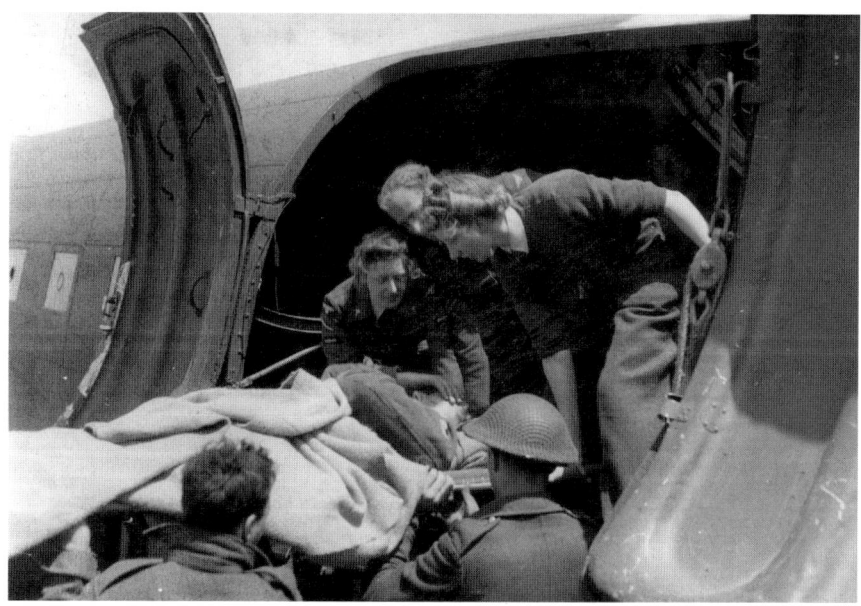

A casualty is lifted onto a Dakota for repatriation to the United Kingdom from France in June 1944. (*Crown Copyright – Air Historical Branch MoD*)

DEVELOPING THE BRIDGEHEAD

1944 that a dedicated casualty air evacuation unit (No.1) was formed at Airfield B.56 Evere in Belgium.[28]

There were also several problems with supplies at this time, despite the herculean efforts that had been made to build up combat stocks prior to a breakout from Normandy. Despite the maximum effort to accumulate sufficient stocks of the vital resources to support air operations, the RAF still found itself short of aircraft bombs in theatre. Much of this problem resulted from the difficulties associated with the handling of such munitions. Every effort was made to break this shortage starting with the use of five special ships each loaded with 350 tons of bombs.

When this still did not meet the need, thirty Dakota aircraft, each loaded with 2.5 tons of 500lb bombs were flown in from the United Kingdom. Hand in glove with the need for these munitions were the accompanying requirements of many other vital consumables essential to get aircraft off the ground. By the end of July 1944, the various air defence flying squadrons and administrative units of No.85 Group were well established within the lodgement area and as prepared as they could be for the imminent breakout and advance.

The RAF Airfield Construction Squadrons Arrive

The end of June and the first half of July 1944 saw the two mobile squadrons of the RAF's No.5357 (Airfield Construction) Wing – Nos. 5022 and 5023 move to France. On 12 July, the wing headquarters and elements of No.5022 Squadron eventually arrived at Bretteville-l'Orgueilleuse, on the outskirts of Caen, just north-west of Airfield B.17 at Carpiquet and dug in. Even though the strategically important city of Caen had been captured on 9 July, their arrival was, as the unit's war diary records 'greeted by the arrival of seven shells in an adjoining field but they were not deterred – they just dug deeper'.[29]

In the days following their arrival, the squadron was involved in a number of repair and maintenance tasks, notably at Carpiquet where they assisted the army's engineers with repairing the heavily damaged airport. Their skills were also put to wider use including the modification of a chateau for use as an RAF club. No.5357 (Airfield Construction) Wing was also involved in a series of trials involving the spraying of oil on airfield surfaces to help reduce the generation of dust by aircraft and vehicles.

No.5023 Squadron had arrived a few weeks earlier at the end of June and had been involved in carrying out maintenance work and improvements to the airfields at B.2, B.3, B.4, B.7 and B.8, which had been built by the army. They also loaned some plant and RAF operators to the army's Royal Engineers to help with the urgently needed earth road from Tilly-sur-Seulles to Bayeux. This plant was working under shell fire and their services were greatly appreciated by the army engineers.[30]

As the bridgehead developed throughout June and July, the RAF's semi-mobile airfield construction wings gradually moved to Normandy and proved to be highly versatile with their civil engineering skills soon in demand. No.5352 Wing, for example, was involved in the by-pass around Bayeux including the construction of a reinforced concrete bridge. The use of air power in the lengthy battles to capture Caen soon reduced much of the town to rubble, literally making it impassable to Allied road traffic. The wing was again tasked with road construction to build a 2.5-mile long by-pass that could carry 8,000 vehicles a day. They were given twelve days to complete the work but completed by 21.00 hours on the eleventh day.[31]

Command and Control

Broadly speaking, the various command and control elements of the higher-level formations in 2nd TAF remained in the United Kingdom until it was safe or timely to move them to the Continent. Elements of HQ No.83 Group though, came ashore quite early in the campaign and provided a local command function for main HQ 2nd TAF until they deployed to Normandy. This was essential in order that all RAF units in the initial lodgement and bridgehead areas had a single controlling formation.

The AOC of No.83 Group also had responsibility for calling into Normandy the required RAF units as and when they were needed. This was critical as it helped minimise the extent of the congestion in Normandy that was experienced following the landings. No.83 Group also needed to establish their presence in Normandy much more quickly than their fellow groups in 2nd TAF as their wings were required to move forward more rapidly in support of the more dynamic daily movements of the British Second Army after the breakout from the bridgehead.

Time was not quite so critical for the command and control of No.84 Group. The commitment to supporting the Canadians did not require such a rapid change of air bases and it was not until mid-July when the advance elements of their main headquarters arrived in Normandy. The group's main headquarters arrived on 6 August and located alongside HQ First Canadian Army. Like many of 2nd TAF's units at this time, the headquarters were sited in one of the many orchards which were so commonplace in the Normandy farmland. The close-siting of HQ 2nd TAF to their supported army formations proved to be vital throughout the campaign as it unfolded.

A small administrative team from No.85 Base (Group) deployed to France at the beginning of July, attaching themselves to the already up and running HQ No.83 Group enabling control of the build-up of its units in what would become the Rear Maintenance Area, predominantly around Bayeux.

Each of the groups within 2nd TAF had its own headquarters comprising the AOC and his support staff. The HQ No.85 Group also had the following elements within it:

> AEAF Postal Command HQ Section.
>
> AEAF Command Salvage Officer.
>
> Command Inspector of Explosives.
>
> RAF Chief Base Censor's Office.

DEVELOPING THE BRIDGEHEAD

Overseas Distribution Centre for the distribution of secret and confidential publications to all AEAF units on the Continent.

No.4 Air Despatch Letter Service Traffic Office. To handle official correspondence and parcels to and from the Continent.

HQ No.5139 Bomb Disposal Squadron. To administer the six bomb disposal flights and advise the AOC on all bomb disposal matters.

The other aspect of the command-and-control requirement for 2nd TAF was the direct control of its aircraft. The Group Control Centres were key to the effective control and directing of 2nd TAF's aircraft, primarily using information provided by mobile radar units. Individual centres were each established for Nos. 83, 84 and 85 groups.

The importance of effective ground control had been one of the RAF's success factors during the Battle of Britain where Fighter Command's Sector Control Centres had been the lynchpin, harnessing the information from the Chain Home radar network and observations made by the Royal Observer Corps outposts. This enabled them to plot the height, direction and position of incoming enemy air attacks and to make important and timely decisions about what fighter squadrons were operationally available and which could be 'scrambled' to meet the threat. The concept, unsurprisingly, was used for the control of 2nd TAF's aircraft.

There was a big difference though – the whole network that enabled this had to be mobile. The control centres were usually situated in a dedicated cabin next to group operations rooms and housed a large table-top map which showed the airborne activity in their area of responsibility (for example, height, numbers and identity of aircraft). Communication was vital in all this, with mobile signals units providing radio telephony, wireless telegraphy, and landline telephone connections from the various types of mobile radar units.[32]

For controlling 2nd TAF's fighter-bomber aircraft in the front-line area, small, mobile visual control posts were deployed. The crew and equipment of each post were carried in two specially modified American made White Scout Cars, which would position themselves at a good vantage point so that the target could be observed, enabling them to control the attacking aircraft. They were equipped with VHF radio telephony for communicating with aircraft, wireless telegraphy for communicating with the respective group control centre and other radio sets to link-up with the army. Requests for air support in the battle area were usually made to the control post which, in turn, fed the requirement to the group control centre, which would then task the best placed flying squadron with the mission. The final briefing of pilots of the attacking aircraft were provided by the visual control post when the aircraft were en-route to the target.

It was soon found that there were two limitations to this method of control. Firstly, it was not possible to cover any sizeable area and, secondly, the positions of the forward troops flanking the brigade that the posts were supporting was not always certain. This led to the visual control posts being replaced by a forward control post that operated from army divisional headquarters. The visual control element was catered for by installing duplicate communications equipment in converted Canadian built Ram tanks, based on the American M3 Medium tank chassis. It was soon found that the actual location of the forward control post was not critical, provided the information received was accurate and timely. Later in the campaign, the visual element was provided by 15CWT armoured vehicles known as contact cars.[33]

Visual control post. (*Crown Copyright – Air Historical Branch MoD*)

DEVELOPING THE BRIDGEHEAD

The Key to the Breakout – Capturing Caen

The key to the breakout from the lodgement area was the capture of the city of Caen. The original plan was that the British Second Army was to secure this important city by the evening of D-Day. Despite attempts by the army and the use of a substantial volume of both strategic and tactical air power, the heavy concentration and fighting strength of the enemy in this area of Normandy effectively prevented a breakout within the planned timescale.

It took many weeks of bitter fighting in two major operations in late June and early July, to move towards and eventually capture Caen on 9 July 1944: Operation *Epsom* on 26 June was the British Second Army's offensive to cross the Odon and Orne rivers south-west of Caen and then the Anglo-Canadian offensive, Operation *Charnwood*, to capture the city itself. There was one further operation that took place between 18 and 21 July, codenamed *Goodwood*, which was intended to be a more limited attack to the south, from the Orne bridgehead, to capture the rest of Caen and the Bourguébus Ridge beyond. Although the operation failed in its primary aim, it did force the enemy to keep much of its forces, especially a large portion of its armoured reserves, on the eastern flank of the Normandy area.

RAF Regiment Reinforcements Arrive

The end of July and early August saw a change in the RAF Regiment's presence in theatre. Up until this point, only the light anti-aircraft roled squadrons had deployed to the Continent and had provided vital airfield defence and, from time-to-time a number of other duties such as perimeter patrolling and assisting with refuelling and rearming aircraft. The rifle and armoured car squadrons had been held back in the United Kingdom until this point but then a further seventeen squadrons and nine mobile wing headquarters deployed to the Continent as reinforcements for Nos. 83 and 84 groups. Additionally, three rifle squadrons were attached to Nos. 2 and 85 groups for special duties.

In total, this brought the number of RAF Regiment units in France to a total of nineteen mobile wing headquarters, eighteen light anti-aircraft squadrons, eight rifle squadrons and four armoured car squadrons. The rifle and armoured car squadrons found themselves involved in a much wider range of duties than they were used to, much of which was engineering in nature. It was not uncommon to see them helping to assemble rocket projectiles for the Typhoon aircraft, preparing belted machine gun ammunition for fighters and helping with a range of airfield construction and maintenance tasks.[34]

Cheek by Jowl

It was not just an operational imperative to breakout of the lodgement area but a logistical must. Large numbers of units and mountains of stores and supplies were literally flooding into Normandy. The overall effect was that the lodgement area started to become highly congested. One of the other factors that contributed to this congestion was that the RAF could not acquire the urgently needed airfields, so it was necessary to increase the number (above those planned) for the area of Ouistreham-Caen-Bayeux-Arromanches.

No.50 Mobile Field Hospital found itself being relocated to a new site at Camilly in mid-July 1944; their war diary commented that:

> It is understood that the move to the West of Bayeux was necessitated by the overcrowding of the BAYEUX - CAEN area as more and more troops arrived in the Beachhead. To fly over the Beachhead is fantastic – every field is packed with stores dumps, MT. tanks, guns, or camps. With the front line now beyond CAEN, the situation has eased, more airfields are being built in the CAEN area.[35]

While unit diaries later in the campaign, when troops had advanced into Belgium, contain many references to a highly welcoming civilian population, some accounts of the experience in Normandy suggest a different story. The war diary of No.50 Mobile Field Hospital contains a most enlightening summary of the unit's experiences in France up to the end of July 1944. In this they commented that they had not received any, 'rapturous welcome from a starving population – instead we have been received, on the whole civilly, by a well fed, prosperous, farming community, who do not look upon our extensive incursions into their carefully cultivated fields, knee high in growing crops, as a heaven-sent blessing, nor do they appear to view with any obvious joy the progressive destruction of their houses, villages and towns.'[36]

At an individual level, the initial, unleashed violence of the invasion was no doubt too much for many French men, women and children in Normandy to bear. As a nation though, there was little doubt it was a price that had to be paid to rid the occupied countries of Nazi tyranny. As the unit moved away from the Normandy area though, they noticed quite a different and contrasting reception from the local population. At Moisville, further north, the No.50 Mobile Field Hospital's diarist noted how, 'Crowds flock round, and through, the hospital in embarrassing numbers, with presents of fruits and dairy produce. One hears occasional atrocity stories, and one has the feeling, for the first time since arriving in France, that one is genuinely welcome.'[37]

By the final week of July 1944, Phase I of the operation had come to a close with the Allies achieving a significant first footing on the Continent. The limiting factor now, was not how much more they could get ashore, but how quickly the ground forces could get on the move. A breakout from Normandy was critical, not just to keep the enemy on the back foot and retreating but to free up the bottleneck of men, machines and supplies that were straining at the leash in the lodgement area.

Chapter 6

Crossing the Start Line – Breakout from Normandy

Phase II of the Allied campaign began on 26 July 1944 and was effectively the starting line for the much-awaited breakout from Normandy. As described in the previous chapter, the British and Canadians had eventually captured Caen. On 27 July the Americans captured the first major port at Cherbourg. Subsequent actions enabled the Allies to capture the Cotentin Peninsula down as far as Lessay and then east through Saint-Lô, to the far end of the SWORD Beach area to the east.

By the time the breakout started, the Allies had become more confident that the 'pendulum of the battle was gradually swinging in the Allied favour'. From here on, the strategic intent for this part of *Overlord*, as described by Coningham, 'was to swing the right flank round towards Paris and to force the enemy back against the Seine, over which all the bridges had been destroyed by air action between Paris and the sea'.[1]

The first major engagement in which 2nd TAF distinguished themselves was during Operation *Bluecoat*, the prime aim of which was the British offensive to capture Mont Pinçon and the area astride the road which ran from Vire, through Vassy to the city of Condé-sur-Noireau, heading east. On 2 August, 2nd TAF Typhoons found and attacked both 9th and 10th SS Panzer divisions, which had been repositioned by General Bayerlein to counter the Allied attack on Caumont, which had been launched by the British Second Army on 30 July. Significant damage was inflicted by the Typhoons, with further highly successful attacks by the aircraft on 7 and 8 August.

The move towards Condé-sur-Noireau saw the need to establish a bridgehead across the city's river Noireau. This operation, codenamed *Blackwater*, was a successor to *Bluecoat* and took place between 1 and 6 August. It was a particularly destructive engagement and is believed to have destroyed in the region of 95 per cent of the city's infrastructure, with much of the damage inflicted by bombers of the United States Eighth Air Force. Such operations though, created a secondary effect in that important communications routes were damaged and remained impassable until they could be cleared. Like the important road clearance work they had carried out at Caen, squadrons of the RAF's airfield construction wings were tasked with clearing a way through Condé-sur-Noireau.

On 17 August, detachments from Nos. 5022 and 5023 (airfield construction) squadrons were called upon to support the army's advancing armour of No.30 Corps, which was unable to move through. The squadron's task consisted of bridging a stream with materials available (mainly masonry and rubble) and clearing roads through demolished buildings to enable 50th Division to move up on 19 August. The destruction was so bad that it took the wings' headquarters reconnaissance party two and a half hours to find them. They eventually traced the routes by broken-off telegraph poles and the odd glimpse of the kerbs. Making full use of their bulldozers, the wing cleared the roads in thirty-six hours, allowing the armour to come through and continue their pursuit of the enemy. The squadron's efforts did not go unnoticed and earned them a commendation from No.30 Corps.[2]

This was a busy time for other units of 2nd TAF as well. The Humber Light Reconnaissance Cars of No.2806 (Armoured Car) Squadron had arrived in Normandy on 29 July and had moved to their first operational location at Airfield B.17 Carpiquet (just outside Caen) the next day. The airfield was the first of the existing airfields to be occupied by 2nd TAF and had been finally captured by the 8th Canadian Infantry Brigade on 9 July, but it was not until 18 July that all enemy opposition in the area was eliminated.

The fight for the Carpiquet airfield, part of Operation *Windsor*, had been costly in terms of Canadian casualties but their sacrifice helped secure an important objective. The site had suffered extensive damage during the assault to capture it and, through the hard work of the army's No.24 Airfield Construction Group, supported by the RAF's No.5352 (Airfield Construction) Wing, had become operational on 25 July. The unit diarist of one of the RAF Regiment armoured car squadrons commented on 31 July that:

> The squadron had dug in both their vehicles and personnel and a great amount of clearing up had to be done as there had been a battle in the area only fourteen days previous. Everyone was glad to be in the Army of Liberation and we were roughly situated about four thousand yards from the Bosche.[3]

In addition to their 2nd TAF primary duties, several of the RAF Regiment squadrons found themselves from time to time being temporarily attached to army formations for specific operations. Such was the case for No.2806 (Armoured Car) Squadron's No.2 Flight on 7 August, which was attached to the British 43rd (Wessex) Infantry Division at La Tromperie, awaiting permission to take over a known radar station at Mont Pinçon. The initial reconnaissance of the site was made by Squadron Leader Garratt and Flying Officer Raggatt under intermittent mortar and shell fire, but permission was not given for the flight to take over the site until three days later, on the 10 August, along with one of the RAF's Air Technical Intelligence teams. Despite the enemy resistance, the radar site was found to be only under construction, had not been used operationally and had no trace of any radar equipment.[4]

The reconnaissance capability of the RAF Regiment armoured car squadrons was soon in demand, and they were particularly useful in supporting the airfield construction groups by carrying out reconnaissance missions to help with the selection of sites for future airfields. Such work, though, was no sightseeing trip as

CROSSING THE START LINE – BREAKOUT FROM NORMANDY

No.2 Flight of No.2806 Squadron found on 4 September. The flight accompanied the army's No.16 Airfield Construction Group to help conduct a reconnaissance at Melsbroek, north-east of Brussels in Belgium. They found that the enemy was still occupying part of the airfield and were using anti-aircraft guns for ground defence.

Consequently, they had to withdraw. Undeterred, the party returned the next day with four Sherman tanks in support which proceeded to fire on the suspected enemy positions, only to find that they had been evacuated during the night. Despite this, there was considerable shooting going on from the nearby woods.[5] Accounts of similar activities are common throughout the war diary of this and other RAF Regiment squadrons throughout the campaign after the breakout from Normandy.

The enlargement of, and security within, the bridgehead at the end of August enabled 2nd TAF's command and control to transfer to the Continent. Its operational headquarters moved to Le Tronquay, near Saint-Lô on 4 August 1944 and by this time most of the aircraft of Nos. 83, 84 and 85 groups were then based in Normandy. The lack of suitable airfields for the heavier aircraft of No.2 Group did not permit them to move to France and most of them were still based in the United Kingdom.[6]

The Falaise Gap

United States forces also broke out from the lodgement area following Operation *Cobra*, initially southwards and then eastwards from Brittany to Argentan. In parallel with the American thrust northwards from Argentan, the British and Canadians attacked from Caen in a southerly direction as part of operations *Totalize* and *Tractable*. Overall, these operations began to squeeze the enemy forces into a 'pocket' with Falaise on the upper side where the British Second Army and the First Canadian Army had pressed down from Caen, and Carentan at the lower end of the pocket where the Third United States Army was squeezing the pocket from below.

By 17 August, the enemy realised that their position was becoming untenable. As such, they stopped trying to move reinforcements in westwards, turning their attention to a withdrawal of its 5th Panzer Army and 7th Army through the ever-narrowing Falaise Gap. The Allied pincer movement converged at Chambois just to the east of Falaise and Argentan. Although the Gap was finally closed on 20 August, it has been referred to as a flawed victory in that the time taken to close this escape enabled over 60,000 German troops to escape. Notwithstanding, the pocket proved to be a killing ground with scenes of horrendous destruction. The rocket firing typhoons of 2nd TAF had played a key part in the decimation of large swathes of the retreating enemy.

Estimates of German losses vary quite considerably but in the region of 10,000 were probably killed and 50,000 captured. The aircraft of 2nd TAF 'claimed to have destroyed or damaged 190 tanks and 2,600 vehicles during its sorties over the battlefield'.[7]

Falaise was, in many ways, the springboard for the breakout from Normandy. It was becoming challenging though for 2nd TAF's aircraft with tactical air power being used almost to its full extent in harrying the retreating enemy. The targets

FORWARD AIR BASES IN EUROPE FROM D-DAY TO THE BALTIC

An RAF servicing commando NCO fitting a warhead to a Typhoon rocket projectile. (*Crown Copyright – Air Historical Branch MoD*)

were many and varied, ranging from tanks and armoured vehicles to supply convoys, barges in canals and bridges.

The highly successful employment of tactical air power at Falaise (and the battle at Mortain before that) was singled out for comment in Conningham's post-campaign report:

> One contribution of the Second Tactical Air Force to the two great victories of Mortain and the Falaise pocket, including the pursuit to the Seine during the month of August 1944, was the destruction of 10,500 of Germany's sorely needed transport and 850 of her first line armoured vehicles. In addition, our army was given complete freedom of interference from enemy air action, whilst the enemy supply lines were continually harassed by day and night.[8]

The Move to the Seine

The Allied advance towards the Seine saw 2nd TAF focusing on three main tasks. The first was what was termed as the smashing of the enemy's potential for any future counter-offensive. Much of this had been achieved during the tactical air power effort carried out against the enemy's best ground formations that had been partially encircled in the Falaise/Mortain pocket. The second task involved the continued interdiction of the river Seine/river Loire line and between the pocket to prevent enemy reinforcements coming in from the north, east or south. The third task was the continual harassment of the enemy's retreat to the river Seine 'with the intention of turning it into a rout'.[9]

While the Allied advance was proving to be a resounding success, 2nd TAF's single-seat fighters and fighter-bomber aircraft were soon beginning to operate at extreme range from their airfields, which were still in the Normandy area. In one case, some of these aircraft, running short of fuel, landed at Lympne on the South Coast of Britain rather than attempting to return to their airfields in Normandy. The need to move forward the advanced landing grounds of Nos. 83 and 84 groups soon became a priority in order that 2nd TAF could increase their range and cover for the advancing ground forces. It had originally been planned to build further airfields immediately east and south-east of Caen but by now this area was too far back and the intent was soon abandoned. The next suitable area with soil that would enable the rapid construction of airfields was on the plateau between Dreux and Lisieux.

It was to prove a challenge as shipping space only permitted half of the required surfacing materials to be sent out to France. Work soon started on clutches of new airfields round Dreux on the right flank for No.83 Group and around Lisieux on the coastal flank for No.84 Group. There were approximately eighteen Allied airfields constructed across this diagonal 'swathe', of which at least eight were to become officially named British B airfields. Whilst this was going on, Airfield B.17 Carpiquet at Caen was upgraded with suitable facilities for use by air transport aircraft and as a base for the night fighter wing of No.85 Group.[10]

Of particular significance for France was the liberation of Paris by the French 2nd Armoured Division and the United States 4th Infantry Division on 25 August. Despite the French and American dominance in this highly significant achievement, 2nd TAF also were involved with a detachment from No.2798 (Rifle) Squadron of the RAF Regiment entering the city with the first Allied elements and, along with the French Maquis (French Resistance), secured the racecourse at Longchamps as a site of interest for possible use as an aircraft landing ground or radar site in the Bois de Boulogne. Additionally, one of the squadron's flights escorted an Air Technical Intelligence team in occupying and investigating some seventy-eight suspected V-1 flying bomb launch sites around the city. Unlike most of the RAF Regiment squadrons, this unit had landed on OMAHA Beach towards the end of July 1944 and was attached to the RAF's No.21 Base Defence Sector situated in the American Sector and seconded to the United States Fifth Army.

This commitment required the squadron to operate further west than the majority of 2nd TAF's units and, throughout the latter part of July and August, it was tasked with protecting several of the mobile RAF radar units operating in this sector from surprise enemy attacks, especially from paratroopers. This protection role usually involved the assignment of one rifle flight, plus a troop of reconnaissance cars for reconnoitring suitable deployment sites for the radars. One of the benefits of operating near the American forces was that it seemed to be much easier for them to obtain army combat supplies. One such example, which greatly improved their mobility and ease of operation in the field, was the replacement of their British issue tents which they found too heavy and bulky for manoeuvrability.

The squadron's CO, apparently with some ease, managed to obtain 200 American two-man pup tents which made an enormous difference. Each man carried his half of the tent (about the size of a standard groundsheet) with his personal kit; this made them much easier to carry and to erect when required. The unit war diary shows that the squadron was constantly on the move, but time was still found to fit in all important off-duty activities. Team sport, especially football, was particularly popular and easy to arrange. The occurrences of such matches were as meticulously recorded in the diary as their operational duties. On the night of 29 July, No.2 Flight was engaged on patrols and sentry duties for three different RAF radar units in its area of operations. Returning to base the next afternoon, the unit diarist recorded 'The squadron played the Royal Corps of Signals at a game of football and won – four goals to two. The flight beer ration was sent out to No.1 Rifle Flight'.[11]

By the end of August, it became possible for off-duty 'liberty runs' to be arranged for personnel in Paris which proved to be very popular. The war diary of No.5 Mobile Field Photographic Section recorded that 'A small minority abused the privilege and went "A.W.L" [absent without leave], resulting in disciplinary action, and a warning was necessary to all ranks against a recurrence of this juisance [sic]'.[12]

Although the primary role of the RAF Regiment was in defence of 2nd TAF's airfields, it quite regularly became involved in wider operations, usually when on route to new locations during the advance. The war diary of HQ No, 1300 Mobile Wing, for example, records in some detail its activities and very close proximity to enemy troops while in the process of moving from Beauvais to Vitry on the outskirts of Paris on 3 September.

Late in the day, reports were received from the Maquis that there was 'still a large number of the enemy in the area between Wingles and Meurchin and it was believed that they were heading in the direction of the airfield'. Both RAF and RAF Regiment personnel were reminded by the RAF commander that they would be required to 'operate in a defensive role should an attack on the airfield become imminent'. Fortunately for the RAF this enemy pocket was soon mopped up by a company of the Durham Light Infantry with supporting artillery fire.[13]

Many of the advancing units soon began to witness the harsh conditions of enemy occupation and the often-brutal reprisals on the civilian population by German SS troops. One of the mobile radar units of No.83 Group arrived at Sainte-Marguerite on 23 August, their fourth operating site since landing in Normandy on 7 June. Despite their occupation of what their diarist described as a perfect site 'among apple trees and clean meadows', they were soon aware of the tragic consequences which often accompanied the local population's enthusiastic support of the liberating Allies.

CROSSING THE START LINE – BREAKOUT FROM NORMANDY

The diarist commented:

> There was grim evidence of the Hun too – a family of five civilians lying dead in a cottage, killed because they had welcomed a BRITISH recce' party, and over thirty other civilians had been shot in the nearby town of LIVAROT for the same reason…there were still a few Huns in the neighbourhood; half a dozen S.S. who had had a hand in the shooting of the civilians in LIVAROT were caught and publicly shot as part of that village's Liberation celebration and very rightly too.[14]

Having reached and crossed the Seine with relative ease between 25 and 27 August 1944 and with Paris liberated, Montgomery issued a new general appreciation and directive on 26 August 1944. In this he expressed the view that the enemy was 'in no fit condition to stand and fight' and that speed of action and movement was vital. The intent, he directed, 'was to destroy all enemy forces in the Pas-de-Calais and to capture Antwerp'. Such was the confidence in the rate of success that a few days later Eisenhower issued a Supreme Commander's directive to Twenty-First Army Group (and Twelfth United States Army Group operating north of the Ardennes) for them 'to secure Antwerp, breach the sector of the Siegfried line covering the Ruhr, and then to seize the Ruhr'.

The role of the Allied air forces in all this was to continue supporting the ground forces. Of note was mention of the newly formed United States First Allied Airborne Army, which was directed to support Twenty-First Army Group up to and including the crossing of the river Rhine and then to engage in large scale operations during the advance into Germany.[15] Once the Seine was crossed the First Canadian Army headed towards the Channel coast and the British Second Army (on the left flank of the First United States Army) continued roughly in in a north-easterly direction towards the city of Amiens on the River Somme.

Into the Low Countries

The speedy advance of British Second Army achieved during the rest of August 1944 enabled them to liberate Amiens on 30 August, with the Belgian frontier crossed on 2 September and Brussels and Antwerp were reached by 3 and 4 September respectively. By 12 September, the British had entered the Netherlands. In parallel with the British advance, the Canadian Army was also advancing rapidly north, gradually taking the Channel ports and capturing or destroying many of the V-1 flying bomb launch sites, which were mostly located in the Pas-de-Calais area. This was particularly welcome back in the United Kingdom where the capital and southern England had been under fire from the 'doodlebugs' for the past two months.

This rate of movement proved particularly challenging for 2nd TAF, particularly for No.83 Group, which was supporting the British Second Army. Coningham's

FORWARD AIR BASES IN EUROPE FROM D-DAY TO THE BALTIC

Part of No.34 Wing convoy passing through a French town on route to Brussels. A Type J mobile photographic processing vehicle is in the foreground. *(Copyright Through Their Eyes)*

staff implemented several special measures to improve the mobility of this group. Firstly, it was decided that not more than three forward operational airfields would be used at any one time. Secondly, certain wings were left behind temporarily, and their transport used to move fuel and munitions to the forward wings. Thirdly, much greater use was made of captured airfields as there was not enough time to build airfields to keep pace with the advance.

Most of these former enemy airfields had to be reconditioned for use following battle damage and invariably had to be cleared of mines and booby traps to make them safe to operate. Wherever possible, airlift was used to move personnel and equipment and forward airfields were moved in 'bounds', each of approximately 100 miles. Further measures adopted included greater use of radio telephone circuits as the provision of landline circuits was somewhat challenging during such rapid movement and the RAF's reinforcement of the army's airfield construction groups.

Despite the robust arrangements that were in place for the provision of aviation fuel, self-help measures were also employed at this time. For example, the night reconnaissance Wellington aircraft of No.69 Squadron had to be used during this time to ferry fuel to their forward airfield to keep the other two squadrons of its parent No.34 (Reconnaissance) Wing in the air. Starting on 6 September 1944, the Wellingtons made forty-four trips in which they moved 15,590 gallons of petrol and 1,180 gallons of oil to Glisy airfield, just outside of Amiens.[16]

All in all, these measures enabled No.83 Group 'to give the furthest possible forward air cover to our rapidly moving columns'.[17] The flexibility provided by

CROSSING THE START LINE – BREAKOUT FROM NORMANDY

the various RAF Regiment squadrons proved of particular benefit at this time and a number found themselves on much wider duties in addition to capturing and occupying new airfields. Alongside of other specialist units they assisted with clearing mines and booby traps, transporting aircraft fuel to forward airstrips and, in concert with the RAF servicing commandos, helping to refuel and rearm aircraft.

On the whole, the advancing Allies were warmly welcomed by local populations even though many had been killed or injured as a result of British and Canadian shelling or aerial bombing as they endeavoured to drive the enemy back.

On 6 September 1944, No.2819 Light Anti-Aircraft Squadron RAF Regiment was on its way to Evere Airfield, Brussels and recorded the experience of the local welcome in their war diary:

> This journey was one which will never be forgotten, for we were acclaimed on every part of the route. In one village in Belgium the convoy was stopped by huge crowds of cheering people, asking for souvenirs and autographs on Red/White/Blue hair ribbon. It was some time before we could get them to move so that we might pass on.[18]

A jubilant scene in Eindhoven town square. Locals welcome No.34 Wing as they pass through. Such scenes were commonplace as the advancing Allies liberated towns and cities during the advance from Normandy. *(Copyright Through Their Eyes)*

FORWARD AIR BASES IN EUROPE FROM D-DAY TO THE BALTIC

Support on the Move

Keeping the flying squadrons and many of the other mobile support units resupplied while on the move remained a challenge throughout the campaign. The key to success were the air stores parks, each of which was a self-contained unit, set up along the lines of a wheel with the hub being the headquarters along with its administrative element. Each spoke of the wheel was a self-contained vehicle, the perimeter being the whole complex. The spokes were each numbered to match a numbered vehicle. Vehicle drivers also had to be storekeepers as well as stores accountants and all records were maintained in a manuscript ledger, with one in each vehicle.

The parks moved in convoy (often at short notice) and would be assigned to support a specific number of flying squadrons operating from newly captured airfields; they were based within a 25- to 40-mile radius of the squadrons they were supporting. When on the move, vehicles were kept in their numerical order in case any spares were required whilst they were re-locating. Should this happen (as was often the case) a despatch rider would be sent down the convoy and the appropriate vehicle pulled out of the line and the spares required would be issued.

When static, the parks were housed under, and operated from, tents which were carefully camouflaged to avoid detection from the enemy. Their personnel were armed, and each park carried several Bren light machine guns with a tripod that enable them to be used for anti-aircraft defence. The parks reported their position daily to group headquarters which, in turn, gave instructions to move forward when required.

The three air stores parks attached to No.83 Group experienced the most turbulence of the parks in the campaign and underwent five to six location moves through France, Belgium and into the Netherlands. At the beginning of September, No.404 Air Stores Park had started to note that the supply situation was becoming tenuous:

> The rapid advance had taken most of our 'customer units' well forward and the units that remained with us were virtually non-operational because of the great distance which separated us from the front line. The immediate priority was for petrol and ammunition, and all other forward movement was held up.[19]

On 15 September the unit was forewarned of a move into Belgium, a process that started two days later and took them 280 miles to a location just west of Brussels. By the end of the month, the park was located on the outskirts of Eindhoven in the Netherlands.[20] The group's supply and transport company (No.309), which was charged with the important role of moving critical stocks of fuel and munitions, from rail and roadheads to airfields, also travelled further, during September 1944, than any other time during the campaign (see Figure 1 below).

The experience of No.84 Group was quite different as it was assigned to support the First Canadian Army that advanced on the left flank, as it endeavoured to liberate the Channel ports. An analysis of the group's squadron locations shows

CROSSING THE START LINE – BREAKOUT FROM NORMANDY

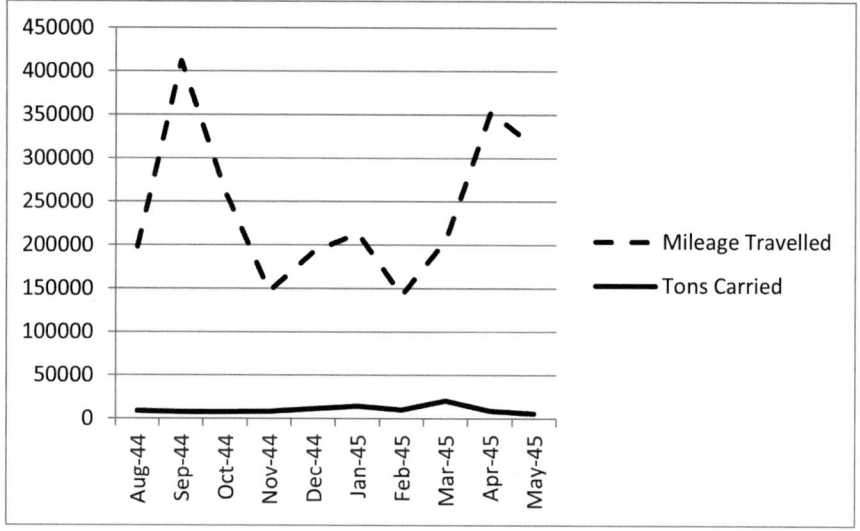

Figure 1. Miles travelled and tonnage carried by No.309 Supply and Transport Column – August 1944 to May 1945.[21]

that the majority by the end of Phase II were located within a radius of 15 miles of Lille in Northern France. This nucleus of airfields was some 200 miles from the Normandy bridgehead. The actual line of communication by road or rail was considerably more than this.[22]

The group's photographic reconnaissance wing (No.35) and its Air Observation Post Auster aircraft squadrons were much farther forward in Belgium near Ghent and north-east of Antwerp. The logistics units supporting the group were located towards the north-east of Brussels and they too had been the subject of almost continual and short notice moves. A remark made in the war diary of No.404 ASP by the CO at the end of September 1944 well illustrates the turbulence during this period:

> This month has been one which has tested our much-vaunted and much-practiced [sic] mobility to the full. When the month opened, we were still in the original 'bridgehead' area in Normandy. At its close half the unit was in Holland – some 500 miles distant! Our stay in Belgium lasted only ten days and, in that time, we had two locations.[23]

While most of the RAF's logistics units were manned by and used their own labour, the war diary of No.422 Aviation Fuel and Ammunition Park assigned to No.84 Group shows that the unit had army pioneers among its number. The sheer bulk, weight and nature of the munitions and aviation fuel, which they carried made their moves to new operating locations a challenging task. Of note is that during the move of No.422 park from Calengeville to Bondues (both in Northern France) during the period 14 to 30 September 1944, the RAF Regiment provided both labour and some ninety, 3-ton lorries to assist with the movement of the unit.[24]

Despite their differences in role, most of 2nd TAF mobile support units spent much of their time being relocated, often at short notice as the operational need dictated. For many, what became known as a leap-frog method was employed. This was particularly significant for the mobile field hospitals where each had to be cleared of its patients before it could advance. The concept was most widely used in Nos. 83 and 84 groups where a rearward field hospital (presumably with spare capacity) would advance, passing the first hospital and camping to cover the new forward area. Patients would then be evacuated from the hospital now in the rear so that it in turn would be ready to leap-frog as soon as further airfields became operational.[25]

On 26 August, an urgent requirement arose for Spitfire and Typhoon 45-gallon drop tanks. In all, over 3,200 tanks were sent by the Forward Equipment Unit at RAF Bicester all within just seven days despite transportation difficulties. Emergency air freight transport was used for this tasking but not in sufficient quantity and the Queen Mary trailer-based service was held up at the crucial time owing to bad weather.

Fortunately, one of the RAF's supply and transport columns was on its way to Normandy and due to travel in larger tank landing ships so some 1,000 tanks went over by this means. The more routine resupply from the United Kingdom to Normandy continued apace and by the end of August 296,374 individual issues had been made to consumer units.

Restoring the Railway Network

The further units moved away from Normandy, the longer the lines of communications back to Normandy became. There was a problem with this though – the Allied air forces had destroyed large parts of the rail infrastructure, locomotives and rolling stock. In western France and Belgium, thirty-seven rail centres had been destroyed and twenty-three heavily damaged.[26] The reconstruction and re-establishment of the rail infrastructure in particular, was important for British and Canadian operations in France, Belgium and the Netherlands, as it enabled supplies, especially heavy and bulky stocks such as fuel and munitions, to be moved in substantial volume from the Rear Maintenance Area and from the smaller channel ports as they were captured and re-opened throughout September 1944.[27]

This targeting of the rail network was a vital, pre-D-Day measure and was a concerted effort, effectively to isolate the Normandy area from potential enemy reinforcement by cutting-off the road and rail routes into the area. It had been acknowledged from the very early days of planning for *Overlord* that the Germans, once the invasion started, would need to rapidly reinforce Normandy in order that they could repel the invasion force to maintain the integrity of the Atlantic Wall defences.

CROSSING THE START LINE – BREAKOUT FROM NORMANDY

An important part of the German reinforcement supply chain was the French railway network and, following a study by Professor Solly Zuckerman, this was known as the Transportation Plan. The aim of this was to isolate the Normandy area, whilst also contributing to the on-going deception plan. It was a process of attrition and started well before D-Day: by the beginning of June 1944, in addition to the destroyed marshalling yards, rail junctions and rolling stock repair shops, 1,500 out of 2,000 steam locomotives had been immobilized. In the six-weeks prior to D-Day, thirty-six Luftwaffe airfields were also attacked in France, the Netherlands and Germany and, immediately before the invasion, fighter-bomber squadrons targeted a number of radar sites along the French and Belgian coastline.

The outcome of the Transportation Plan was to be a double-edged sword. While it effectively cut-off Normandy from outside reinforcement, it destroyed valuable transportation network that the Allies would need as part of their movement away from the coast following the breakout from the bridgehead when it came. The greater priority though was to isolate Normandy – the repair of railways and roads would be done in slightly slower time. The breakout from Normandy allowed greater access to the damaged network and Twenty-First Army Group soon put to work several specialist organisations to tackle this, including four railway construction and maintenance groups; three railway operating groups; two railway workshop groups and one Canadian railway operating group.

Managing the People

Amid all this activity, there remained a need to manage RAF personnel posted to 2nd TAF units on the Continent and those returning to the United Kingdom for various reasons. As originally planned, the coordinating of this fell to No.85 Group's Base Personnel Centre, which landed in France in late August 1944. Their work was not glamourous, if indeed anything in war can be ever considered as such.

It was important though and they were the funnel through which reinforcements/replacements to 2nd TAF units flowed, as well as holding what were classed as non-effective personnel. This latter category usually consisted of those somewhere in or just out of the medical system or being processed through the RAF's disciplinary system. In August, the unit also took on responsibility for the RAF's leave transit camp at Arromanches. By all accounts, the staff of the Base Personnel Centre took great pride in their role despite the challenging conditions as an entry in their war diary for the end of August 1944 indicates:

> It is worth recording that since the arrival of the Unit on the Continent personnel have adapted themselves very well to the new conditions. During the period of erecting tents, building latrines, digging soak away pits, building roads and doing other heavy tasks, there was not one grumble. It is obvious that the unit is going to be a very contented one in carrying out the very important function of transmitting personnel and holding non-effective personnel on the Continent.[28]

The throughput of personnel handled by the personnel centre was no small beer. During the three-month period from October to December 1944 they received and processed just over 7,000 officers and other ranks coming into Normandy.[29]

The administration of discipline during times of war has always been important and remained so during the campaign. Absence without leave appears from time to time in various unit diaries and could often attract quite significant sentences by district court martials. One leading aircraftman in the convalescent section, for example was tried on a charge of absence and received a sentence of fifty-six days' detention.

Luckily for the individual concerned, this sentence was suspended by the AOC of No.85 Group for reasons unknown. Other disciplinary incidents provide a somewhat colourful depiction of unauthorised activities at the time. In February 1945, for example, another leading aircraftman was being investigated for failing to stop at the Belgium-Netherlands border and accused of smuggling goods over the border.

Eyes in the Sky

Air reconnaissance was an important capability in 2nd TAF, and photographic reconnaissance wings were included as part of HQ 2nd TAF (No.34 Wing) and within No.83 Group (No.39 Wing and No.84 Group (No.35 Wing). In the weeks following D-Day and throughout the build-up period before the breakout, much of the reconnaissance effort was directed at monitoring what the enemy forces were up to.

A variety of aerial reconnaissance cameras were fitted to the specially modified photographic reconnaissance aircraft and, after a sortie, film from aircraft cameras had to be processed and printed so that the resulting images could be examined by highly specialised photographic interpreters. The resulting information enabled a detailed picture to be built-up of the battle area, enabling enemy dispositions to be identified and for the intelligence and operations staffs to brief both air and ground commanders.

For No.34 Wing, still largely based at RAF Northolt on the outskirts of London, the daylight work consisted of three main tasks. The first was a requirement directly from Supreme HQ Allied Expeditionary Force to monitor the principal railway lines in Northern France to detect any movements which might constitute enemy reinforcements. This was always a very risky operation as, following the RAF and US Army Air Force's attacks on the network as part of the Transportation Plan, the Germans had deployed anti-aircraft defences both on the trains and at the principal towns along the lines. On one stretch of line between Somain and Montdidier, the wing lost three aircraft and crews in four sorties.

Eventually Supreme HQ Allied Expeditionary Foce was persuaded to ask for cover of only the important stations along the lines unless the whole could be covered at high-level. The second task was to monitor the main railway marshalling yards in Northern France. These were being kept unserviceable by the bombers and

CROSSING THE START LINE – BREAKOUT FROM NORMANDY

Photographic reconnaissance Wellington of No.69 Squadron. *(Copyright Through Their Eyes)*

cover over each of them was essential to monitor the enemy's efforts to repair them. It was a considerable task and usually involved a list of some twenty-five sites provided by Supreme HQ Allied Expeditionary Force each evening for cover on the following day. The third task was part of an overall effort to provide an up-to-date order of battle of the German Luftwaffe and to watch for construction of new airfields or extensions to old ones.

Again, it was a sizeable task and there were usually about forty airfields on the task list at the beginning of each day. In addition to these three tasks there were many other requirements such as monitoring key river lines of communication, woods and bridges as well as carrying out bomb damage assessment for No.2 Group. Despite the strengthening of enemy defences in specific areas that were the attention of Allied air attacks, these photographic reconnaissance missions were always risky. An unofficial diary produced by No.34 Wing describes what happened when five aircraft took off to photograph several river bridges between Chartres and the Seine:

> Over France, they ran into very low cloud, the whole circus [*sic*] flew over the middle of Paris and the 'natter' on the R/T as they tried to keep in touch with each other caused much amusement, especially when one pilot was heard to exclaim, 'gosh! did you see that lightning?' and the reply came back, 'that's not lightning – it's flak!' However, some useful photographs were taken, and all returned

without damage except the hood of Willy Willshaw's aircraft was blown off by flak.[30]

All these missions produced large quantities of film which required urgent processing if the information gained was to be of value. The nature of the missions and the difficulty of capturing enough detail of course dictated how many exposures needed to be made but an example of the sheer quantity of material produced comes from the record of some thirty-one Mosquito reconnaissance sorties back in February 1944, which produced 7,451 negatives and 23,466 prints.

Speed was therefore vital if maximum use was to be made of the imagery gained from all these sorties, the processing of which relied on mobile field photographic sections. Each of these self-contained units consisted of seven main work vehicles and several auxiliary vehicles. The operational 'heart' of each unit was a group of articulated lorry vehicles (usually Crossley prime movers), each connected to a flat-topped caravan type trailer, which resembled a railway carriage but with fewer windows. The visual appearance of these convoys earned them the affectionate nickname of 'The Blue Train'.

Unlike the relative ease of providing digital imagery, which air forces of the twenty-first century have become used to, the processing of 'wet' film required considerably more resources so the field photographic sections included: a continuous film processing vehicle which contained chemical baths and a roller transport mechanism that enabled the continuous film strips to be developed, fixed and dried; two multiprinter vehicles; a contact printer vehicle; a photograph enlargement vehicle; a storage and chemical mixing vehicle and an administration vehicle which housed the CO's office with desks for other administrative tasks. In addition to the range of specialist photographic processing chemicals that these units carried, they required vast quantities of water, which was carried in two water bowsers, each with a water pump driven by a separate power take-off from the engine.

Several thousand litres were required each day which required continual replenishment from lakes, rivers and streams. A diesel generator vehicle provided electrical power and three further vehicles (usually 3-ton Bedfords) carried spares, domestic supplies and personal equipment. The most important vehicle, from the personnel's perspective, was a mobile cooking facility. For communications, primarily for transporting processed imagery to group headquarters or airfields, two motorcycle despatch riders were used.[31]

The workload of the mobile field photographic sections was considerable. No.4 Section for example, landed at 10.00 hours on JUNO Beach on 18 August 1944, setting up camp at Airfield B.4 at Beny-sur-Mer. By 17.00 hours that day they were fully operational and over the next 24 hours processed some 30,000 photographs. Up to the end of the month the unit completed 236,00 photographs.

The figures rose further in September with the unit processing 250,000 photographs and producing 2,200 enlargements. Their work was critical, especially to the ground forces, and even by the end of September 1944 had attracted personally conveyed appreciation from HQ First Canadian Army. There was an

CROSSING THE START LINE – BREAKOUT FROM NORMANDY

A 2nd TAF radar unit convoy stops for a break somewhere in the Low Countries in 1944. This photograph clearly shows the diverse range of vehicle mounted radar structures, which were typical of these units. *(Copyright Through Their Eyes)*

excellent working relationship between No.4 Section and the Canadians with the latter going out of their way to develop this. Indeed, in late October 1944, an intelligence officer from 1st Division, First Canadian Army visited the unit (then at Deurne, north-east of Antwerp) to give a talk on the value of air photographs to First Canadian Army at that stage of the war.[32]

The war diary of No.5 Mobile Field Photographic Section, which worked in support of No.39 (Reconnaissance) Wing in No.83 Group, tells a very similar story. They had landed in France in late June or July 1944 and in their first month of operation had produced 302,000 prints, enlargements, and various other types of photographic copies. This, they commented, 'completely eclipses anything achieved in the previous 7 months in the Unit's history'. This achievement, they went on to record, was only possible by the 'hard work, keenness, and the encouraging assurances from Second Army that the photographs were being rushed to the battle area and were, in APIS [Air Photo Interpretation Section] "priceless" to the planning and fighting men'.[33]

The fruits of photographic reconnaissance were valued at various levels within the operational hierarchy, whether it was to enlighten the generals as they planned the next stages of the campaign, or the operational commanders as they prepared for specific battles or tasks. Not long after their arrival in France the RAF's mobile photographic sections started to receive demands from the army for special photographic mosaics (a collage of overlapping photographs) be used in place of maps.

By the middle of July 1944, the demand for these mosaics increased substantially and had become so valuable that the distribution list for them extended right down to platoon level. No.5 Section recorded in its war diary that they 'had the satisfaction of producing some mosaics one evening while an army captain waited, which were taken straight away to General Montgomery'. Little surprise then that the diarist added 'Unit personnel really felt they were contributing directly to the war effort'.[34]

The constant need to watch out for the movement of German reinforcements into Normandy remained a high priority well into August 1944 and formed a sizeable component of the night-time photographic reconnaissance tasking. The focus of much of this work was keeping an eye out for the movement of German reinforcements into the area immediately behind their forward troops and it was therefore potential detraining stations that became the principal targets. The effectiveness of the RAF's night work at this time was commented on in an intelligence report on the German Panzer-Lehr-Division, which observed that the dropping of flares, flashes and bombs severely hampered the enemy divisions' movements and sleep at night. Cumulatively, this all helped to the wearing down of the Germans, weakening their resolve and undermining their fighting capability.

The reconnaissance aircraft of No.34 Wing continued to play a vital part in the campaign and on 31 August 1944 the main party of its headquarters back at RAF Northolt in the United Kingdom deployed to France and moved to the American

The crew of a No.34 wing photographic processing section posing in front of their Type J vehicle at Amiens airfield in September 1944. Note the airman just to the left of the doorway holding up a German steel helmet. *(Copyright Through Their Eyes)*

landing strip at A.12 Lignerolles/Balleroy about 10 miles south-west of Bayeux where they were joined by the aircraft and crews on 1 September.

The small rear party from Northolt was expected to follow a few days later but all the Dakota transport aircraft were required for the forthcoming Operation *Market Garden*, the ill-fated but heroic venture to seize the Rhine bridges up to the Dutch town of Arnhem. This restriction on the availability of transport aircraft was to have a much wider effect on campaign logistics and is discussed in more detail in the next chapter.

Air Base Expansion

With most of the early airfields in Normandy having been constructed by the army, the RAF constructed its first overseas operational landing ground at what would become Airfield B.19 Lingèvres. The site was approximately 1 mile north of the village of Lingèvres, due south of Bayeux and just north-west of Tilly-sur-Seulles. The village had been badly damaged during the armoured battles on 11 and 15 June.

Work commenced at midday on 1 August 1944 with No.5022 (Airfield Construction) Squadron under orders to complete the task by first light on 8 August – just over a week for a 5,000 foot airstrip covered with square mesh track. Work progressed well although the unit war diary commented that this was 'despite frequent incidents caused by plant and motor transport detonating explosive objects. There were no squadron casualties however'.[35] The evidence of battle was ever present as the RAF moved into such locations and the personnel of A Flight, amidst their labours of building the airfield, volunteered to bury the bodies of both Germans and English soldiers that were in the clearance area.

Although the square mesh track used for the runway surface was an innovative solution, it was not an easy material to work with. Provided in sheets (12 x 6 feet) or rolls (7 feet and 3 inches wide x 77 feet total length) it did enable large areas to be covered relatively quickly. The rolls, for example, enabled some 175 square feet to be laid per man hour, but only 80 square feet with the sheets. The track was edge jointed but held taut whilst metal stakes were driven in to hold it in place. Despite the backbreaking work to clear, level and prepare the site with tracking, the work was completed on 6 August, enabling aircraft landings to be made that very day. Airfield B.19 Lingèvres became the home to No.125 Wing (mainly Spitfires), albeit for just twenty days until the wing moved to Airfield B.40 Beauvais on 2 September.[36]

The remainder of August and for much of September 1944 (up to the end of Phase II of the campaign) proved to be particularly busy for the squadron as it moved up through Northern France and into Belgium. Between 26 August and 30 August, it completed the airfield at B.30 Créton with a 5,000ft untracked grass strip used as a staging point for the aircraft of No.124 Wing, which would eventually move into the squadron's next construction project at Airfield B.48 Amiens/Glisy and then Lille where, despite the proximity of an enemy 'pocket' equipped with the fearsome 88mm gun, they repaired the airfield at Vendeville, which had been heavily cratered as the Germans withdrew. The squadron was on the move again the next day, moving into the grounds of a chateau at Hal near the city of Brussels.

Proximity to the city was particularly welcome for many of the support units of 2nd TAF, a place which the diarist of No.5022 Squadron described as 'a city with a people who gave us a great reception'. The rapid advance of the Allies at this time, though, was already stretching the lines of communication, mainly still from Normandy (the port at Antwerp was not opened to Allied shipping until late November).

Among the many urgently needed supplies fuelling the Allies offensive, there was one precious component which is often commented on in memoirs of the time – mail from home. By the time No.5022 Squadron reached Brussels though, they had not received any post for nearly two weeks, a point not lost on the unit diarist who commented:

> The task [construction work at Diest] went well despite changed specifications and the local reception – our first Flemish contact – overwhelmed us with dairy produce. The latter assisted in disguising our unhappiness at having received no mail for 13 days.[37]

This was, however, a situation which had been influenced by operational realties and not planning. As early as D+1, the planners had factored-in a daily sea service of mail to and from the United Kingdom, using field post offices on the Continent. Most units had an appointed postal orderly responsible for the collection and delivery of mail.

Importance of Air Transport

Notwithstanding the difference in how far Nos. 83 and 84 groups had advanced since the breakout from the Normandy bridgehead, both had started to experience supply problems because of the lengthy supply lines from Normandy. This was not just a challenge for the RAF but one which had become a significant problem for Twenty-First Army Group as a whole.[38] The inflow of equipment and supplies from the minor ports and scheduled supply-by-air service, however, was not enough to solve the supply crisis. Problems continued with bad weather in early September, causing reliability problems with the air freight service, resulting in a hold up in the despatch of urgent equipment to the Continent.

The use of air transport became ever more important as the Allies rapidly advanced into France and Belgium and the transport aircraft could be landed much closer to the line of advance. Indeed, during August alone, the aircraft of the RAF's No.46 Group (predominantly Dakotas of Nos. 48, 233, 271, 512 and 575 squadrons) were particularly active in supporting the campaign, with almost daily flights from the United Kingdom carrying freight and passengers as part of the scheduled supply-by-air service. Surviving records from this period are somewhat patchy in terms of their usable detail but the war diary of HQ No.46 Group shows that some 215 tons of scheduled service RAF freight was flown to the Continent for 2nd TAF units during the month.[39]

In his report to the Air Ministry in 1945, Coningham commented how 'owing to the length of the line of communication the continued advance of the ground forces seemed likely to be hampered by the lack of supplies' and he therefore ordered the maximum use of air transport to bring in supplies to various airfields in Belgium.[40]

Much of this was critical *materiel* for the army such as fuel for vehicles, ammunition and rations, but also included aviation fuel. Whilst Supreme HQ Allied Expeditionary Force was generally happy with the physical quantity of aviation fuel available on the Continent in mid-August, the exceptional advance made and the greatly extended lines of communication by the first few weeks of September had challenged fuel transportation to the utmost. Airlift was needed to reach flying squadrons in the forward areas.[41]

From his experience as the commander of the Desert Air Force, Coningham was acutely aware of the importance of air transport and knew that it could be required at any stage of a campaign. Despite his attempts to secure dedicated air transport for 2nd TAF, Coningham had no transport under his operational command. Apart from instances where he had used his own aircraft such as the photographic reconnaissance Wellingtons to move fuel to Amiens earlier in September, bids for additional air transport had to be submitted to the Combined Air Transport Operations Room at RAF Bentley Priory in the United Kingdom. The fly in the ointment though, from 2nd TAF's viewpoint, were the growing demands of the United States First Allied Airborne Army, especially for aircraft from the RAF's Nos. 38 and 46 groups.

Casualty Air Evacuation

The evacuation of casualties by air really came into its own during the rapid advance from Normandy into Belgium and the Netherlands, and saved countless lives. With many units on the move a long time often elapsed before base hospitals could be moved forward from Normandy and when there were no ports in the Low Countries in which hospital ships could be berthed. Based on the Continent, these aircraft were able to operate in the forward areas where they knew the country and were able to fly at low altitude without escort. This freedom of movement would not have been possible for transport aircraft not under the direct control of 2nd TAF.

The Handley Page Sparrow (ambulance flight) aircraft were on loan from RAF Transport Command and proved to be particularly valuable, especially as their local operational control came under 2nd TAF's Principal Medical Officer who, in turn, had a close working relationship with his counterpart in HQ 21st Army Group. On outward flights the Sparrows carried mainly medical supplies to the forward airfields and then returned with casualties to hospitals in the advanced base or in the rear area. Not surprisingly, the value of such a service was one of several recommendations for future campaigns which Coningham made.

Interestingly, though, he did recommend that they not be marked with red crosses in order that they could also be used as resupply aircraft to carry urgently required supplies to the forward areas.

Market Garden – the Disruption

The story of the ill-fated, but remarkable Operation *Market Garden* was Montgomery's ambitious plan to propel troops and vehicles across the river Rhine and into Germany. It was, he asserted 'the lightning stroke needed to topple the Third Reich and effect the end of the war in 1944'.[42] Numerous historians and authors have written about this operation, and, despite its strategical failure, the operation is replete with numerous examples of courage and fortitude, from individual acts of heroism to the British Parachute Regiment's stoical, gallant defence of the Arnhem road bridge.

In essence, the operation comprised two parts. Market was the airborne element involving the capture of key bridges in the Netherlands by the United States 82nd and 101st airborne divisions and the British 1st Airborne Division, landing by parachute and glider. The ground element, *Garden*, involved the British No.30 Corps advancing over the key bridges at Eindhoven, Nijmegen and Arnhem, and then the Rhine. Its overall intent was to liberate the Netherlands, outflank the German Siegfried Line and enable armoured forces to strike at Germany's industrial centre, the Ruhr.

The operation was launched on 17 September 1944 but failed to achieve its overall objective due to the inability of No.30 Corps to reach Arnhem before its British defenders were overwhelmed by fierce German opposition. Just over a week later, some 2,100 troops of British 1st Airborne Division were evacuated back across the Rhine, leaving 7,500 killed or taken prisoner by the enemy. It is worthy of note that 2nd TAF aircraft played a significant part during this period intercepting enemy aircraft activity directed against the bridges. Indeed, aircraft under the control of No.83 Group's control centre accounted for seventy-six enemy aircraft destroyed and fifty-four damaged.

Of the many factors that contributed to the failure of the operation, the availability of air transport often attracts comment. The simple fact is that, for the operation itself, there were not enough aircraft to carry all three airborne divisions into the Netherlands in a single airlift.[43] To meet the need, a high proportion of the airlift required for the *Market* component of the operation was frozen at a time when it was urgently needed for day-to-day airlift on the Continent. So strongly did Coningham feel about this that he made specific comment in his post-war report, commenting that,

> a review will show that a 'freezing' of air transport during a week of fine weather, with ample ground suitable for landings, when the Americans and British armies were only halted through lack of fuel and ammunition supply, was the decisive factor in preventing our armies reaching the Rhine before the onset of winter.[44]

Thus, a conflict of air transport resource requirement arose between the needs of the British airborne forces in Operation *Market Garden* on the one hand and those of the British Second Army (and 2nd TAF) as they advanced towards Germany, on the other.

It was not any easy issue to resolve, and most bids submitted by 2nd TAF for the RAF and the army had to be met using whatever aircraft could be released from No.46 Group, along with emergency support provided by RAF Bomber Command's No.4 Group. In the case of the latter, an average of seventy Halifax aircraft per day (at 5-minute intervals) flew in 1,445 tons of motor transport petrol in jerry can, from RAF Pocklington in Yorkshire to Melsbroek, near Brussels during the 8 days following 25 September 1944. These were not purpose designed transport aircraft and were effectively 'misemployed' bombers.

Additional help was provided by a wing of Liberator aircraft of the United States Eighth Air Force.[45] Up until the opening of Antwerp, an average of 800 tons was flown in.[46] This period, from the peak in mid-September through until the end of November 1944, is illustrated quite clearly in the graph below. Of note is that the greater tonnage of freight moved during this time was by special service, supply-by-air aircraft.

In his campaign report, Coningham made specific comment about these air transport difficulties, remarking that 'the fact that 21st Army Group and 2nd TAF had no air transport aircraft at their own immediate call was a very definite handicap throughout the campaign' and both he and '21 Army Group ... as experienced operational users, are firmly convinced that an army and air force operating in the field should have control of a definite number of transport aircraft'. This could

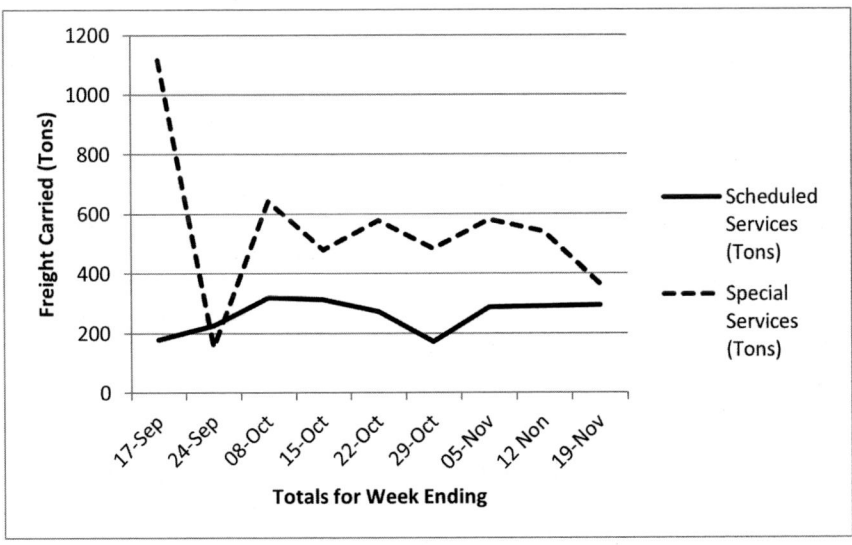

Figure 2. Air freight carried by Dakotas of No.46 Group – scheduled and special services – 13 September to 19 November 1944.[47]

have been achieved, suggested Coningham, by the allocation of certain squadrons from RAF Transport Command, with aircraft being withdrawn when required for airborne operations. By contrast, the United States Ninth Air Force in the Allied Expeditionary Air Force had its own air transport resources (seventy-five Dakota aircraft in IX Troop Carrier Command) which were under local control and not diverted to airborne operations.[48]

Thankfully, the availability of RAF transport aircraft improved considerably after the Arnhem airborne operation and towards the end of September 1944 the number of aircraft employed daily on the schedule was increased to eleven; with few exceptions this number was maintained.

The Advance Continues

Overall, September 1944 saw the rapid advance of British and Canadian forces across France, Belgium and into the Netherlands. Lille was reached on 2 September, Brussels on 3 September, and eventually the strategically significant city of Antwerp on 4 September. By this time, 2nd TAF had developed a particularly close working relationship with the ground forces and was able to provide virtually on-call ground attack where determined enemy resistance was encountered. As with the attacks on enemy vehicles at Falaise, rocket firing aircraft such as the Typhoon were particularly useful in providing such support.

As the ground troops moved forward, the support units of 2nd TAF often found themselves involved in what might be described as 'mopping-up' operations, invariably involving rounding-up enemy troops that had become cut off from their units during the German retreat and were in hiding. Such an instance was experienced by No.2874 Squadron RAF Regiment which in mid-September 1944 was in the process of moving from Airfield B.35 at Godelmesnil, just inland from the port at Le Tréport (north-east along the coast from Dieppe) to Airfield B.53 at Merville much further north towards the border with Belgium. As with most moves during the advance, units usually relocated in what were known as advanced or main parties. Often these were discrete sections of a unit such as a flight or squadron. In the case of this RAF Regiment squadron, its B Flight remained at Godelmesnil whilst the rest of the squadron took to the road.

On 14 September, the OC of B Flight was informed by the mayor of the nearby town of Eu that a small party of the enemy was raiding farms in the local area. A small section from the RAF Regiment went to carry out a reconnaissance of the area, most of which was dense woodland. Although they came under enemy small arms fire, they were unable to locate the offenders. Later that evening, in conjunction with some French Resistance fighters (then known as the French Forces of the Interior), a further foray into the area enabled them to capture two Germans in civilian clothes. Both were handed over to the Resistance at Neufchâtel under armed escort. A relatively small-scale incident but typical of many at the time which invariably proved to be a time-consuming use of resources.[49]

CROSSING THE START LINE – BREAKOUT FROM NORMANDY

A 15ft, Type II radar vehicle just gets under a bridge. This photograph was probably taken somewhere in the Netherlands during the advance. *(Copyright Through Their Eyes)*

By this stage of the campaign with the advance now in the Netherlands, some of the RAF Regiment's armoured car and rifle squadrons found themselves located alongside army troops on the front line.

Significance of the Ports

Air transport could not solve the logistics problem alone and the key to success was the availability of the Continental ports. Their use had been considered by the planners as early as 1941 as part of the Operation *Roundup* planning. The landings in North Africa in 1942 and mainland Italy in 1943 had both shown the importance of capturing ports as early as possible. A British Port Organisation Committee was formed in September 1943, which did much important work regarding the finer detail of port operations on the Continent. Over a four-month period, several meetings were held and, along with wider analysis, enabled the Committee in February 1944 to produce for Supreme HQ Allied Expeditionary Force a highly detailed paper entitled *Details of Operation and Control of Captured or Liberated Ports*. The analysis considered the technical workings of the ports at Antwerp, Rotterdam, and Hamburg, but purely from a port-operating perspective.[50] How the ports were operated was one thing, but how their capture was prioritised in the broader operational plan was another matter altogether.

Many of the minor Channel ports were progressively captured throughout September 1944 with their usage enabling some pressure to be taken off the greatly extended line of communication. On the left flank of the advance, No.84 Group operating in support of the Canadians, was heavily involved in major actions which succeeded in capturing the Channel ports at Dieppe on 2 September, Ostend on 9 September, Le Havre on 12 September and Boulogne on 24 September.

Up until late November 1944, the largest tonnage of stores came into France through the port at Cherbourg, although the majority of this was for the Americans,

FORWARD AIR BASES IN EUROPE FROM D-DAY TO THE BALTIC

with just 500 tons a day allotted to the British.[51] There was certainly an RAF interest in this port operation as the RAF's No.87 Embarkation Unit (part of No.85 Group) was stationed there from 29 June 1944. Given the position of Cherbourg at the tip of the Cotentin Peninsula, well to the west of the Normandy beaches, its value to British operations diminished after the breakout and subsequent advance. By far the most significant port for the British during September and October 1944 was Dieppe and it took just five days from its date of capture to the date of opening. By fifty-five days after its opening, Dieppe was discharging just over 5,000 tons of cargo per day.

The RAF's No.93 Embarkation Unit was based at Dieppe from the date of its opening through until the beginning of November 1944 and some 11,678 tons of RAF fuel and 4,587 tons of munitions were unloaded there during September and October 1944.[52] Dieppe's smaller satellite port at Le Tréport also proved to be valuable to the RAF, used for the return of crashed aircraft to the United Kingdom for repair and as an inward route for urgently required RAF stores.[53] A detachment of RAF personnel from No.93 Embarkation Unit was based at Le Tréport from 22 October 1944.

Despite the great strides that had been made with capturing what were termed the minor ports, the keystone to the logistics problems which were emerging throughout September was the port at Antwerp. The city itself fell to the Allies on 4 September, but their failure to cross the Albert Canal before the bridges across it were blown-up, enabled the retreating Germans to regroup and to occupy defensive positions in the Beveland peninsula. This effectively prevented Allied shipping

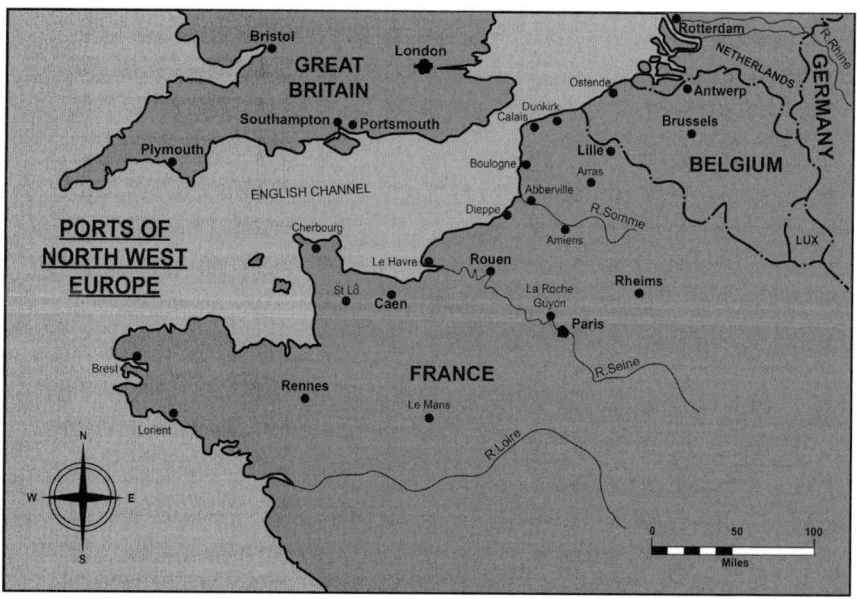

Map 3. North-west Europe Ports Utilised by the British, 1944–1945.[54]

CROSSING THE START LINE – BREAKOUT FROM NORMANDY

from using the river Scheldt to access Antwerp from the North Sea. Any further advance could not be maintained without the city's port being opened to Allied shipping. By the end of September 1944, this need had become a vital necessity.

The tactical errors of the Allies which enabled the Germans to establish control of the Scheldt and deny Antwerp's use as a port to the Allies, commonly referred to as the great mistake, denied the use of a much-needed sea line of communication into the Continent at a critical time of the campaign.[55] Despite what would appear to have been a clear priority, matters took a different line of travel and the logistical significance of Antwerp became lost as the senior commanders, notably Montgomery, squabbled over the broad front/narrow thrust strategy.

There are various views about Montgomery's perspective, but he does seem to have been indifferent about the capture of Antwerp. Indeed, just before the commencement of Operation *Market Garden* in mid-September, it was recorded in the log of Twenty-First Army Group that 'From a purely British point of view Antwerp had never been a vital necessity'.[56]

Interestingly, in his post-war memoirs, Montgomery does acknowledge the significance of the Channel ports to logistics, especially the benefits gained from the capture and subsequent opening of Dieppe on 8 September 1944. His recollection of the situation regarding Antwerp, despite what actually unfolded in terms of supply problems and the actual significance of the port to the British, is somewhat bizarre, claiming that 'the American armies in particular were greatly hampered in their operations by lack of resources, and the solution of their difficulties lay in opening the port of Antwerp'.[57] Why he should have avoided including the British need in that remark is not clear, but perhaps he was carefully avoiding any share of blame for not attaching enough importance to Antwerp in his original strategy.

Not all British senior commanders shared Montgomery's view. Admiral Sir Bertram Ramsay, the naval C-in-C for Operation *Neptune*, understood the importance of the Channel ports and had expressed concern throughout 1944 that insufficient effort was being paid to their early capture. In a high-level meeting of the various commanders-in-chief chaired by Eisenhower on 5 October 1944, Ramsay took the opportunity to express his concern regarding the critical significance of Antwerp which had become all too apparent by that point. In his diary entry for that day, he wrote:

> Very interesting exposition of situation on Army Group fronts. Monty made the startling announcement that we could take the Ruhr without Antwerp. This afforded me the cue I needed to lambast him for not having made the capture of Antwerp the immediate objective at the highest priority & I let fly with all my guns at the faulty strategy we had allowed. Our large forces were now practically grounded for lack of supply & had we now got Antwerp & not the corridor we should be in a far better position for launching the knockout blow.[58]

Despite what was flowing into the Continent through the minor Channel ports, the lion's share of supplies was still being transported by road (and where possible, by rail) from the Rear Maintenance Area in Normandy – thus stretching transport resources to the limit. As a result, the logistics effort was beginning to struggle by the tail end of summer 1944. Coningham later wrote:

> On our part, we had reached a position where we had so extended our lines of communication from the original base ports in western France that, in spite of the benefits of air transport afforded by our air supremacy, our logistical position was critical. Even after the capture of Havre [sic], we could not maintain the momentum of any further advance without the use of Antwerp, which lay intact in our hands, secure from air attack but with its approaches denied to us by the enemy who had taken up firm positions on either side of the Scheldt Estuary.[59]

Phase II Ends

The tail end of September 1944 saw Phase II of the operation end. It was a point in the campaign where the enemy was making desperate efforts to consolidate the natural barrier of the Meuse. The German Luftwaffe had largely withdrawn to bases in north-west Germany and eastern Netherlands. Every indication was that a 'decisive penetration of the Meuse-Rhine barrier … would probably cause the complete collapse of his military machine'.[60]

Although the breakout from Normandy had taken much longer than originally planned, the speed of advance was greater than expected. The HQ 2nd TAF had moved to its winter quarters in Brussels and had been joined by its rear headquarters which had only moved to the Continent in mid-August. Unit moves, typically, were long journeys. On 29 September 1944, for example, No.2874 Squadron RAF Regiment had to travel approximately 230 miles from its base at Airfield B.53 at Merville in Northern France, to a new location at Airfield B.80 Volkel in the Netherlands, roughly mid-way between Eindhoven and Nijmegen.

Their war diary for September 1944 recorded:

> The operational moves of the Squadron have proved very successful, and the main problems have been administrative. The lengthening lines of supply have caused some difficulties in obtaining petrol and rations from time to time. The Squadron has had to carry out operational moves over very long distances at short notice, and ingenuity and enterprise in obtaining vital supplies has been necessary. During the month the Squadron has not been in action against enemy aircraft.[61]

While the support units of 2nd TAF had clearly trained hard and were generally well equipped, the journey from Normandy had been a continuous learning experience. Leigh-Mallory's campaign despatch makes the point that,

CROSSING THE START LINE – BREAKOUT FROM NORMANDY

throughout June and July most of the squadrons operated from new-made landing strips only a few miles from the front line, and that dust on these Normandy airfields was, in the opinion of many experienced campaigners, worse than that in the North African desert campaigns.[62]

With that alone as a backdrop, it is remarkable that a high degree of average serviceability was maintained as the data in the table below shows.

The resources to keep the aircraft flying were substantial. During July alone, Allied Expeditionary Air Force dropped 750 tons of bombs and more than 200,000 rounds of ammunition. Fuel consumption alone reached nearly 30 million gallons of petrol – almost 1 million gallons a day. Whilst these figures cover the Allied air force's consumption, 2nd TAF's share would have been considerable.

Throughout August and September, No.83 Group was highly successful in pursuing the retreating enemy forces, much of which was aided by the relatively open rolling nature of the land they moved over: it was ideal terrain over which their low flying fighters and fighter-bombers could operate. Coningham remained conscious of the need for the tactical air force, especially No.83 Group which was providing the main air support for the British Second Army, to keep pace with the ground forces.

The RAF's official history of the campaign relates how the group moved in 'a series of leapfrog advances across Northern France to the Dutch frontier'. Wherever possible, only three operational airfields and those captured from the enemy were used at any one time. Coningham made as much use of air transport as possible to move ground crews and fuel and apparently there were occasions when 2nd TAF aircraft were also used in the transport role. The group, and of course its support units, did not pause for any appreciable length of time until they reached their planned winter locations around Eindhoven.

The group's airfields by the end of Phase II shows that they were then occupying a broad, wedge-shaped zone, from the east of Brussels and Antwerp at the broad end in Belgium, to Eindhoven and Nijmegen in the Netherlands at the other. Most of the group's support units were also well forward and mostly concentrated around Eindhoven.

Month	Fighters			Bombers		
	Average Strength	Average Serviceability	Percentage	Average Strength	Average Serviceability	Percentage
June 1944	1156	954	82.5%	272	231	85.0%
July 1944	1058	946	89.5%	265	232	87.5%
August 1944	1077	930	86.4%	277	240	86.7%
September 1944	1250	1093	87.5%	253	214	84.6%

Figure 3. 2nd TAF average aircraft strength and availability – June to September 1944.[63]

Chapter 7

Logistics at Breaking Point – The Autumn Crisis

Phase III of the Allied campaign began on 27 September 1944. The resolve of the enemy was increasing as they now knew that the Allied advance was coming ever closer to their fatherland. The advance though, had slowed, mainly as a result of poor weather – the priority now was to stabilise a line which could be held during the winter months. With Operation *Market Garden* having failed to establish a bridgehead over the Rhine at Arnhem, the Allied front line at the end of September 1944 was lying west of the river Meuse and extending northwards and westwards in an arc through Nijmegen, to include Antwerp. The latter of course was not yet in operation as a fully functioning port.

Broadly speaking, 2nd TAF's No.84 Group was working in conjunction with the Canadians to open up the Scheldt. No.83 Group's main role was to maintain air supremacy on the front of Montgomery's Twenty-First Army Group and to prevent enemy road and rail movement by interdiction missions in the north-east of the Netherlands and Germany, in front of the Second Army. The heavier aircraft of No.2 Group were active in attacking the man bridges on the river Ijssel, along with assisting No.84 Group on the front of the Canadian Army. The grouping of airfields that 2nd TAF had now secured in the Netherlands between Eindhoven and Nijmegen were now key locations which would enable the tactical aircraft to continue their critical support of Twenty-First Army as they were pushing forward towards Germany.

In his post-war report, Coningham makes several interesting observations about the wider benefits which the Allied air supremacy at this time brought about. The vehicle convoys of 2nd TAF were allowed to move almost head-to-tail along roads which were beyond the reach of enemy artillery. Within 2nd TAF, Coningham ordered the return of all camouflage netting to the base depot as they were then seen to interfere with unit mobility.

Indeed, the whole process of camouflaging units in field locations was time-consuming and needed careful consideration, let alone the time taken to take down the nets and pack them for transport. A greater number of aircraft were based on airfields than earlier in the campaign, sometimes as many as six squadrons on each, but with the corresponding loss of dispersal. It was also more common to see communications and transport aircraft flying more freely within the Allied area.

The advance into the Netherlands, coupled with the precarious position towards Nijmegen and Arnhem, established following Operation *Market Garden*, found several RAF Regiment squadrons in action throughout the area. Many of these

LOGISTICS AT BREAKING POINT – THE AUTUMN CRISIS

A road convoy of German prisoners of war in Normandy, 1944. *(Author's collection)*

were in the Canadian area of operations including what was known as the Breskens Pocket on the southern side of the Scheldt Estuary, an area of resistance held by the isolated German 64th Infantry Division under Generalmajor Eberding.[1]

Despite the overwhelming air supremacy, many of the forward 2nd TAF units which were based much closer to Germany, began experiencing sporadic attacks by Me 262 jet fighters, albeit these were being misemployed in a bomber role at Hitler's direction. Several forward airfields started to report the presence of these aircraft during October 1944 but, flying at approximately 15 to 20,00 feet, they were invariably out of range of the RAF Regiment anti-aircraft guns.

This was, as recorded by the diarist of No.2874 (Light Anti-Aircraft) Squadron RAF Regiment 'much to the disgust of the gun crews!' Its sister squadron, No.2875, had more success and was credited with destroying the first of these jet fighters by ground fire. These forays by the new Me 262s became increasingly confident, not just because of the altitude they operated at but also because they outclassed the RAF's piston-engine aircraft.

The RAF Regiment's anti-aircraft guns did get to grips with the new enemy jet though. On 26 November 1944, an Me 262 attacking Airfield B.86 Helmond, near Eindhoven was shot down by the 40mm Bofors guns of No.2875 Squadron. This was the first time an enemy jet aircraft had been shot down by ground fire.

It was not just attacks by manned enemy aircraft that presented an ever-growing danger. At just after 19.00 hours on 14 October what was believed to be an V-1 flying bomb landed just 60 yards from the HQ B Flight No.2874 Squadron at Airfield B.80 Volkel in the Netherlands. The resulting explosion set fire to one of the squadron's 3-ton trucks which was loaded with Bofors gun 40mm high explosive and armoured piercing ammunition.

In the darkness 'the light from the fire was very considerable and invited further attention from the enemy, but the ammunition exploding in all directions and the absence of any cover, made approach extremely dangerous'. Given the

FORWARD AIR BASES IN EUROPE FROM D-DAY TO THE BALTIC

RAF Regiment 40mm Bofors gun. (*Crown Copyright – Air Historical Branch MoD*)

danger to which the airfield and nearby personnel were now exposed, it was not surprising that the vehicle blaze needed to be brought under control. Two senior NCOs from the RAF Regiment squadron, Warrant Officer Patrick Maguire and Sergeant Archibald Brown, both voluntarily took a firefighting 'foam' hose to within 5 yards of the fire, completely disregarding the danger from the flames, exploding ammunition and the possibility of further enemy attack. Very quickly they were able to extinguish the fire but not before they had suffered burns to their hands and 'extreme discomfort from the heat'. Both men were subsequently decorated for their bravery.[2]

Proximity to the front line brought several of the RAF Regiment's squadrons close to the enemy. On a day in October 1944, Flying Officer John Wild was in command of a contingent of armoured reconnaissance cars, on the south bank of the Wilhelminakanaal. His unit received a warning that an enemy patrol was working its way across the canal towards his position. Not wasting any time, he immediately set out to meet the oncoming patrol, covered by two of his men. Very shortly he encountered four of the enemy and, despite coming under heavy fire, threw a hand grenade at them. He then worked his way round to the enemy's flank, throwing another grenade, which wounded a German officer and two men.

Wild then moved on the German position, killing the officer with his revolver, but the other men escaped, leaving their weapons behind. The RAF Regiment men endeavoured to track down the other enemy soldiers, but the rest of the patrol had escaped across the canal. For this action, in which he personally accounted for at least six of the enemy, John Wild was awarded the Military Cross. The citation for the award related how he 'displayed courage and skill of the highest order ... and at all times set a magnificent example to his men.[3]

Menace of the V-weapons

Despite the relative security of the major towns and cities during late 1944, the enemy remained conscious of the significance of Antwerp to the Allies and the city and from its capture it became a regular target of attempted attacks by V-1 flying bombs and V-2 long range rockets. The V-2 offensive alone lasted from September 1944 through until March 1945. Nearly 2,500 V-2 rockets were launched during this time with some 500 hitting London with several hundred more landing on surrounding counties.

Initially, London and Antwerp were the main targets, but a number also fell around Ipswich and Norwich plus a number of Allied sites in France, Belgium and the Netherlands. Most of these were being launched from well camouflaged ramps, which could be quickly erected on widely dispersed sites. Firing sites against London were clustered around the Hague (V-2s) and those against Antwerp were largely in a triangular area of between Zwolle, Deventer and Almelo.

V-1 flying bomb on display in Brussels after the city's liberation in September 1944. *(Copyright Through Their Eyes)*

FORWARD AIR BASES IN EUROPE FROM D-DAY TO THE BALTIC

The rocket attacks claimed 2nd TAF casualties on both sides of the channel. On 18 November, the CO of No.2811 (Rifle) Squadron RAF Regiment, Squadron Leader Blatherwick and his driver Leading Aircraftman Skeet were caught up in the blast from one such attack. The CO was injured and admitted to hospital but tragically his driver was killed.

By December the rate of fire was considerable. Within 24 hours, 148 flying bombs were fired at Antwerp alone. An attack on the city on 16 December had tragic consequences when a V-2 rocket struck the Rex Cinema in Antwerp killing 567 with 291 wounded. Of these, twenty-six RAF personnel were killed, including four airmen of No.2757 (Armoured Car) Squadron RAF Regiment who were killed in the resulting explosion.[4]

Logistics – The 'Achilles' Heel

Of the many pressing issues which needed to be addressed at this time, the most critical was logistics. Without a major port, supplies and reinforcement were still having to come from Normandy or through some of the minor ports. A point does need to be made here about the rate of advance (and forward basing) between Twenty-First Army Group and 2nd TAF. Whilst aircraft of the tactical air force were operating at the front line, its airfields were farther back than the field locations of the army (and their at-hand combat supplies). Moreover, the RAF occupied its airfields much longer than the army occupied its positions during the advance.

Consequently, during Phase II and the early part of Phase III, the distance over which RAF supplies needed to move forward from the Rear Maintenance Area in Normandy, was less than that of the army. A rough comparison between the British front line on 10 November and the majority of 2nd TAF airfields at that time (excluding air observation post squadrons) was some 20 to 30 miles. Nonetheless, the shorter distance between the field locations of Twenty-First Army Group and 2nd TAF proved to be insignificant given the overall length of the line of communication. It became difficult for both ground and air forces. The opportunity was taken though for both the army and the RAF to establish an advance base in the vicinity of Brussels.

At the end of October 1944, Coningham set about trying to secure dedicated air transport support as an emergency measure. In a letter to HQ Allied Expeditionary Air Force he asked if he could retain No.575 Dakota Squadron under his local control (as part of 2nd TAF) on the Continent (then based at Brussels/Evere airfield, having flown re-supply missions to Arnhem as part of Operation *Market Garden*.[5] He was not successful, largely as a result of the views of the AOC-in-C Transport Command, Air Chief Marshal Sir Frederick Bowhill, who was content for it to remain on the Continent under local control of 2nd TAF, but firmly remaining in No.46 Group.

In his response to HQ Allied Expeditionary Air Force and defending his view, Bowhill made specific reference to several principles laid down by the Air Council which, inter alia, specified that 'transport aircraft allotted to any theatre must be regarded as part of a common pool of Transport resources'. With the arrival of No.2 Group on the Continent the daily scheduled lift of air freight was increased from eleven to thirteen aircraft giving a lift of approximately 29 tons per day. Additional aircraft to this scheduled lift were also arranged during November 1944 to deal with backlogs caused by bad weather and special commitments which arose from time to time.

Opening of Antwerp

On 28 October 1944, Eisenhower had issued his directive for the crossing of the Rhine but had made it quite clear that 'without the use of the port … forces could not be maintained during the winter months'. The Supreme Commander directed that 'the securing and placing in operation of Antwerp was our first and most important immediate objective'.

Operations to clear the Scheldt leading up to the port at Antwerp proved to be lengthy and took between 1 October and 8 November 1944 for combat operations, up until 28 November to sweep the Scheldt and its approaches of sea mines and to repair the port infrastructure. It was also costly, and the First Canadian Army lost nearly 13,000 officers and men killed, wounded, or missing. Almost half of this figure was entirely Canadian, whilst the rest were British, Polish, American and other Allied units under command.[6] The RAF Regiment was also actively involved in these operations, the 3-inch mortars of No.2816 (Rifle) Squadron operated side by side with the 2nd Canadian Infantry Division. On 7 October, HQ No.1313 Wing and Nos. 2757 (Armoured Car) and 2816 (Rifle) squadrons were in action on the Leopold Canal and remained in the line for fifteen days until relieved by Nos. 2777 (Armoured Car) and 2717 (Rifle) squadrons.

Flight Sergeant Albert Greening of No.2816 (Rifle) Squadron was in command of a 3-inch mortar flight at Moerkerke and close to the enemy lines. His flight was under continual enemy mortar and sniper fire, as well as periodical shelling. There was one incident when the church tower at Moerkerke, from which Greening was observing, was hit, and set on fire. Undeterred, he competed the shoot he was spotting for before escaping from his observation post. Greening spent some fourteen days involved in this dangerous but essential work and was awarded the Military Medal, the citation for which commented:

> The accuracy of the fire he directed undoubtedly caused the enemy to lose the initiative in an area where our own positions were very thinly held. The offensive spirit and good shooting of Flight Sergeant Greening's detachment successfully discouraged the enemy from preparing for a series of local attacks.[7]

Flying Officer Norman Page was in command of a rifle flight of No.2816 (Rifle) Squadron RAF Regiment and was involved in several actions, which led to him being awarded the Military Cross. On one occasion his flight went to the aid of twenty men of an army Royal Artillery unit that had been surrounded by the greatly superior enemy forces who were in well concealed positions in a wood north-east of Vaeke, south of the Leopold Canal.

On another occasion his flight was,

> beset on three sides by heavy enemy machine gun fire and fairly heavy mortar fire taut, by outstanding skill and leadership, Flying Officer Page withdrew his flight without loss, inflicting casualties on the enemy. For about fourteen days Flying Officer Page's flight occupied the left flank of a forward defence locality at Moerkerke. During this period, he was tireless in his devotion to duty. He frequently led patrols to enable mortar fire to be brought to bear on the enemy and, by night, he directed counter measures against enemy patrols.[8]

A number of men also distinguished themselves in other ways. Leading Aircraftman Thomas Davies of No.2798 (Rifle) Squadron RAF was at the village of Wamel, just south of the river Waal, west of Nijmegen. He was part of a mortar section that was given a section of the front line to hold. The enemy, in strength, was on the opposite bank of the river. Around mid-afternoon on 28 October his section opened fire on a factory site where several instances of either parachute flares or various signals had been reported. Soon after the bombardment started a bomb from one of the mortars failed to leave the muzzle completely and was in danger of falling to the ground. Recognising the danger, Davies, grabbed the precarious mortar bomb and threw it into a pond at the rear of their firing position. He then carried on firing the mortar and so 'enabled his team to complete a rapid attack and to withdraw before counter-fire was brought to bear against them'. Davies was awarded the Military Medal for his courage and sense of duty. The citation for his award commented that his swift action 'saved the lives of his colleagues and enabled an important enemy objective to be destroyed.'[9]

Another RAF Regiment rifle squadron, No.2726, fought for a while under the command of 2nd Armoured Battalion, Irish Guards. By this stage of the campaign, the RAF Regiment had developed a much wider operational role than just airfield defence. Whilst some nineteen squadrons were assigned to light anti-aircraft duties, the RAF Regiment also sported twenty-one rifle and six armoured squadrons in 2nd TAF at the end of 1944.[10]

Once the port was opened for business, the effect on logistic operations was dramatic, a change of fortune which was described in one of the official histories as 'nothing less than a complete revolution in the Allies' position'.[11] The port received its first convoy on 27 November. Despite the targeting of the city by the German V-1 flying bombs and V-2 rockets from October 1944 to March 1945, the port became busier day by day. The amount received at Antwerp reached a peak on 29 March 1945 when the port received 66,500 tons of cargo and 733 vehicles in just one day.[12]

LOGISTICS AT BREAKING POINT – THE AUTUMN CRISIS

As part of the operating organisation, the RAF based its No.85 Embarkation Unit here in November 1944 along with some twenty-five personnel from No.93 Embarkation Unit after they had finished operations at Dieppe.[13] Unfortunately, the war diary for this unit covering its time at Antwerp did not survive and it is therefore difficult to assess port operations from an RAF perspective. The official history of Twenty-First Army Group does make one of the more detailed, albeit generic, statements on Antwerp:

> Tonnages discharged on British account rose rapidly reaching an average of 8,600 tons per day at the end of December and in January had increased to over 10,500 tons per day. Bulk petrol installations within the port were developed as a joint project and during December 160,000 tons of bulk petrol were discharged. The opening of Antwerp made it possible to accept shipping direct from the US and from the Middle East.[14]

Part of the problem in ascertaining the value of Antwerp to the RAF is that most of the sources make generic reference to fuel or supplies – as such, these could be

Aerial view of the port at Antwerp showing the extensive number of quaysides and cranes. This photograph was taken just after unloading operations began at the port by the Allies on 28 November 1944. *(Copyright IWM)*

army or RAF related. Given the fact that the aviation fuel was transported to the Continent by sea tanker vessels, it is highly likely that much of this was coming in through Antwerp after its opening to shipping in late November 1944. Not surprisingly, the Germans recognised the significance of the port and aimed to recapture Antwerp as part of their Ardennes offensive in mid-December 1944.

The Tragedy of Tank Landing Ship 420

The period up to December 1944 saw a number of units join the support organisation of 2nd TAF. Many of the base units having been phased in as and when space became available within the Rear Maintenance Area. One such organisation was the Base Signals and Radar Unit, originally destined for Normandy. In the event, it was not until November 1944 that it was scheduled for departure, largely due to the successful support provided by mobile signals servicing units and that the Allied front line was by then in Belgium. The revised plan was for the unit, its vehicles and personnel to move to Ghent in Belgium.

The story of this unit, as one of 2nd TAF's many support units, might have been unremarkable, except for the fact that a large number of men who formed part of the advanced party were to be lost at sea in what is believed to be the largest loss of life from a tank landing ship sinking during the war. The unit sailed from the United Kingdom aboard Tank Landing Ship 420 bound for the Belgian port at Ostend on 7 November 1944 as part of a small convoy of other vessels. There are differing accounts as to exactly what happened, but it seems that the ship was not granted permission to enter the port due to a storm and the captain therefore turned the vessel around and headed for the Thames Estuary where they could shelter until the following day.

It was on this return journey, and still within sight of Ostend, that, at 15.00 hours, the bow section hit a powerful German sea mine, which tore a substantial hole in the hull resulting in the ship breaking in half. The stern section was enveloped in flames caused by petrol from damaged vehicle fuel tanks being ignited by the fires in the ship's galley, which had been lit to cook the evening meal. The ship sank rapidly and, sadly, only larger vessels nearby could attempt to rescue survivors in the water due to the heavy sea conditions. The exact number of those who died is difficult to ascertain with any degree of accuracy, but one estimate suggests that as many as 320 lost their lives that November afternoon. It is certain though that at least 232 members of the TAF signals unit perished including 14 officers, three warrant officers, 31 senior NCOs and 189 airmen. Among these were five men of the Royal Canadian Air Force.[15]

The grim and heart-breaking task of recovering many of the bodies fell to the men of the RAF Base Personnel Centre, many of whom had only been in Normandy a couple of months. On 8 November, fifty-five bodies had been washed up on the beach near Ostend, with only two survivors having been found. The next day, the officer commanding the Base Personnel Centre had the rather unpleasant task of recovering a copy of the unit's nominal roll from the body of its CO, Wing Commander William Wendon to help ascertain who was on board the ship. A

LOGISTICS AT BREAKING POINT – THE AUTUMN CRISIS

further forty-one bodies were washed up on the beaches over the next few days, most of which were buried at Ostend.[16] Mines, both on land and at sea, continued to claim lives even in the absence of the enemy.

By the beginning of December 1944, the Allied front line had extended to a point between Nijmegen and Arnhem, with its left flank along the river Maas and right flank along the river Meuse. The airfields in use, along with a number under construction, were behind this line in the Netherlands, Belgium and Northern France. By the end of Phase III, the airfields of No.83 Group were more spaced apart between Nijmegen in the north and Brussels to its west, but slightly closely to the Rhine; its logistic units by this time were largely around Eindhoven. No.84 Group was furthest west with its airfields and logistics units close to a line drawn north-east/south-west running through Antwerp.[17]

Airfield Consolidation

Autumn turned out to be wet and cold, which led to numerous problems with maintaining the airfields in a safe and operational condition. Up until this point in the campaign, 2nd TAF had relied on what was termed as 'hasty' airfield construction. Essentially this consisted of three principal methods:

> Graded earth strips made of compacted earth, intended only for the short duration use by fighter aircraft types.
>
> Surfaced runways, taxiways, standings, and aprons. These were constructed using square mesh track, pre-bituminised surfacing, or pressed steel planking.
>
> Reconditioned enemy airfields. These were improved to RAF specifications and dimensions but were usually constructed or repaired with hard materials such as concrete, macadam, hardcore with a steel planked surface or laid in brick.[18]

This general lull in the Allied advance also enabled the heavy field force wings to carry out much needed repairs to several captured airfields in France and Belgium and restore them to use for heavy aircraft. The two runways at Airfield B.71 in the Belgian North Sea coastal town of Coxyde had around 320 bomb craters. With the assistance of approximately eight hundred local civilians, one of the heavy wing squadrons repaired the runways and 2 miles of taxiway, along with laying new hard-standings for forty aircraft in three months.

Further up the coast at Knokke, Airfield B.83, needed much attention. During its German occupation the airfield had been used for the training of anti-aircraft units. Although several aircraft hangars had been built, it had not been used as an active Luftwaffe airfield. It was liberated by Canadian army forces in October 1944, although the previous 'tenants' had dug numerous trenches to destroy the runway and the area was intensively mined.

One of the squadrons was involved in extensive work to bring this site online. After the clearance of some 12,000 land mines, 3 runways were brought back into

FORWARD AIR BASES IN EUROPE FROM D-DAY TO THE BALTIC

Royal Engineers constructing a landing strip somewhere in Normandy, 1944. (*Crown Copyright – Air Historical Branch MoD*)

use. Further inland at Airfield B.55 Wevelghem, near Courtrai, south of Bruges, 50,000 square yards of hardstanding and a runway were built for the RAF's aircraft repair depot. Again, the venture was supported by a local labour force, with 2,000 civilians and 600 horse and carts boosting the military effort.[19]

The real maintenance challenge came when the winter rains came. Many of the airfields experienced serious flooding problems, much of this caused by previous damage to drainage systems or through sabotage by the retreating enemy. This put many of 2nd TAF's airfields out of action. Much work was needed to get them operational again and often necessitated the more widespread use of steel planking or other surfacing materials so that runways could stand up to aircraft usage when the water level was high. Airfield construction work remained the dual responsibility of the army's Royal Engineers (airfield construction groups) and the RAF's airfield construction wings; a close and highly successful working relationship was maintained between them throughout the campaign. Much of this was greatly aided by the fact that the Twenty-First Army, deputy chief engineer airfields and his staff had been co-located with Coningham's HQ staff since it was first established on the Continent.

The most important airfield to be captured in the Netherlands was Eindhoven which was to become 'home' to many of 2nd TAF's units during the period of consolidation during the autumn and winter of 1944 and 1945. Situated approximately 5 miles to the west of the city centre, the airfield was originally a grass airstrip, opened in 1932. It was occupied by the Germans earlier in the war (renamed Fliegerhorst Eindhoven) who had carried out extensive development work of the site including new, paved runways (the longest of which was 1,750 yards long) with dispersal sites for up to 130 aircraft. Additionally, several defensive bunkers were built around the airfield perimeter, some of them disguised as civilian houses.

The airfield had been equipped as a first-class bomber station used by all types of aircraft up to and including the Dornier Do 217. It became an important base for bomber and bomber reconnaissance units that were engaged on night bombing and mine laying sorties, as well as for transport aircraft for the Germans. It had also frequently been used as an alternative airfield by bomber units and defensive night fighters from Gilze-Rijen, Leeuwarden and Deelen. With these facilities, it is easy to understand why it was an attractive prize for 2nd TAF. The airfield was captured by the United States 101st Airborne Division during Operation *Market Garden* and was named Airfield B.78 in common with the airfield naming convention, which had been used throughout the campaign.

When 2nd TAF moved in, though, the airfield was in poor shape. Its significance as a key Luftwaffe installation, had made it a target for Allied attack, the heaviest of these being on 15 August 1944, followed by minor attacks just before the re-occupation. The greatest damage had been inflicted by the retreating Germans with their demolition squads setting to work as early as the night of 5/6 September. Their work was thorough, causing widespread destruction of hangars, buildings and installations. Much of the site land drainage was beyond repair, all but one of the hangars had been blown apart, three quarters of the buildings were beyond repair and most of the aircraft standings had their blast walls partially destroyed. Ironically, it was the Allied bombers which had damaged the runways. Approximately 10 per cent of the main runway surface had been cratered or shattered, 24 per cent of runway No.2 and 18.5 per cent of runway No.3 was similarly affected.

Eindhoven soon became the focus of extensive work to make it operational again with the RAF's Nos. 5022 and 5023 airfield construction squadrons carrying out the work, along with civilian labour. The first echelon of No.5023 (Airfield Construction) Squadron moved in to commence work as soon as 19 September. The priority was to effect emergency repairs to enable initial operations. The wider repair would take much longer.[20]

Given that the Operation *Market Garden* airlift was still underway at this time, the men of the airfield construction squadron were so close to the front line that half of the men were required to mount guard whilst the other half started work. The Air Ministry's official history remarks that 'within 36 hours the strip was ready and those who worked on the job had the satisfaction of watching RAF Typhoons take off, fire their rockets into enemy concentrations and land for rearming, all in one circuit'.

The number of civilians employed under contract was quite sizeable, rising from just 25 men in November 1944, to a peak of 280 by March 1945. As can be appreciated from the extent of the damage, the scale of repair and new construction work was enormous and involved the filling of bomb craters, laying of various new surfaces, clearance of rubble, new laying of drainage and numerous other work. A small bomb disposal party was attached to the advanced echelon of

FORWARD AIR BASES IN EUROPE FROM D-DAY TO THE BALTIC

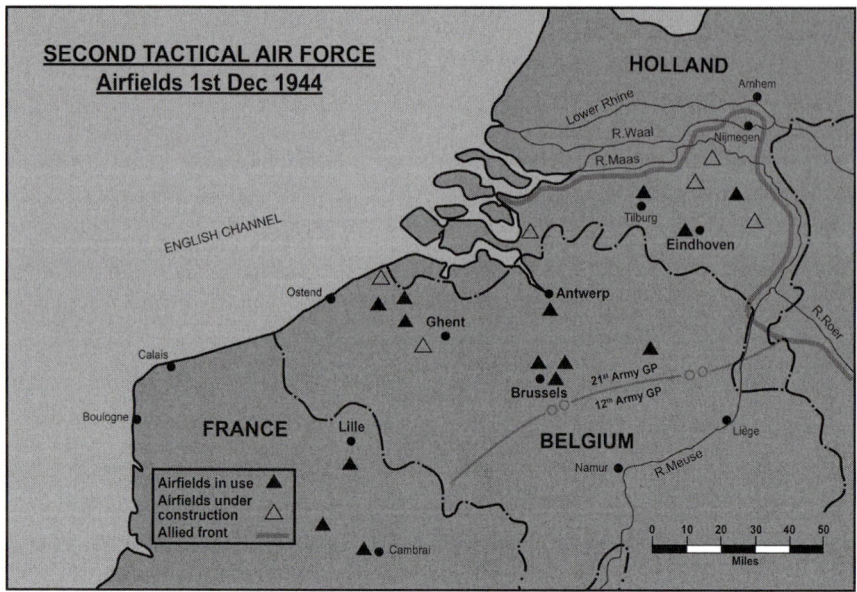

Map 4. 2nd TAF Airfields (in use and under construction), 1 December 1944.[23]

No.5023 Squadron, engaged solely with the removal of Allied unexploded bombs ordnance.[21]

The men, skills and plant of both the army and RAF airfield 'constructers' remained much in demand throughout the autumn and winter of 1944/1945. There were times, though, when conflicts of priority arose between airfield work and other 'pressing' tasks. One such need came about when roads and other hard standings required attention during the preparations for the Rhine crossings. This led to the diversion of assets away from airfield maintenance/construction work and resulted in delays to the airfield construction programme. Such was the give and take required in the highly uncertain conditions of mobile warfare. Pushed and pulled they might have been, but their work attracted great praise and appreciation from 2nd TAF's commander who remarked in his post-campaign report that 'their achievement in providing all-weather air bases for the Second Tactical Air Force during this period deserves the highest praise'.[22]

Communications

One aspect of support that was particularly challenging during the advance from Normandy was communications. The control of flying squadrons from the various group headquarters and their respective control centres to airfields was, wherever possible, carried out using both landline and radio telephones and teleprinters. For the landline work, 2nd TAF was supported by army air formation signals units;

men of these units did an incredible job in maintaining a complex communications network.

From HQ 2nd TAF forward to the wings, every telephone, every teleprinter, nearly all lines and switchboards and all the complicated apparatus were provided and maintained by these army units. With the frequent moves of the composite groups, this was a difficult job and invariably involved laying and relaying what turned out to be thousands of miles of all types of cabling to keep the various elements connected. Indeed, by May 1945, they operated landlines which would go twice around the world. Additionally, these units also provided a despatch rider letter service as well as their personnel manning and maintaining all the switchboards and teleprinters. The despatch riders alone, from June 1944 to May 1945, would carry over six million packages, over 6 million miles, without any loss.

In the early days of the campaign, especially within the lodgement area and just after the initial breakout from Normandy, Coningham's tactical air force had to rely entirely on the military provision of such communications as the civil and German equivalents were almost entirely destroyed. As the speed of the advance accelerated, the enemy had less time to sabotage its and the civilian networks, so opportunities did arise for 2nd TAF to make use of them. This proved to be particularly useful during the rapid advance into Belgium and the Netherlands. The slowing down of the advance by the autumn/winter period enabled a much greater use of the civil network. Coupled with the use of military resources, this enabled a much larger scale of command and lateral flow of communications, not just to 2nd TAF's control centres but also those of the United States Ninth Air Force. Coningham found this particularly valuable in mid-December when the Germans launched their counter-offensive in the Ardennes.

Despite the outstanding support provided by the air formation signals units, it became clear that radio-based communications were a vital necessity in modern mobile warfare, albeit that security of transmission content was difficult and such means could easily be intercepted by the enemy. Coningham highlighted this point in his post campaign report commenting that 'the development of automatic cyphering and de-cyphering facilities on radio teleprinter circuits and scrambler facilities on radio telephone circuits should be developed at the highest priority'.[24]

Settling in for the Winter

By early November the Allies had advanced more than 400 miles across France, Belgium, and the Netherlands. Some seventy-five airfields had been established and by late November 1944, many of 2nd TAF's units had begun to bed down for the winter period. The move into the low countries had gradually enabled many of 2nd TAF units to use, wherever possible, various buildings as billets, rather than the tentage that had been such a familiar part of their day-to-day life since landing on the Continent.

It became increasingly difficult to find accommodation in an area which had been badly damaged, and which was subject to more severe winter conditions than those generally experienced in England. Moreover, there was also a growing number of displaced persons desperately trying to find somewhere to shelter from the elements.

To address this, 2nd TAF started a programme to construct hutted accommodation in conjunction with Twenty-First Army's director of works. The programme was highly successful: on 1 October 1944 60 per cent of 2nd TAF was living under canvas but by 20 November 1944 only 9.8 per cent of Coningham's 100,000 officers and other ranks were still living in tents. This achievement was to make an enormous difference to the well-being and fighting efficiency of the tactical air force during the harsher than normal weather conditions during the winter of 1944–1945.[25]

Much consolidation took place; it proved to be good time to carry out much needed maintenance to vehicles which had endured a punishing time since the breakout from Normandy. The war diaries for many of 2nd TAF's units at this time provide an interesting view of day-to-day operations. No.7 Mobile Field Photographic Section, for example which supported No.34 Wing, captured four Germans who had been hiding since September near Perck (north-east of Brussels), following information provided by local civilians.

The winter, and indeed the early spring of 1945 saw severe weather in the Low Countries, which had a noticeable effect on road conditions. Moreover, it also became difficult for 2nd TAF to maintain all weather airfields which would enable aircraft on the forward bases to keep up offensive operations let alone escort long range bombers from the United Kingdom. It was also a challenging time for personnel, especially providing them with winter accommodation in an area, which had suffered heavy war damage. It was also recognised that health and morale needed to be maintained ready for the spring offensive.

Rest and Recuperation

Coningham and his commanders placed great importance on the welfare of their men, and latterly women, throughout the campaign, conscious that the facilities available were generally of a much higher standard than those available during the First World War. Indeed, in his post campaign report Coningham made the point that:

> On the principle that the human being directs the machine, and must be equally or more efficient, it is essential, if best results are to be achieved, to feed, clothe, house and entertain the force at the standard necessary for full efficiency.[26]

The change in tempo of operations did enable the men of 2nd TAF to have some rest and recuperation so Brussels and Antwerp became popular hotspots. Broadly speaking, each of the TAF groups was responsible for the welfare of its own men but No.85 Group was overall responsible for setting up rest camps, Malcolm

Clubs and NAAFI canteens. Supplies for the latter were obtained through the army HQ.

There were many talented individuals amongst the ranks of the ground crews. No.418 Air Stores Park, for example had its own dance band and had brought musical instruments with them from home, carefully hidden in various lorries. Leave 'hostels' were also established in Brussels and other large towns where personnel could spend time away for short periods of leave in pleasant surroundings away from their units.

The ability for personnel to mix more freely with larger numbers of very grateful liberated civilians in the larger cities did of course bring with it a risk of sexually transmitted disease. It was a fact of life which senior commanders had been cognisant of before D-Day. The official medical history of the campaign makes the point that it was known that there was a very high level of venereal disease among prostitutes on the Continent, especially in the occupied countries and Germany itself. This high level of pre-war incidence had increased significantly during the war due to poor conditions and a shortage of the drugs required to treat the condition, along with available medical personnel. The incidence of venereal disease contracted by RAF personnel while in Normandy was low. Apparently of forty-five personnel requiring treatment in August 1944, only two of these had contracted venereal disease while in Normandy.

After the breakout from Normandy, and as units neared the larger centres of population such as Lille, Amiens and Brussels there was a surprising and very sudden increase in infection rates. In 2nd TAF this rose to 162 notified cases in September 1944 alone and represented an incidence rate of 1.84 per 1,000 as opposed to 0.62 in August 1944. There was of course a much larger proportion of 2nd TAF that did not succumb to the temptation of the 'ladies of the night' but it was a problem that has befallen armies since antiquity.

Interestingly, and despite the stipulation of non-fraternisation with the German population after their surrender in May 1945, incidences of venereal disease once again became an area of concern, and much effort was put into publicity to educate the occupying troops.

The German Counter Offensive in the Ardennes – Battle of the Bulge

The other highly significant event during Phase III that posed a risk to the support of 2nd TAF was the German counter-offensive which was launched against the American front in the densely forested Ardennes region between Belgium and Luxembourg on 16 December 1944. Commonly referred to by the Allies as the Battle of the Bulge, the German code named Operation *Autumn Mist*, had two key purposes.

Firstly, the enemy was trying to obtain the initiative and disrupt Allied preparations for crossing the Rhine north of the Ruhr.

FORWARD AIR BASES IN EUROPE FROM D-DAY TO THE BALTIC

Secondly, they recognised that Antwerp was vital to the Allies as a supply source and there was a clear intent to break through to the port by using the blitzkrieg method of surprise and concentration. In doing this they also would effectively drive a wedge between American and British forces. The Germans achieved a total surprise when they launched the attack, the brunt of which was borne by American forces who incurred their highest casualty rate of any operation during the war. The battle also significantly depleted German armoured forces and aircraft and they also took a high number of casualties. At this stage of the war, the enemy was unable to replace such losses.

The enemy offensive was launched against a weakly defended section of the Allied line, taking advantage of poor weather conditions that grounded the Allies' superior air forces. The attack though, met with stiff resistance and this, notably at the Belgian town of Bastogne, effectively denied the Germans access to key roads to the west and north-west, which they needed for success. Bastogne, a town that commanded several important roads in the area, attracted concerted enemy action and saw American forces hold out during a siege which was to last until 26 December when the lead element of General Patton's Third United States Army reached Bastogne from the south. This disruption to the use of major roads put the German advance well behind schedule and allowed the Allies to move in reinforcements.

Whilst ground action in and around Bastogne was predominantly an American affair, 2nd TAF ground units found themselves involved. Several mobile radar units of No.72 Wing were deployed in the area of La Roche-en-Ardenne and came close to being overrun by the enemy offensive but were safely evacuated thanks to the endeavours of the RAF Regiment squadrons providing defence (Nos. 2770 and 2811 (Rifle) squadrons, along with No.2804 (Armoured Car) squadron). The HQ No.2811 (Rifle) Squadron together with four of its flights had arrived around La Roche-en-Ardenne on 6 December 1944 and were dispersed at a number of locations, including the town of Malmedy, which became infamous as the site of the massacre of 362 American prisoners of war and 111 Belgian civilians during December by German Waffen SS troops under the command of Kampfgruppe Peiper.

The war diary of No.2811 Squadron for the period is particularly busy but notably on 17 December when the unit diarist recorded that enemy parachutists had been dropped at a crossroads in the area of Malmedy around midday. All squadron sites were brought to full readiness and all three squadrons of the RAF Regiment assisted with the emergency evacuation of the RAF's mobile radar units which became endangered by the enemy advance.

The German thrust managed to reach as far west as the village of Foy-Nôtre-Dame, south-east of Dinant, but was halted by the United States 2nd Armoured Division on 24 December 1944. The poor weather that had worked to the enemy's advantage began to improve on Christmas Eve 1944, which enabled Allied air attacks on German forces and supply lines. Whilst the offensive was effectively broken by 27 December, the battle continued for another month before the front line was effectively restored to its former position.

Coningham was particularly concerned that both British and American Allied supply dumps could be overrun if the enemy advance was sustained. As a

LOGISTICS AT BREAKING POINT – THE AUTUMN CRISIS

precaution, 2nd TAF increased stocks of fuel and explosives in northern Belgium and the Netherlands by diverting such stocks from the port at Antwerp, leaving base stocks around Louvain (directly on a possible German north-west line of advance towards Antwerp) as low as possible.[27] The salient created by the German offensive in the Ardennes was eliminated by early February 1945 through a combination of Allied air and ground force operations.

2nd TAF Consolidates

It was during this phase of the campaign that the mainly bomber squadrons of No.2 Group moved from the United Kingdom to airfields in Northern France and eastern Belgium. Unlike the single engine aircraft of Nos. 83 and 84 groups, the Boston, Mitchell and Mosquito aircraft were multi-engine bombers that were more demanding in terms of the aviation fuel they consumed and munitions they carried. This proved to be particularly demanding for the RAF's supply chain, so the opening of Antwerp was particularly important for the import of these vital supplies.[28]

The night fighter squadrons of No.85 Group had moved out of the Normandy bridgehead area and were now located at Amiens and Lille in Northern France, with their supporting air stores park close to Brussels. By the end of December 1944, Twenty-First Army Group had established a whole series of main depots in advance bases at Brussels and Antwerp.

With good road and rail links, along with the port at Antwerp in operation for Allied shipping, the logistics position was stabilised, enabling concentrations of stores and supplies to be accumulated for the forthcoming advance into Germany. Whilst the opening of the port at Antwerp and subsequent build-up of a supply base provided much needed relief to the advancing forces, a challenge remained for the requirements in Phase IV of the campaign. As with the supply difficulties that had resulted from the extended line of communication from Normandy, an advance from the new main base at Antwerp brought a similar problem.

In his campaign report, Coningham highlighted the point that, for the crossing of the Rhine and subsequent advance, the lines of communication would be further lengthened and that 'railways were almost bound to be non-existent'.[29] The question of what supplementary ports could be used beyond Antwerp became a concern for 2nd TAF, with Bremen or even Hamburg as the next option; this concern was shared by Montgomery's Twenty-First Army Group which had identified Hamburg as its next advanced base.

Christmas 1944

Whilst the Allied landings and advance towards Germany had been a resounding success, it had been nearly six months since they had first set foot on the Normandy beaches. Many hard battles had been fought and the relatively stable position that they occupied at the end of 1944 enabled many units to make some arrangements for their men to celebrate Christmas, albeit many miles away from their homes and families. No.2834 Squadron of the RAF Regiment, then based at Airfield B.80 Volkel in the Netherlands, like many 2nd TAF units in theatre, worked hard to provide as good a Christmas to their men as possible.

In the week or so before Christmas they had learned that leave was to be started on 1 January 1945, which led to much excitement amongst all ranks, especially as each man was to have seven clear days at home. As far as practicable, Christmas was celebrated by as many units as possible. There must have been many mixed feelings, as they were separated from family and friends and still a very uncertain future ahead of them.

The diarist of No.2834 squadron RAF Regiment provides a snapshot of the squadron's Christmas Day in 1944:

> It was a pity the Squadron could not have been [all] together for the occasion but operational requirements decreed otherwise, in spite of that a good time was had by all. The Christmas fare had been augmented as far as possible by purchases with PSI funds of all the extras offered by NAAFI, BIS and Welfare. A good supply of beer had also been procured in Brussels. Dinners were held in each Flight Headquarters (two in each in relays) and one in SHQ [station headquarters]. The meals were served as is customary by the officers and Senior NCOs and afterwards in the NAAFI huts of each HQ a singsong and other forms of amusement went on until 6 a.m. Pianos had been borrowed from the local inhabitants for the occasion. As already mentioned, a good time was had by all.[30]

Good relations were not just fostered between the military. Where possible, units looked out to local civilian populations and were acutely aware of the hardships and often brutality they had faced under Nazi occupation. One touching example of the kindness that was extended was the initiative taken by No.4 Mobile Field Photographic Section on Christmas Eve 1944. Then based at Gilze Rijen in the Netherlands, the unit collected children from an orphanage at Breda, brought them to their camp for tea and entertainment and gave each child a present.

The ground units of 2nd TAF had established a sizeable footprint on the Continent by the end of 1944. The RAF Regiment alone comprised sixteen mobile wing headquarters and forty-five squadrons.[31]

New Year's Greetings from the Luftwaffe – Operation *Bodenplatte*

On New Year's Day 1945 the Luftwaffe launched a carefully planned, surprise low-level attack against seventeen Allied airfields in Belgium, the Netherlands and France. Comprising a total of some 850 fighters and fighter-bombers, the raids

LOGISTICS AT BREAKING POINT – THE AUTUMN CRISIS

were carried out by mainly by Me 109s and Fw 190s, but also Me 262s. The overall purpose of the attacks was for the enemy to try and regain dominance in the air by destroying as many Allied aircraft on the ground as possible, along with supplies and airfield facilities.[32] Roughly half of the attacking enemy force was directed against eleven RAF airfields.

Although the enemy had the benefit of both surprise and good weather conditions, the attacks were not as successful as they might have been, and the Germans lost over 200 first line aircraft and pilots. By contrast, the British and Americans lost about 122 operational aircraft, 84 more damaged with only 6 British pilots being killed. The RAF lost its six Sparrow casualty air evacuation aircraft in the attack. The German attack, carried out between 09.00 and 10.30 hours that morning, also managed to destroy numerous vehicles, stores and fuel dumps, although it is not clear from primary sources how serious these losses were.

Casualties amongst RAF personnel were not as high as they might have been although 40 were killed and 145 seriously wounded. There were a few 'close shaves'. At Airfield B.56 Evère, Brussels, many patients awaiting casualty air evacuation had been kept in a holding area prior to boarding Dakota transport aircraft. The attack came in before they could be loaded, but all the allocated Dakotas were lost in the enemy attack. It was a day that the RAF Regiment came into its own with mainly its light anti-aircraft squadrons engaging the enemy raiders at many of the RAF's airfields.[33] An idea of the fast-moving action can be gleaned from the unit war diaries of a few of these squadrons.

At Airfield B.80 Volkel in the Netherlands the Bofors gunners of No.2874 Squadron RAF Regiment were quick to engage the enemy. At 09.10 hours one of the unit's gun posts saw anti-aircraft fire to the south-west and at five minutes later an Me 109 flew across the airfield at 20 to 30 feet firing guns and dropping two bombs. Over the next half an hour, the airfield was subject to sporadic attacks by a total of ten enemy aircraft comprising Me 109s, Fw 190s and Me 262s.

During the action, the RAF Regiment claimed, and was credited with shooting down two of the enemy raiders at the expense of just 108 rounds of their 40mm ammunition. The squadron's diarist recorded the action:

> At 0935 hours a F.W.190 was seen flying towards the Airfield from the East at zero feet, carrying one large bomb. No.3 Post opened fire and obtained a hit. The enemy aircraft then went into a steep right hand climbing turn to about 600 feet. Several of the Squadron guns opened fire and it appeared to be hit twice, one hit being claimed by No.7 Post and the other by No.8 Post. The enemy aircraft did not drop the bomb. Smoke was pouring from it and it was then attacked by an R.A.F. Tempest just before turning upside down and exploding on the ground.[34]

The Bofors anti-aircraft guns of No.2834 Squadron RAF Regiment, also stationed at Volkel, saw extensive action during this attack as their war diary entry records:

New Year's Day 1945 and Jerry, whether he considered that the RAF would be suffering too badly from the night before or what will never be known but 1010 hours the airfield was attacked by Me 109s, Fw 190s and a 262 [the Messerschmitt twin jet engine aircraft]. All the gunners were on their toes, all guns, when a target presented itself opened up and a number of hits were registered and eventually claimed for three destroyed and two damaged were sent in.[35]

The RAF Regiment units based at Eindhoven (No.1302 Mobile Wing and Nos. 2817, 2773 and 2703 anti-aircraft squadrons) also went into action:

At approximately 0920 hours formations of very low flying enemy aircraft numbering approximately 60 plus and consisting of a variety of types including Me 109s, Fw 190s, He [Heinkel] 110s, Ju [Junkers] 87s and Me 262s, attacked the airfield. The aircraft came in from the east and breaking formation proceeded to machine gun aircraft about to take off and dispersals, installations, parked vehicles, and RAF Regiment gun sites. The three AA squadrons… consisting of 36 Bofors guns, immediately engaged the enemy. The action continued to approximately 0950 hours. The task of the gunners was not too easy because of the low altitude at which the enemy aircraft were attacking – often the guns were unable to engage targets because they were below the safety angle. Altogether the guns fired 2,750 rounds during the engagement. Five enemy aircraft were definitely shot down by the AA guns and there is no doubt that a good many others were damaged. Casualties were comparatively light considering the intensity and duration of the attack – No.2817 Squadron having one killed, No.2773 Squadron two injured and No.2703 Squadron five injured. Airfield losses of personnel were slightly greater approximately fifteen being killed and forty injured.[36]

To modern ears, such an experience seems terrifying but, at the time, the effect on the men was quite the opposite as the unit diarist describes:

There can be no doubt that an action like that which took place this morning was a most wonderful tonic that could have been administered to the Gunners who had not had any action for months and are living in desolation with a little or no entertainment and lousy weather conditions. Coupled with the knowledge of leave soon to come, the spirits of all rose perceptibly.[37]

While the RAF Regiment had distinguished itself in many other theatres of war prior to the campaign in north-west Europe, their conduct on 1 January 1945 was a classic example of the reason they had been formed back in early 1942. That cold day in 1945 they lost two airmen killed in action and a number more were wounded. Several men distinguished themselves that day with Sergeant George Toye of No.2701 Squadron at Melsbroek and Corporal Hugh Adair of No.2876 Squadron at Ophoven being awarded the Military Medal for bravery in the field.

Many other 2nd TAF support units related experience of and tragedies resulting from the surprise Luftwaffe attacks.

The war diary for No.5022 Airfield Construction Squadron, then based at Eindhoven, recorded:

> The first day of 1945, and the year in which it is expected Nazi Germany will finally be crushed, started with a daring attack by the Luftwaffe on our airfields – 60 aircraft attacked Eindhoven and 'hell was let loose' for 30 minutes. As far as the squadron was concerned, there were two fatal casualties and several seriously wounded personnel amongst the flights working on the airfield at the time, while the transport and plant suffered minor damage. Immediately following the attack, all efforts were made to remove debris and wreckage from the runways, and flying was not seriously hampered.[38]

The Winter Bites

January 1945 saw heavy snow begin to fall. It was a time in which 2nd TAF was having to operate in the extremely trying conditions of a continental winter. Units based in and around Eindhoven began to record in their unit diaries that heavy falls persisted for almost three weeks with intermittent falls keeping a constant depth of some 3 inches or so. Roads became treacherous due to ice.

Such conditions lasted until the end of January when a much-awaited thaw set in but with the result that the melt waters led to further problems with maintaining airfields and roads in a serviceable condition. The saving grace was that adverse weather conditions for the rest of January 1945 enabled flying squadrons to re-equip and for supplies to be replenished.

Chapter 8

Over the Rhine and into the Reich

The beginning of 1945 marked the turning point of the war in Europe. The Allies were at the door of Germany in the west and the Soviets had started their offensive in Germany from the east on 12 January. Enemy resistance soon began to collapse, and the Soviets entered East Prussia. They captured the capital of Poland, Warsaw, on 17 January and within a matter of weeks Soviet troops were amassed along the east German border along the river Oder, with Berlin just 30 miles away to the west.

In his directive of 19 January, Eisenhower highlighted the point that with the enemy withdrawing in the Ardennes, and despite having suffered tactical defeat and severe losses in men and *materiel*, he would probably manage to withdraw the bulk of his formations. The key message from the Supreme Commander was that the Allies now needed 'to regain the strategic initiative by launching strong offensives north of the river Moselle.

The objective for this next stage of the advance was to be the Rhine, north of Düsseldorf, with two main operations involving Twenty-First Army Group and the Ninth United States Army Group, both under the command of Montgomery – operations *Veritable* and *Grenade*. Speed was now of the essence as the Russian offensive from the east had forced the enemy to withdraw troops from the Western Front.

Considering this, Eisenhower modified his earlier directive and now considered it 'of paramount importance that we should reach the Rhine north of Düsseldorf with all possible speed and that Operation *Veritable* should be mounted not later than 8th February, and Operation *Grenade* not later than 10th February'.[1]

This all set the scene for Phase IV of the campaign, which was to embrace the crossing of the rivers Meuse and Rhine, and what was termed as the 'final disruption and pursuit'. For 2nd TAF, the winter and spring of 1945 was to be quite different from the second half of 1944 which had been a period of significant mobility and lengthening of the lines of communication. The weather continued to be a major problem during February 1945.

Although a welcome thaw came in the early part of the month, the resulting conditions became a major handicap. Many of the roads became virtually impassable due to the slush and mud, a situation which deteriorated further with the movement of heavy or armoured vehicles. Conditions at Nijmegen were apparently particularly serious and there are accounts of stacked ammunition and heavy stores irrecoverably sinking into the sodden ground. The Allies were not alone in suffering such conditions – the enemy too experienced similar difficulties. Conditions did improve towards the end of February although many of 2nd TAF's airfields continued to suffer from flooding and the resultant difficulties of keeping airfields operational.

Battle of the Reichswald – Operation *Veritable*

Having pushed the enemy back, the Allies immediately launched Operation *Veritable* on 8 February 1945 – the Battle of the Reichswald. This was part of an Allied 'pincer' movement attack by the British during which the Twenty-First Army Group advanced through the Reichswald forest and the Rhine plain. The southern part of the attack (Operation *Grenade*) was carried out by the United States Ninth Army.

Lasting until 5 March 1945, the operation enabled the Allies to clear the area between the rivers Maas and Rhine, driving German forces east of the Rhine.[2] The wise decision was taken by 2nd TAF to concentrate its stores and supplies in a new forward area at Goch (just across the border into Germany and across the river Maas); this was as close to the Rhine as possible and on the main line of communication for the support of Phase IV operations.[3]

This long-awaited offensive was preceded by a substantial artillery bombardment and an attack by over 900 heavy bombers on the German towns of Goch and Cleve. Ground crews had worked around the clock to help ensure that virtually every aircraft was made available. These were used to strike at twelve pre-arranged targets on the first day, many of which included ammunition dumps, defensive positions, bridges, and roads. Indeed, some 552 sorties were flown with most of them in direct support of the ground troops. Progress in the early stages was good and all the first objectives were reached on schedule. The poor winter weather, however, soon took its toll. The heavy frost which had made the roads particularly treacherous in the first few days gave way to a thaw which turned much of the battle area into a quagmire. A key road towards Cleve collapsed entirely and heavy rain led to the comment being made that the British and Canadian troops engaged 'were conducting amphibious operations'.[4]

Operation *Veritable* did not require much, if any additional movement for the majority of 2nd TAF's support units. They were, however, heavily involved in keeping the tactical aircraft operational as they flew their vital missions in support of the ground effort. The supply and transport columns though, continued their vital work in conveying the vital supplies of fuel and ammunition for the flying squadrons. Most of their work was carried out using the ubiquitous 3-ton truck – a true workhorse but they were consuming considerable volumes of fuel, averaging just under 6 miles per gallon per vehicle.

Although much of their valuable work was unglamorous and largely behind the scenes, it could still be hazardous. No.309 Supply and Transport Column, for example, supporting units in No.83 Group, suffered their first fatal casualty on 8 February 1945 when Leading Aircraftman Thomas Lynch, a vehicle driver of A Section was killed whilst on convoy duties for a tasking involving the movement of rear HQ No.83

Group. The incident occurred during the morning near Berg in the Netherlands, just after the convoy, in which Lynch was driving the second vehicle, had crossed the Juliana Canal. The unit's war diary entry for the day takes up the story:

> As the leading vehicles were turning a bend, an aircraft, hitherto unseen and unheard, dived on to them and sprayed them with bullets. There is no evidence to show what type of aircraft was concerned. Leading Aircraftman Lynch was driving very slowly at the time, approaching a bend, and after LAC Lynch was killed the vehicle came to a stop without leaving the road.

Thomas Lynch was buried the next day at St Andrew's Military Cemetery, Ophoven, near Sittard. Thomas was a much-valued member of the unit and had been with it since its formation. He was, as commented on in the unit's war diary, extremely popular with the men and the officers and he always did a good job of work. Although no recompense for her loss, a collection was made on the unit and the sum of £179 7s 6d sent to his widow back in the United Kingdom.[5]

The poor weather kept the participating squadrons from 2nd TAF grounded for many days and it was not until 14 February 1945 that it cleared sufficiently for air operations to resume. It was a tough battle to push the enemy back and it was not until 10 March 1945 before the west bank of the Rhine was finally cleared. The period following *Veritable* was one of consolidation for the Allies, with a build-up of supplies and forces in preparation for the final assault on Germany.

Crossing of the Rhine – Operations *Plunder* and *Varsity*

The rate of effort in early 1945 was rapid. Just a month after the launch of *Veritable*, Eisenhower issued his directive to Montgomery to begin Operation *Plunder*, with a target date of 24 March. This came on the night of 23–24 March 1945 with the Anglo-American-Canadian crossing of the river (Operation *Plunder*), with the accompanying airborne forces operation (Operation *Varsity*) on 24 March 1945 and an objective of gaining a firm bridgehead over the Rhine, north of the Ruhr, as a base for further operations to isolate the Ruhr.

There were five principal tasks entrusted to the air forces for these operations. First, and most important of all, was to maintain dominance in the air, particularly in the area of the assault and the airborne forces landing zones. Second, neutralising anti-aircraft defences; third, providing fighter protection to the transport aircraft carrying the parachutists; fourth, close air support on the battlefield; and fifthly, prevention of any enemy movement towards or in the battle area.[6]

By and large, the crossing of the Rhine was a notable success. The airlift element alone in Operation *Varsity*, was enormous, comprising the combined resources of the United States XVIII Airborne Corps and the British 6th Airborne Division with much of its airlift provided by Nos. 38 and 46 groups. By nightfall on D-Day 24 March 1945, 21st Army Group had established a bridgehead of nearly 30 miles wide. The Allies wasted no time in establishing bridges across the Rhine and by 26 March 1945 there were twelve bridges in service across the mighty river. By 27 March, the Allies had fourteen divisions on the Rhine's east bank.[7]

By this time, the enemy was very much fighting on the back foot and the Ruhr completely encircled. Eisenhower though, and despite opposition from Churchill and the British Chiefs of Staff, now intended to direct his main attack (with the First United States Army and Ninth United States Army) towards the Leipzig area, almost due east. Further south the Third United States Army and Seventh United States Army would move from the area of the Saar towards Austria. To do this, the Supreme Commander had to remove the Ninth United States Army from Montgomery's command and directed him and his Twenty-First Army to 'cross the Weser, Aller and Leine, capture Bremen, pass the Elbe and then move up to the Baltic coast'.[8]

The crossing of the Rhine was a real milestone on the journey into the Reich as the diarist of No.2834 Squadron RAF Regiment, then still based at Volkel, commented: 'D-Day today, the battle of the Rhine commenced, which has caused a wave of excitement to pass through all on the airfield'.[9] The outcome of these operations effectively placed the Allies on the North German Plain.[10] Coningham remained conscious of the need for 2nd TAF to secure more forward airfields so that his aircraft could continue to provide the vital air support to Twenty-First Army. This was particularly important as it was becoming clear that an advance to the Baltic was likely to be rapid. He was pushing at an open door as Montgomery had emphasised the importance of this priority to his commanders.

Logistics remained a difficult challenge following the crossing of the Rhine as the advancing forces continued to outpace the rate at which they could be resupplied. Much of this was caused by the difficulties caused by the bridge limitations across the river itself and the fact that the railway infrastructure had been almost completely destroyed. Of the *materiel* required by the RAF, shortages of airfield construction materials became a growing concern.

Advance to the Elbe

On 5 April 1945, Montgomery issued his Directive M.567 which made several alterations to his intentions following the withdrawal of the Ninth United States Army from his command. The British Second Army, supported by 2nd TAF's No.83 Group, was to secure the line of the river Weser and capture Bremen. Having achieved that initial goal, it was then to secure bridgeheads over the rivers Weser, Aller and Leine, and advance to secure a bridgehead over the river Elbe, which, next to the Rhine, was the widest river in Germany. The First Canadian Army, supported by No.84 Group, was to clear the west of Netherlands and then to move northwards to clear north-east Netherlands and then eastwards to clear the coastal belt and all enemy naval bases up to the line of the river Weser. The Canadians would eventually take over Bremen and protect the left flank of the British Second Army during the advance to the Elbe.[11]

FORWARD AIR BASES IN EUROPE FROM D-DAY TO THE BALTIC

Coningham's air plan for increasing the range of 2nd TAF aircraft and providing suitable air bases, especially north-east of the river Rhine, was to improvise as much as possible, a similar approach to the strategy he employed during the rapid advance from the river Seine to Brussels. Broadly speaking, the basing of the composite groups was to maintain the maximum number of wings, which the logistical situation allowed, as far forward as possible along the axis of advance of the British and Canadian armies.

At the beginning of April 1945, HQ 2nd TAF was still in Brussels with its No.34 (Photographic Reconnaissance) Wing under its direct control, at the Airfield B.58 Brussels/Melsbroek, along with No.1401 Meteorological Flight. To keep in touch with the advance of Nos. 83 and 84 groups, Coningham moved his main headquarters on 7 April 1945 to Suchteln, near Krefeld in Germany, where it remained until the German surrender in May. Interestingly, and given the chaos of the world at the time, the irony of HQ 2nd TAF being in a former, (then known as) lunatic asylum, directly alongside the main HQ 21st Army Group, was probably not lost on many of its new occupants!

The two composite groups at this time were in the Netherlands. The HQ No.83 Group was located at Eindhoven, with its Group Control Centre at Erp. The group's six airfields were located at: B.80 Volkel, B.78 Eindhoven, B.88 Heesch, B.100 Goch, B.86 Helmond and B.90 at Petit Brogel. The HQ No.84 Group was located further north at Grave, with its Group Control Centre at Hatert. The group had just four airfields, which were located at: B.91 Kluis, B.77 Gilze Rijen, B.85 Schijndel and B.89 at Mill. No.85 Group with its broader, largely air defence responsibility, had its headquarters at Ghent, with two night fighter wings at Airfields B.51 Lille/Vendeville and B.48 Amiens/Glisy, with another wing at B.83 Knokke, controlling one anti-aircraft cooperation squadron, one Coastal Command (Albacore) squadron and one air sea rescue squadron. HQ No.2 Group was in Brussels with its aircraft occupying five airfields at: B.71 Coxyde, B.50 Vitry, A.75 Epinoy, B.58 Melsbroek and B.87 at Rosieres.[12] The main and rear HQ 2nd TAF itself but, to keep in touch with the further advance of Nos. 83 and 84 groups, moved to Suchteln, near Krefeld in Germany on 7 April 1945, remaining there until the German surrender in May.

A 2nd TAF radar unit convoy passing over a Bailey bridge on the river Ems at Lingen, Germany. *(Copyright Through Their Eyes)*

Above all, it was the ever-increasing evidence of the cost of war and Nazi inhumanity that many units started to experience as they moved into Germany. The men of No.2874 Squadron RAF Regiment moved from the Netherlands to Airfield B.109 at Quakenbrück, south-west of Bremen, on 16 April 1945. Although the unit was first and foremost an anti-aircraft unit, they were given instructions 'to operate in any role considered necessary'.

It was thus that the squadron found themselves mounting guard on 3 German military hospitals housing approximately 200 wounded German soldiers. These were soon moved to two of the hospitals and the third was readied for the reception of sick Russian workers, a move carried out by the squadron using its own vehicles. The transfer of about 100 Russians of both sexes was overseen by a German civilian doctor, aided by 6 male civilian workers. About twelve of the Russians were in a terrible condition. When brought to the attention of the doctor he commented that:

> They had recently been brought from a Nazi prison camp and were suffering from an advanced state of Tuberculosis, which he thought had been caused through lack of food, medical treatment and over-work. Their bodies were in a pitiful state of emaciation and shrunk to the size of a child. The stench was overpowering. The Doctor stated that they would live only a few days, and the vast majority would not live more than a few months.[13]

The armoured cars of the RAF Regiment continued to prove their worth as a valuable reconnaissance asset. One day in April, a troop of Humber Light Reconnaissance Cars of No.2781 (Armoured Car) Squadron was on patrol round the perimeter of the airfield at Osnabruck in the vicinity of a maintenance working party on the airstrip and alongside flights of another RAF Regiment squadron. The latter had been ordered to 'neutralise enemy fire which might be directed at them from beyond the Ems Weser Canal'.

It was not long before the enemy engaged with Spandau machine guns and snipers opening fire, killing an officer and an airman and seriously wounding four others. The armoured car patrol rushed to the scene, under the command of Flying Officer John Millar who took charge. The following action, which was to earn Millar the Military Cross, is described in the citation for his award:

> In spite of the proximity of the enemy, he succeeded in removing the dead and wounded in the reconnaissance cars and gave sufficient covering fire to the remainder of the flight to enable them to withdraw. All this time his troop was under concentrated fire from the enemy at a range of under 100 yards.[14]

The armoured car units also continued to support the work of the Air Technical Intelligence units as the Allies pressed further into Germany. From 3 to 12 April 1945, Flight Lieutenant Walter Jay was in command of a flight of armoured cars from No.2804 (Armoured Car) Squadron working 'as an armoured reconnaissance unit to a "special force" whose speedy advance was only made possible by his determined and efficient handling of the flight'.

On 8 April 1945, Flight Lieutenant Jay was ordered to carry out a reconnaissance with a troop of armoured cars which necessitated proceeding between two strongly held pockets of resistance. His actions were to earn him the Military Cross, the citation for which describes the action:

> He was frequently under fire and once had to join battle with the enemy, giving covering fire to an American detachment in difficulties. His determination, courage, and complete disregard of personal danger, enabled the force to gain its objective without casualties. The operation resulted in the capture of the entire designing staff of the Focke-Wulf Aircraft Company, together with many valuable secret documents.[15]

A number of the RAF Regiment's missions with the technical intelligence gathering operation at this time proved particularly valuable in understanding the enemy's capability. In the dying throes of the Third Reich, a final throw of the dice was always a possibility and an appreciation of what he might be capable of was always going to be of value.

One such venture involved the capture of the Focke-Wulf aircraft design offices at Bad Eilsen, just south-east of Minden. It was quite clear that there would need to be a much longer-term occupation force in Germany following what was now an unquestionable collapse of the Third Reich and its surrender. With this in mind, HQ 2nd TAF had its eye on the spa town of Bad Eilsen as its post-war headquarters site and was keen to lay claim to it before the army could do the same. The RAF Regiment quickly assembled a small task force comprising No.2804 (Armoured Car) Squadron, along with Nos. 2729 and 2807 (rifle) squadrons to tackle the task.

Fighting was still in progress and the RAF Regiment task force still needed army permission to pass through its forward lines. Eventually they reached the town having taken on several enemy roadblocks as they raced to their prize. The icing on the cake was that they were able to take prisoner Focke-Wulf's chief designer, Professor Kurt Tank, at the company's design offices. Along with several of his technical assistants, Tank was interrogated, a process which eventually revealed that, in terms of design, the German Luftwaffe was probably ahead of the Allies in this respect. It was a 'busted flush' though. By this stage of the war, the Luftwaffe had lost large numbers of its aircraft and pilots and was sustaining heavy casualties every day. It was no longer able regenerate its force strength in anywhere near the numbers it needed. Moreover, its airfields had become heavily congested as its units had retreated to the homeland and it was desperately short of fuel.

It was not surprising that many of the RAF Regiment came into such proximity to the enemy due to their role, but other members of 2nd TAF's support units also faced considerable danger and displayed great bravery. One such example is Leading Aircraftman Cyril Fones who was working with No.662 Squadron in No.83 Group, an air observation post unit flying Auster reconnaissance aircraft.

OVER THE RHINE AND INTO THE REICH

On 13 April 1945, Fones was the member of an advanced ground support party at Vechta airfield to the south-west of Bremen, Germany, awaiting some of their Austers to land. Just as soon as the first aircraft arrived, the enemy opened fire with an 88mm gun from just 1,500 yards away. The pilot in the lead aircraft ordered Fones to start the engine to enable him to take off. Fones had some difficulty doing this but persisted, despite the constant shelling around him. Once he had succeeded, Fones guided the pilot through the shell fire to the runway. For his bravery in the face of great danger, Fones was awarded the Military Medal. The citation for his award stated that by his cool action and devotion to duty he was 'largely responsible for saving the aircraft from serious damage or destruction'. It says much of his courage that Fones only took cover when the aircraft was airborne.[16]

By 24 April 1945, the advanced elements of the British Second Army had reached the west bank of the river Elbe. Montgomery's intent was for a crossing similar to the Rhine with a battalion of the First Airborne Division being dropped on

A survivor amongst the ruins. A low-level aerial reconnaissance photograph of Cologne Cathedral taken in July 1945. *(Copyright Through Their Eyes)*

its east side. The fall of Bremen on 26 April 1945, though, led to a much welcome weakening of the enemy's resistance and an airborne operation was not required. The aircraft of No.83 Group though were required to take out several German railway guns that were hindering the engineer's work to construct bridges across the river.

Towards the end of April and into early May, the basing of No.83 Group had changed quite dramatically. By 23 April 1945, the group's headquarters had moved to Mettingen near Osnabruck, with its Group Control Centre at Sohneverdingen. By 1 May it had moved again to Bispingen, with the main HQ Second Army. Its Control Centre remained in situ. The group's airfields on 1 May were now at: B.152 Fassberg, B.118 Celle, B.116 Wunstorf, B.154 Reinsehlen, B.150 Hustedt and B.120 at Langenhagen. The airfield at B.156 Lüneburg was being opened to replace Langenhagen. No.84 Group's role continued in support of the First Canadian Army and mainly involving operations to eliminate pockets of enemy resistance from Bremen westwards to the Hook of Holland. The group's main headquarters was located at V.3008 Delden alongside the HQ Canadian First Army, with its Group Control Centre at V.7440 Brögbern. The airfields of No.84 Group were situated so that they could best support operations along the coast to protect the port at Antwerp and a new shipping lane, which was to be opened along the coast from Antwerp to Bremen. The group's airfields during this final stage of the war were at: B.103 Plantlunne, B.113 Varrelbusch, B.109 Quakenbrück, B.105 Drope, B.111 Ahlhorn and B.106 at Twente. It was not easy, nor necessary, for No.2 Group to move its aircraft as far forward as the composite groups, if anything they needed much longer runways for their heavily bomb laden, multi-engine aircraft.

The group headquarters remained in Brussels and operated from five airfields: B.80 Volkel, B.77 Gilze-Rijen, A.75 Cambrai/Epinoy, B.110 Achmer and B.58 at Melsbroek. No.85 Group with its vital night defence role as far as Denmark, was now having to cover the port of Antwerp and the shipping lane to Hamburg. To meet this, the group had to move its two night fighter wings to B.108 Rheine and B.77 at Gilze-Rijen, whilst the Coastal Command general reconnaissance wing still operated from B.83 at Knokke, where the air sea rescue and anti-aircraft co-operation squadrons were still based.[17]

Many of 2nd TAF's units were beginning to observe mounting evidence of the dying throes of Germany's Third Reich. No.2834 Squadron RAF Regiment had moved to Airfield B.152 Fassberg (roughly midway between Hanover and Hamburg) on 24 April 1945 and observed that there were 'hundreds of [enemy] aircraft, many of which are quite serviceable, a sure sign that Germany was short of Octane'. The advance from here was rapid. The Elbe was crossed by the British VIII Corps on 29 April and on 2 May the British Second Army was on its way to Lübeck, Germany's second-largest city on the German Baltic coast in the state of Schleswig-Holstein.

Logistics Remains a Challenge

Although the opening of Antwerp's port at the end of November 1944 had considerably eased the Allies supply difficulties, the line of communication from northern Belgium was to increase further following the crossing of the Rhine and the advance into Germany. By and large, Antwerp remained the main supply base for operations at this stage.

With it now becoming clear that the Twenty-First Army would be heading north towards the Baltic after they entered Germany, it was evident that no further supplementary ports could be opened until Bremen was captured. The army was considering that the area around Hamburg was likely to the next location of the advanced base. The RAF therefore decided to concentrate as much sustainment stocks of equipment and supplies as they could, as close as possible to the Rhine and on the main line of communication. Once again, the advance (and 2nd TAF's new airfields) began to outpace the rate at which stores and supplies could be moved along the line of communication, primarily due to completely wrecked railway systems and bridge limitations over the Rhine.[18] Again, supply by air became crucial. Throughout March 1945, scheduled air transport continued to fly in supplies to the Brussels area, although problems were experienced with aircraft availability due to the operational needs of the airborne forces element of the Rhine crossing, which were remarkably like the problems experienced during Operation *Market Garden* in mid-September 1944.

By April 1945, the supply difficulties had become more acute and special supply-by-air services were once again required to provide 2nd TAF with urgently required petrol, oil and ammunition. By the middle of the month, a significant number of sorties were being flown by Nos. 38 and 46 groups with, not just what was needed for the tactical air force, but also for the ground forces as well.[19] During the month of April, No.46 Group transported some 7,000 of supplies along with No.38 Group which carried 514 tons to the Continent. It was not just a one-way transport operation as the Dakota, Stirling and Halifax aircraft repatriated to the United Kingdom 27,277 British and American prisoners of war and 5,986 casualties.[20]

Surviving archival sources on this period are quite sparse but, it is clear that, in addition to the requirement for some 200 tons of motor transport petrol for the army, much pre-stocking of new No.83 Group airfields was also carried out. The availability of airlift worked on some days, but not others. In the case of No.83 Group, assistance was sought from the army's road transport resources.[21] The availability of air transport at this time was also more difficult due to the pressing requirements of Twelfth United States Army Group on the right flank and the non-availability of airfields in north-west Germany; those airfields, which were available, were either required for 2nd TAF aircraft or were not suitable for transport aircraft. Of note is that the US Ninth Air Force, which was operating on the right flank in support of the Twelfth United States Army fared much better than the RAF with regards to transport aircraft and had some seventy-five Dakotas under their direct control. Access to these aircraft remained 'frozen' for American air transport needs and were not diverted to airborne operations, unlike the RAF's arrangement at the time of the Arnhem operation and the crossing of the Rhine.

The special service airlift requirement at this time for 2nd TAF was substantial and required some eighty flights by No.46 Group transport aircraft alone. The total weight of freight carried by the group to Europe during April 1945 was almost double the total for the preceding month.[22] Although data is only available for selected dates during the period January to April 1945, the graph below shows quite clearly the significant increase in special service supply by air.

Although the logistical problems, and how many of them were solved, might suggest a haphazard approach, it was not the case. Certainly, 2nd TAF was well placed with experienced personnel in this discipline. The RAF had developed a highly proficient supply organisation in the form of its Equipment Branch for officers and related trades for its non-commissioned ranks. Many of these had earned their spurs and gained vital experience of supporting mobile operations during the operations following the invasion of North Africa and mainland Italy earlier in the war. Of notable value was that a number of these people had become specialists in the supply, storage and movement of fuel and munitions.

As the RAF also gained a more effective and capable air transport fleet, their logistics personnel also started to gain expertise in the movement of air cargo. In this respect, the Normandy campaign and subsequent operations was the first time that the RAF had movements' staff in its various headquarters to coordinate movement activities by air, rail, road and sea. This approach was particularly successful because the movements staff worked closely, not just with the RAF equipment staff, but also with their counterparts in Twenty-First Army Group. It did not wave a 'magic wand' at logistics, but went a long way towards keeping the vital supply lines flowing.

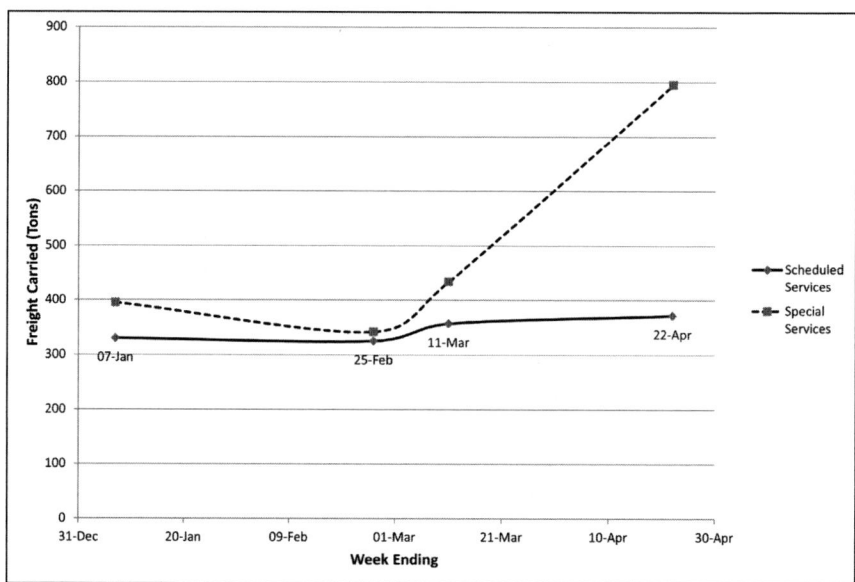

Figure 4. Air freight carried by Dakotas of No.46 Group – scheduled and special services – selected dates – January to April 1945.[23]

OVER THE RHINE AND INTO THE REICH

Schleswig-Holstein

One of the last major operations before the German surrender, which involved the RAF Regiment, took place in the operation at the beginning of May 1945 to occupy the German province of Schleswig-Holstein, the northernmost part of the country bordering Denmark. This was a sizeable area, extending some 93 miles from Hamburg and the Elbe to Flensburg and the Danish border.

At this time, the province was home to a number of Luftwaffe airfields along with a number of army garrisons and naval bases. Notwithstanding the not insignificant enemy presence, the Twenty-First Army was more focused on the drive east to link up with the Soviet army – Schleswig-Holstein was a matter for later in its view. Conscious of the valuable air-related technical material, which had already been seized to date, HQ 2nd TAF was keen to secure what was believed to be a further haul of such material in the province. It was thus that just four days before the war ended that nine task groups made up of RAF Regiment rifle, armoured car and light anti-aircraft squadrons moved into the province with orders to capture as much Luftwaffe equipment as possible, to disarm enemy troops and to arrest senior Nazi officers.

The operation was a major success and saw the RAF Regiment occupy 16 major airfields, taking the surrender of some 50,000 enemy personnel at Schleswig alone. The real 'prize' was the capture of Grand Admiral Karl Dönitz at Flensburg who had been appointed as the official successor to Adolf Hitler. The RAF Regiment was also able to secure the release of over 1,000 Allied prisoners of war but their greatest challenge was the feeding, clothing and housing of large numbers of Russian prisoners found in terrible conditions at numerous slave labour camps throughout the province.[24]

Victory in Sight – Spring 1945

Vienna, the capital of Austria, fell on 13 April, and just three days later the Battle for Berlin began. By this stage of the war, Hitler had retreated to his Führerbunker deep underground beneath the Reich Chancellery in Berlin. He was not to leave this subterranean world after 20 April but continued under the delusion that Germany could still fight it out. By 30 April, the Soviets were less than 0.5 miles from his bunker. At 15.30 hours that day, Hitler, and the mistress he had recently married, Eva Braun, both committed suicide. Leadership of the Nazi Party then passed to Grand Admiral Karl Dönitz. The German High Command endeavoured to broker a peace deal, but this was rejected by the Soviets who demanded unconditional surrender. On 2 May 1945, the city of Berlin was finally surrendered by its commandant Lieutenant General Karl Weidling.[25]

Notwithstanding the moves towards achieving a complete surrender, units of 2nd TAF continued to play their part in keeping the enemy at bay. On 2 May 1945, No.2874 Squadron RAF Regiment then at Airfield B.113 Varrelbusch (south-west of Bremen), was to have what was probably its last engagement with an enemy aircraft. Just before 17.30 hours, a Ju 88 aircraft approached the airfield at about 300 feet from the north-west and appeared to be trying to land, albeit the aircraft's undercarriage was still retracted. The squadron's war diary comments:

> In accordance with the rules of engagement, in force at the time, eight of the squadron guns opened fire. Two hits were obtained, and the aircraft disappeared to the South-West at tree top height. The aircraft subsequently crash landed, and the pilot and crew of two were captured by the Canadian Army. The destruction of this aircraft has been claimed.[26]

Unconditional Surrender and Victory in Europe

The diarist of No.2834 Squadron RAF Regiment recorded on 4 May 1945 that 'at 1810 hours it was agreed that the cease fire would be from 0800 hours on May 5th.[27] Now the end is near feelings are very mixed. It is a case of being too good to be true.' Such was the effect of over five years of war.

On 5 May 1945, Eisenhower issued his final directive that reflected the proximity of Soviet ground forces, which had advanced from the east. Essentially, the Allied Expeditionary Force was to launch an operation across the lower Elbe to establish a 'firm operational flank on the approximate line Wismar-Schwerin-Domitz, the exact line, depending on local adjustments, when contact with the Soviet forces was made'. After this, the expeditionary force was to drive north into Denmark. That same day, a patrol from No.2717 (Rifle) Squadron operating along the Elisabethfehnkanal to the west of Bremen, encountered a group of civilians who, through a local schoolmaster acting as interpreter, informed them of the locations of several minefields in the area.

During this exchange, the schoolmaster mentioned that another civilian who had spent several years in a concentration camp wished to speak with the RAF Regiment officer commanding the patrol. It turned out that he had important information concerning a 'Werewolves' hideout in the woods covering their route forward. The Werewolves had been initiated by Heinrich Himmler in the late summer/early autumn of 1944 as a group of supposedly elite volunteer forces to operate secretly behind enemy (i.e. Allied) lines.

Despite Nazi Germany's Propaganda Minister Joseph Goebbels' efforts to put an alarming 'spin' on their capability and role in the dying days of the Third Reich, the initiative never amounted to a serious threat and there is little evidence of a coordinated plan for these units to cause major disruption to the Allied advance. The regiment patrol soon discovered a foxhole that connected with a well-built underground room approximately 8 feet square with two bunks set in the wall and sufficient food and cooking materials to last two men up to about two months. Interestingly, they also found all sorts of clothing, including complete sets of women's clothing. Other supplies included tools, maps, books, a wireless set, typewriter and duplicator plus a bicycle outside. Despite extensive searches in the local area over the next few days, no further Werewolf connected personnel or equipment were discovered.[28]

By 7 May 1945, Montgomery's Twenty-First Army Group had cleared the Netherlands and north Germany up to the river Elbe and the Danish border. The unconditional German Instrument of Surrender was signed at a ceremony in Berlin at 00.16 hours local time on 9 May 1945 by representatives of the three German armed services, the Allied Expeditionary Force and the Supreme High Command of the Soviet Red Army. So ended the Second World War in Europe.

With the enemy laying down arms in vast numbers, virtually all the Allied units found themselves in one form or another involved in the chaotic process of handling prisoners and abandoned equipment. No.2834 Squadron, recorded how on 10 May 1945 at 17.30 hours an Me 262 landed, followed by four more at 19.00 hours. The pilots gave themselves up on instructions from the Luftwaffe after carrying out a final sortie on the Russian front.

By the end of Phase IV of the campaign, the squadrons of No.2 Group had moved to new air bases in northern Netherlands, whilst Nos. 83 and 84 groups had crossed the Rhine and were occupying several former Luftwaffe airfields in north-west Germany. No.83 Group's airfields were nearly all east of the river Weser,

A group of RAF groundcrew pose on an abandoned German armoured vehicle in Normandy, 1944. *(Author's collection)*

extending roughly on a line from Lübeck in the north to Hanover in the south. No.84 Group's airfields were further back to the west, mostly between the rivers Emse and Weser and roughly on a line extending south-west from Bremen.

The air defence squadrons of No.85 Group were divided between northern Netherlands (providing cover for the Forward Base conglomeration in the Brussels/Antwerp area) and just north of Munster (for the airfields of No.84 Group).[29] The logistics units of 2nd TAF had also moved to locations which were geographically convenient for supporting their respective Groups.

During the period from D-Day to VE Day, 2nd TAF flew 259,369 sorties and destroyed 1,574 enemy aircraft, albeit at the loss of 1,942 aircraft of their own.

- THE SECOND TACTICAL AIR FORCE WAS FORMED IN THE UNITED KINGDOM ON THE 1st JUNE 1943.

- IT TOOK PART IN THE AIR OPERATIONS OVER EUROPE WHICH PRECEDED THE INVASION OF THE CONTINENT.

- IT COMMENCED TO LAND ON « D » DAY THE 6th JUNE 1944 AND FOUGHT WITH 21 ARMY GROUP OVER FRANCE, BELGIUM, HOLLAND AND INTO THE HEART OF GERMANY IN THE CAMPAIGN WHICH LIBERATED EUROPE FROM NAZIDOM.

The following is a personal message to relatives and friends of all members of 2nd T. A. F., from Air Marshal Sir Arthur Coningham, K. C. B., D. S. O., M. C., D. F. C., A. F. C., Air Officer, Commanding-in-Chief, 2nd T. A. F.

To you, our relations and friends go our first thoughts of gratitude for the victory in Europe.

It is your courage and steadfastness that have sustained us.

A. Coningham.
a. m.

V. E. DAY, MAY 8th 1945

Coningham's personal message to members of 2nd TAF on the occasion of VE Day, 8 May 1945. *(Author's collection)*

OVER THE RHINE AND INTO THE REICH

For many in 2nd TAF, the relative silence which came with the final surrender was a strange experience. Five years of war had changed the lives of many. Day-to-day life had been filled with a heady mix of often conflicting emotions: excitement and fear, sorrow and joy. The unofficial account of No.84 Group's experience in the campaign contains a paragraph in its closing summary which could equally apply to the tactical air force as a whole:

> It was a strange feeling ... to go down to Twente airfield where 35 Wing were stationed and to see Spitfires standing silent in serried line. Suddenly they seemed to be aware that their work was done and the urgency past: but in their silence they wore a quiet dignity and sober pride. They seemed indeed to realise that all was over more quickly than did we who were unable to adjust our minds to the simple fact that the struggle was done, the conflict past.[30]

By the time of the surrender of German forces in Europe, 2nd TAF was occupying forty-one serviceable airfields in north-west Europe. The work to establish new and refurbish existing air bases had been the joint efforts of both the army and RAF's airfield construction units. Between D-Day in June 1944 and VE Day in 1945, these units had built or repaired 127 airfields, invariably under quite hazardous conditions and invariably still under enemy attack. Such was the significance of this air base development work that both Coningham and Montgomery were of the same view that 'on occasions, the requirements for transportation for airfield stores may even have to take priority over those of fighting troops'.[31]

It had been a long and uncomfortable journey for many of the units, but morale remained high. Whilst little of their story was to be told after the war, many units in 2nd TAF seemed content that they had played their part. No.418 Air Stores Park, which had accompanied No.84 Group had several talented individuals amongst their numbers, one of which penned this short 'ditty' entitled *What a Convoy*:

> Bags of petrol, bags of oil,
> Bags of sweat, bags of toil,
> Bags of gunfire, bags of flashes,
> Bags of bumps, and bags of smashes.
>
> Petrol leakings, springs acreaking
> Linings hot and brakes a squeaking,
> Dust screens here, dust screens there,
> Monty's smoke screens everywhere.
>
> Still the Crossleys strain and whine,
> Nearly swim the river Rhine,
> On their knees they onward go,
> As their loads swing and fro.

> On they went, and some had hitches,
> Some thought it safer to drive in ditches,
> Went on their [way] and thanked their maker
> It may have been a Studebaker.
>
> Then our journey was completed,
> Never more to be repeated.
> The time the convoy had got through
> Drivers and passengers both felt blue.
>
> Thanks to fitters and "B" class drivers,
> And the passengers sat beside us,
> All deserved thanks – they gave their best,
> What about Brussels, and a well-earned rest.[32]

The Role and Achievement of 2nd TAF 1944 to 1945

The 2nd TAF had been formed to operate in association with Montgomery's Twenty-First Army Group with three key purposes. It was required to achieve air supremacy in the army group area and as far as possible beyond it when they could. This gave both the ground and air forces freedom of movement and minimised enemy interference. Secondly, it was to deny the enemy land forces freedom of movement in their rear areas and thirdly to provide 21st Army Group with close air support. In the words of Coningham, his tactical air force 'fulfilled these functions to the letter'.

In his post campaign report, Coningham summed-up the extraordinary achievements. From D-Day to VE Day, 2nd TAF flew 259,369 sorties and, as mentioned above, was responsible for some 1,574 enemy aircraft being destroyed of which 1,368 were in the air and 206 on the ground. Despite this crippling impact on enemy air capability, it came at a cost and 2nd TAF themselves lost 1,942 aircraft. Despite this imbalance in loss figures, 2nd TAF remained on the front foot.

The Allies could make good what they had lost, Germany could not and their ability to wage war, particularly by the beginning of 1945 had diminished significantly. The overall achievement of 2nd TAF is best summed up by the following message sent to Coningham by Prime Minister Winston Churchill on 16 May 1945:

> Now that Germany has been well and truly defeated, I wish to express to you, on behalf of his Majesty's Government, the deep sense of gratitude felt by all our people for the glorious part which has been played by the Second Tactical Air Force.
>
> Their mastery of the skies above our armies, their ever-vigilant reconnaissance, their interventions in the land battles and their devastating attacks against the enemy's vital communications,

concentration areas and supply organisation have made the tasks of our Armies far easier and far less costly in casualties.

I know that our Armies are deeply conscious of these achievements, and I know, too, how much they appreciate the care and skill with which your operations have been planned and executed.

The great deeds of the Second Tactical Air Force bear eloquent testimony to the high morale which has sustained your aircrews and to the devotion with which their efforts have been supported by their comrades on the ground. The Nation will not forget the decisive part which your officers, airmen and airwomen have made to the victory.[33]

With the war over in Europe and with the RAF needing to maintain a presence in Germany, 2nd TAF which had by then occupied a whole series of new airfields in Germany, was disbanded and replaced by the British Forces of Occupation on 15 July 1945.

It was resurrected, however, on 1 September 1951 to reflect the role it then had as part of the NATO alliance. The 2nd TAF reached its peak post-war strength in late 1955 when it had a compliment of thirty-five squadrons. With the 'tripwire' strategy of massive nuclear retaliation and the growing dominance of the United Kingdom based V-bombers, the need for a tactical force had diminished and from 1 January 1959 became a command as RAF Germany.

In time, with the demise of the Soviet Union and the reunification of Germany, British defence policies changed significantly, and the command was progressively run-down, eventually being disbanded in 1993. RAF forces remained in Germany under No.2 Group until 1996, then No.1 Group. At the time of writing, the RAF no longer has a deployed presence in Germany, but the identity and spirit of some of the old 2nd TAF support units proudly lives on in the naming and roles of some of the RAF's deployable support units, mainly based at RAF Wittering, near Peterborough in Cambridgeshire.

APPENDICES

Appendix I

Timeline of Key Dates and Events – June 1944 to May 1945

Phase I (6 June 1944 – 25 July 1944):

6 June 1944	Operation *Neptune*, D-Day assault landings.
11 June 1944	Mulberry B at Arromanches opened for Allied shipping.
26 June 1944	Operation *Epsom*, British Second Army's offensive to cross the Odon and Orne rivers south-west of Caen.
27 June 1944	Capture of Cherbourg.
8–9 July 1944	Operation *Charnwood*, Anglo-Canadian offensive to capture the city of Caen.
9 July 1944	Capture of Caen.
18–21 July 1944	Operation *Goodwood*, British Second Army's offensive south-east of Caen.

Phase II (26 July 1944 – 26 September 1944):

26 July 1944	Breakout from Normandy.
30 July 1944	Operation *Bluecoat*, British Second Army's offensive towards Mont Pinçon and Vire.
8–11 August 1944	Operation *Totalize*, First Canadian Army's offensive towards Falaise Phase I.
14–16 August 1944	Operation *Tractable*, First Canadian Army's offensive towards Falaise Phase I
20 August 1944	Falaise gap sealed.
25 August 1944	Paris liberated.
3 September 1944	Normandy beaches closed.
3 September 1944	Brussels liberated.
4 September 1944	Antwerp liberated.
17–26 September 1944	Operation *Market Garden* (Arnhem).
22 September 1944 – 4 October 1944	Fuel pipeline to Cherbourg operational (Operation *Bambi* – part of Operation *Pluto*).

TIMELINE OF KEY DATES AND EVENTS

Phase III (27 September 1944 – 14 January 1945):

1 October 1944 – 8 November 1944	Combat operations to clear the Scheldt.
26 October 1944	Fuel pipeline to Boulogne operational (Operation *Dumbo* – part of Operation *Pluto*).
3 November 1944	Mulberry B closed for discharge of British stores. The harbour itself was finally closed on 1 December 1944.
9–27 November 1944	Mine sweeping operations along the Scheldt.
28 November 1944	Antwerp port opened to Allied shipping.
16 December 1944	German ground offensive (Battle of the Bulge).
1 January 1945	German air offensive (Operation *Bodenplatte*).

Phase IV (15 January 1945 – 8 May 1945):

8 February 1945	Battle of the Reichswald (Operation *Veritable*) and advance to Xanten (Operation *Blockbuster*).
23/24 March 1945	Crossing of the Rhine: ground forces under Operation *Plunder* and airborne forces under Operation *Varsity*.
March 1945	Advance to the Baltic.
4 May 1945	Unconditional surrender of all German forces.
8 May 1945	Victory in Europe (VE) Day.

Appendix II

Channel Ports used by the Allies – Key Data

Port	Date Captured	Date Opened for Allied Shipping	Remarks
Antwerp	4 September 1944	28 November 1944	
Boulogne	22 September 1944	14 October 1944	Became redundant following opening of Antwerp. Closed on 13 January 1945.
Calais	30 September 1944	21 November 1944	Developed for personnel traffic and as a train ferry terminal.
Cherbourg	2 July 1944	16 July 1944	US port
Dieppe	1 September 1944	6 September 1944	
Le Havre	12 September 1944	4 October 1944	US port
Le Tréport	1 September 1944	2 September 1944	Satellite of Dieppe used by the RAF for return of crashed aircraft to UNITED KINGDOM and inbound urgent stores. Not used after Boulogne was developed.
Mulberry Harbour "B"	First caissons planted 10 June 1944	11 June 1944	Construction was progressive from 10 June through to 17 July when the LST pier was completed. Closed for discharge of British stores on 3 November 1944.
Ostend	9 September 1944	28 September 1944	Port for intake of stores and fuel until Antwerp was opened.
Port en Bessin	8 June 1944	11 June 1944	Small port mainly used for fuel transfer from ocean tankers to on-shore pipeline to the RMA.
Rouen	1 September 1944	16 October 1944	

CHANNEL PORTS USED BY THE ALLIES – KEY DATA

Main Channel Ports Discharge Data – June to September 1944

Port	Date of Opening	Average Daily Discharges in Tons (0 = Date of Opening)			
		0 to 0+13	0+14 to 0+27	0+28 to 0+41	0+42 to 0+55
Cherbourg	16 July	1,828	5,509	9,837	8,906
Le Havre	4 October	662	3,744	5,095	4,246
Rouen	16 October	1,656	3,518	3,924	4,850
Dieppe	7 September	3,655	5,247	4,965	5,017
Boulogne	13 October	523	1,609	2,385	2,580
Ostend	28 September	998	1,907	2,366	2,946

Appendix III

Alphabetical Listing of 2nd TAF Support Units 1944 to 1945

This alphabetical listing includes the types and identities of the various 2nd TAF ground support units employed throughout the campaign from the landings in June 1944 through to the end of the war. It is difficult to list all 2nd TAF support units accurately and comprehensively as no overall master document was produced and identities have had to be gleaned from numerous operational records and from The National Archives search engine *Discovery*. Where possible, additional reference details have been included such as deployment or movement details and geographical locations. Unless otherwise specified, all formations listed are RAF units. Where units were formed especially for employment with 2nd TAF, their identity numbers were prefixed with a figure 4 for example, No.401 Air Stores Park. This listing is as accurate as possible but any readers who have additional information or corrections are asked to contact the author via his website at https://www.trevorstonelogistics.co.uk.

Air Formation Signals (Army – Royal Corps of Signals)

Each of these units included landline, teleprinter and DR communications of the RAF. Each had a headquarters (two companies), a line section, a line maintenance section, tele ops section, DR section, construction section, tech maintenance section and a light aid detachment. Eight units were attached to 2nd TAF:

No.11 Unit assigned to No.83 Group

No.12 Unit assigned to HQ 2nd TAF (main and rear)

No.13 Unit assigned to No.84 Group

No.14 Unit assigned to No.72 (Radar) Wing

No.15 Unit assigned to No.2 Group

No.16 Unit assigned to No.85 Group

No.17 Unit assigned to No.85 Group

No.18 Unit assigned to Air Staff Supreme Headquarters Allied Expeditionary Force and No.87 Group (formed in February 1945 to assimilate RAF units Paris)

ALPHABETICAL LISTING OF 2ND TAF SUPPORT UNITS

Air Stores Parks

    No.34 Air Stores Park supporting No.85 Group

    Nos. 401, 404 and 406 (Royal Canadian Air Force) Air Stores Park supporting No.83 Group

    Nos. 402 and 408 (Polish) and 418 air stores parks supporting No.84 Group

    No.414 Air Stores Park supporting No.2 Group

Airfield Construction Wings
Mobile:

    No.5357 (Airfield Construction) Wing comprising Nos. 5022 and 5023 squadrons, each with six field flights

Semi-Mobile (Heavy Construction):

    No.5352 (Airfield Construction) Wing comprising Nos. 5001, 5013, 5014 and 5202 (plant) squadrons

    No.5353 (Airfield Construction) Wing comprising Nos. 5005, 5008, 5012 and 5203 (plant) squadrons

    No.5354 (Airfield Construction) Wing comprising Nos. 5006, 5007, 5016 and 5204 (Plant) squadrons

    No.5355 (Airfield Construction) Wing comprising Nos. 5002, 5009, 5017 and 5205 (plant) squadrons plus No.4857 Quarrying Flight

Home Based:

    No.5351 (Airfield Construction) Wing comprising Nos. 5003, 5004, 5011, 5015 and 5201 squadrons

    No.5356 (Airfield Construction) Wing comprising Nos.5010, 5018, 5027 and 5206 squadrons

Repair Unit (Plant):

    No.52 Unit remained under command of No.85 Group

Airfield/Wing Headquarters

    Nos. 121 to 150 (inclusive); Nos. 126, 143 and 144 were Royal Canadian Air Force units; No.131 a Polish unit; No.132 a Norwegian unit and No.134 a Czech unit

FORWARD AIR BASES IN EUROPE FROM D-DAY TO THE BALTIC

Aviation Fuel and Ammunition Parks

> No.407 Aviation Fuel and Ammunition Park assigned to No.83 Group; consisting of a headquarters element, five ammunition and Petrol, Oil and Lubricant (fuel management) sections
>
> No.422 Aviation Fuel and Ammunition Park assigned to No.84 Group; consisting of a headquarters element, five ammunition and Petrol, Oil and Lubricant (fuel management) sections
>
> No.423 Aviation Fuel and Ammunition Park assigned to No.2 Group; consisting of a headquarters element, five ammunition and Petrol, Oil and Lubricant (fuel management) sections
>
> No.424 Aviation Fuel and Ammunition Park assigned to No.85 Group; consisting of a headquarters element, five ammunition and Petrol, Oil and Lubricant (fuel management) sections

Base Communications and Radar Unit

> No.1 Unit assigned to No.85 Group; some primary sources indicated this might have originally been formed as the Base Signals Unit at RAF Chigwell in the United Kingdom.

Base Defence Sectors

> No.21 Base Defence Sector manned by No.21 Wing; situated in the American Sector; was seconded to the United States Fifth Army.
>
> No.24 Base Defence Sector manned by No.24 Wing; landed in Normandy on 12 July 1944; was based at Meuvaines, inland from GOLD Beach; moved to Boves, south-south-east of Amiens on 17 September 1944; and then to Ghent on 16 January 1945; was disbanded soon after this final move.
>
> No.25 Base Defence Sector manned by No.25 Wing; landed in Normandy at OMAHA Beach on 28 August 1944; then initially based at Rennes/Vannes; responsible for defence of the Brittany port areas of Brest, Lorient and St Nazaire; moved to Eveberg, east of Brussels on 5 September 1944; responsible for the night air defence of British Second Army and First Canadian Army; disbanded on 16 March 1945 with control passing to No.85 Group Operations Room.

Base Signals and Radar Unit

In addition to their repair and overhaul capability, these units held reserve stock of complete signals units and vehicles, along with various equipment types including Type 15 Ground Control Intercept units and light warning sets. In addition to their

ALPHABETICAL LISTING OF 2ND TAF SUPPORT UNITS

repair work, they also were responsible for installing fixed wireless and radar stations in the base area and along the lines of communication and acted as the central communication centre for all W/T traffic in Allied Expeditionary Air Force. They were also a switching centre for all landline speech and teleprinter circuits for RAF units on the Continent. Like many of the base units, it was intended they would deploy to Normandy when the Rear Maintenance Area was more fully established, probably in the autumn of 1944.

Beach Balloon Squadrons and Flights, RAF

> No.974 Beach Balloon Squadron consisting of Nos. 51 and 52 Beach Balloon flights; attached to No. 2 RAF Beach Squadron in 102 Beach Sub Area (JUNO)
>
> No.976 Beach Balloon Squadron consisting of 50 and 53 Beach Balloon flights; attached to No.1 Beach Squadron in 101 Beach Sub Area (SWORD)
>
> No.980 Beach Balloon Squadron consisting of Nos. 54 and 55 Beach Balloon flights; attached to No.4 RAF Beach Squadron in 104 Beach Sub Area (GOLD)
>
> No.991 Beach Balloon Squadron consisting of Nos. 56 and 57 Beach Balloon flights; detached with its own headquarters, operating at Arromanches Mulberry B
>
> No.103 Port Balloon Flight
>
> No.104 Port Balloon Flight deployed to Normandy on 18 June 1944, specifically to provide balloon cover at Port-en-Bessin-Huppain
>
> *Note: there is an indication in some archival sources that there were also Nos. 965, 967 and 997 beach balloon squadrons along with an 'M' Balloon Unit.*

Beach Squadrons, RAF

Each of the RAF beach squadrons was divided into three flights and an administrative responsibility for a fourth beach balloon flight. Each of the beach flights was subdivided into six sections covering: landing, fuels, ammunition, equipment, provost and motor transport repair. The general concept of operations for these new units was that they would train alongside and be used with the main Beach Group to which they would be assigned. As far as possible, all personnel were volunteers and drawn from the RAF's Equipment Branch and trades. Due to the arduous nature of the work, they had to be of a strong physique and meet the fitness standards required for combined operations' training. They were armed with the same type of weapons as the army, with 70 per cent of the unit being issued sub-machine guns and the remainder with rifles. Initially, RAF beach squadron personnel were kitted out with army khaki battledress, but at the beginning of April 1944 authority was granted for them to wear RAF blue battledress and to fly the RAF Ensign whilst on the Continent. Additionally, authority was granted by HQ Combined Operations in March 1944 for them to wear the Combined Operations Badge on the upper sleeve of their battledress. A small provost section was included within each of the beach flights of the RAF beach squadrons, along with an RAF Police unit attached to 2nd TAF. Additionally, dedicated police units were also included as part of the three component groups. Broadly speaking, they were established to undertake police and security duties including security, provost, special investigation, and traffic control. Four squadrons were assigned to Operation *Overlord*:

No.1 RAF Beach Squadron

No.2 RAF Beach Squadron

No.3 RAF Beach Squadron held in Reserve at RAF Old Sarum in the United Kingdom

No.4 RAF Beach Squadron

Bomb Disposal Squadrons

No.5137 Squadron consisting of Nos. 6220 and 6225 flights

No.5138 Squadron consisting of Nos. 6214, 6228 and 6337 flights

No.5139 Squadron consisting Nos. 6205, 6206 and 6210 flights

Casualty Air Evacuation Units

No.1 Unit formed at Airfield B.56 Evere, Belgium in November 1944, with a detachment at Airfield B.70 Antwerp

No.4 Unit formed in France August 1944 and Belgium September 1944

Note: both primary and secondary sources are sparse in detail on these units. There is a mention of a No.5 in the official medical history of the RAF but no corresponding war diary in The National Archives.

Concealment and Decoy Units, RAF

No.1 Unit assigned to No.83 Group

No.2 Unit assigned to No.83 Group

No.3 Unit assigned to No.84 Group

No.4 Unit assigned to No.84 Group

Note: further units were formed for HQ TAF and No.2 Group, but their identities cannot be ascertained at the time of publication.

Dental Unit, Mobile

No.104 Unit assigned to No.84 Group

No.106 Unit assigned to No.84 Group

ALPHABETICAL LISTING OF 2ND TAF SUPPORT UNITS

No.150 Unit

No.151 Unit

No.152 Unit

Embarkation Units

No.85 Unit formed in March 1944; landed in Normandy on 18 August 1944; detachments at Caen and Ouistreham, France.

No.86 Unit formed in March 1944; Operations Record Book is missing but the unit was believed to be at Hamburg, Germany in January 1946, with a detachment at Cuxhaven.

No.87 Unit formed in February 1944; landed in Normandy (OMAHA Beach and Courseulles) on 15 June 1944; moved to Cherbourg, France on 2 July 1944, with various detachments at French ports from July to September 1944; moved to Blankenberge, Belgium on 7 January 1945 and disbanded 18 January 1945.

No.89 Unit landed in Port-en-Bessin-Huppain, Normandy on 9 June 1944; initially tasked with supervising RAF cargo landed at Port-en-Bessin-Huppain and Mulberry B at Arromanches; detachments to Caen and Tracy-sur-Mer, France in September 1944; moved to Calais on 25 November 1944.

No.93 Unit formed on 1 June 1944; landed in Dieppe on 7 September 1944; initially operated at this port with a detachment at Le Tréport, France from 22 October 1944.

Field Photographic Sections, Mobile

No.1 Section supported No.35 (Reconnaissance) Wing in No.84 Group

No.4 Section supported No.35 (Reconnaissance) Wing in No.84 Group; landed in France on 18 August 1944

No.5 (RCAF) Section supported No.39 (Reconnaissance) Wing in No.83 Group

No.6 (RCAF) Section supported No.39 (Reconnaissance) Wing in No 83 Group

No.7 Section supported No.34 (Reconnaissance) Wing in HQ 2nd TAF

Fighter Direction Tenders

Converted from the standard tank landing ship structure, work on the vessels was carried out at John Brown's shipyard on the River Clyde, just west of Glasgow. Work on all three was complete by the middle of February 1944. The newly converted vessels were literally crammed with the latest technology. Above deck there was a host of various antenna, masts, and aerials, whilst below deck, there

FORWARD AIR BASES IN EUROPE FROM D-DAY TO THE BALTIC

were various rooms which received, interpreted, and forwarded the collected data. On board there were eight components:

> Type 15 Ground Control Intercept Radar; to monitor all air activity in the area; the rotating antenna for the set was located on the bow of the ship some 30 feet above the water line.
>
> Type 11 Radar; known as the German radar; the antenna for this unit was located on the middle, upper deck.
>
> 'Y' Section; a variety of radio monitoring equipment to intercept enemy radio command and control communications, especially those between ground control units and their aircraft.
>
> Radio communications for ship-to-ship, ship-to-shore, and ship-to-aircraft.
>
> Radio counter measures.
>
> Plan Position Indicators; to counter the effects of 'window' aluminium strips dropped from aircraft to confuse radar.
>
> Mark 3 Identification Friend or Foe; used when the air movements liaison section were unable to confirm the identity of a particular aircraft.
>
> Airborne Interception Beacons; to aid control of Allied night fighter aircraft.

Each of the tenders was manned by personnel from all three services, but predominantly the Royal Navy with seven officers and fifty-three seamen to operate the ship and typically nineteen officers and 157 other ranks (NCOs and airmen) RAF/RCAF operators to maintain and operate the specialist equipment on board. Three vessels were used in the campaign:

> No.13 vessel was held in reserve and anchored approximately forty miles offshore in the main shipping lane approach to the beaches.
>
> No.216 vessel was anchored just off JUNO Beach, between SWORD and GOLD beaches and covered the British and American sectors.
>
> No.21 vessel was anchored just off OMAHA and UTAH beaches covering the American sector.

Forward Equipment Unit

Established in the United Kingdom under the control of No.85 Group, initially at RAF Stapleford Tawney in Essex, but moving to RAF Bicester in February 1944. The unit made up of an administrative headquarters and six specialist groups responsible for various types of storage, a packing case-making section and a provisioning (i.e. stock control) office. It was staffed with between 200 and 300 personnel and established for some sixty vehicles. This unit was dedicated to the support of the Allied Expeditionary Air Force and was able to accumulate stocks from the myriad storage depots of RAF Maintenance Command and forward them to the Continent.

ALPHABETICAL LISTING OF 2ND TAF SUPPORT UNITS

It was originally envisaged that the unit would relocate to Normandy and set up in the Rear Maintenance Area, but in the event, it remained at Bicester for the duration of the war. In addition to supporting the various units which would remain in the base area and the base defence sectors, its main role would be to resupply the various mobile units that would eventually move out of the lodgement area when 2nd TAF joined the advance from Normandy. The unit was reconstituted as a transit centre under the control of No.57 Maintenance Wing, No.40 Group, Maintenance Command in January 1945, becoming No.246 Maintenance Unit in May 1945.

Forward Repair Unit

Although initially based in the Rear Maintenance Area, the forward repair unit was designed and equipped to be a transportable unit and could be moved in stages. In addition to its prime responsibility of supporting 2nd TAF, the unit was also responsible for providing repair and salvage support for aircraft of Bomber Command, Transport Command and No.38 Group on the Continent when required. Towards the end of 1944 sub-units were formed including a base aircraft repair unit and a base area salvage unit.

Ground Control Intercept Convoys

Each of these units was a sizeable entity consisting of some twenty-seven vehicles (mainly 3-ton Crossley, Thornycroft and Austin heavy haulage vehicles) and a jeep. Amongst this mixed fleet were the various radars, the command-and-control vehicle, the operations room, diesel generators and various support vehicles. At the heart of each of these mobile intercept units were four types of equipment, collectively known as Air Ministry Experimental Station Type 25, consisting of:

> The long-range Type 15 system.
>
> The Type 13 centimetre height-finding equipment.
>
> The Type 14 centimetre plan-position station, which provided detection of low-level aircraft.
>
> The Type 11 mobile radar.
>
> The last of these was known as the 'German' radar, which had been designed and built by the TRE using parts recovered from the German Wurzburg radar, captured during the famous Bruneval commando raid (Operation *Biting*) in February 1942.

The units formed for the campaign were as follows:

No.83 (Composite) Group:

> GCI Convoy No.15053
>
> GCI Convoy No.15054

GCI/COL Convoy No.15055

GCI Convoy No.15056

No. 21 Base Defence Sector:

GCI Convoy No.15072

GCI/COL Convoy No.15073

GCI/COL Convoy No.15074

GCI Convoy No.15081

GCI Convoy No.15082

No.24 Base Defence Sector:

GCI Convoy No.15083 (Type 25)

GCI Convoy No.15121 (Type 15)

GCI Convoy No.15128 (Type 25)

GCI/COL Convoy No.15129 (included Air Ministry Experimental Station (AMES) 14039 Type 14)

GCI/COL Convoy No.15130 (included AMES 14051 Type 14)

No.25 Base Defence Sector:

GCI Convoy No.15119

GCI Convoy No.15120

GCI Convoy No.15122

GCI/COL Convoy No.14014 (AMES)

GCI/COL Convoy No.14052 (AMES)

Group Control Centre

No.483 part of No.83 Group

No.484 part of No.84 Group

No.485 part of No.85 Group

Group and Wing Support Units

No.2 Group Support Unit formed at RAF Swanton Morley on 1 April 1944 and moved to RAF Fersfield on 17 December 1944

ALPHABETICAL LISTING OF 2ND TAF SUPPORT UNITS

No.83 Group Support Unit formed at Redhill on 1 March 1944 and moved to Bognor, Westhampnett and Dunsfold by February 1945

No.84 Group Support Unit formed at Aston Down on 14 February 1944 and moved to Thruxton and Lasham on 21 November 1944

No.34 Wing Support Unit; formed at RAF Northolt on 1 August 1944 and moved to Blackbushe on 16 October 1944

Hospital, General

No.8 RAF General Hospital served all of 2nd TAF but part of No.85 Group; formed at Aston Down, Gloucestershire in early August 1944; landed in France in late August 1944; and operational under canvas in the Rear Maintenance Area at Bayeux, France on 30 August 1944; relocated to Brussels, Belgium on 19 September 1944.

Hospital, Mobile Field

No.50 Mobile Field Hospital attached to No.83 Group; formed in February 1943 at RAF Wroughton; landed in France on 14 June 1944

No.52 Mobile Field Hospital attached to No.83 Group (RCAF) formed in August 1943 at Detling; landed in France on 8 June 1944

No.53 Mobile Field Hospital attached to No.84 Group; formed in September 1943 at Sawbridgeworth; landed in France on 17 August 1944

No.54 Mobile Field Hospital attached to No.84 Group; formed in September 1943 at Sawbridgeworth; landed in France on 21 August 1944

No.55 Mobile Field Hospital attached to No.2 Group; formed in January 1944 at Fontwell; landed in France on 23 August 1944

Note: each of the hospitals had an attached casualty air evacuation unit which worked in conjunction with RAF Transport Command's forward staging posts to return casualties to the United Kingdom.

Motor Transport Light Repair Units

No.70 Unit attached to No.83 Group; landed in Belgium in September 1944; Eindhoven in October 1944; and then in Germany in April 1945

No.71 Unit attached to No.83 Group; landed in France in June 1944; Belgium in September 1944; Eindhoven in October 1944; and in Germany in April 1945

No.72 Unit

No.73 Unit

No.74 Unit attached to No.84 Group

FORWARD AIR BASES IN EUROPE FROM D-DAY TO THE BALTIC

Personnel Centre, Base

Formed within No.85 Group; landed on 20 August 1944 in Creully in the Rear Maintenance Area; moved to Blankenberge, Belgium on 5 October 1944. The unit was made up of two sections. The first, known as the Transit Section, was responsible for the documentation and initial control of all RAF personnel destined for Allied Expeditionary Air Force units. These were likely to be individuals coming in as replacements or reinforcements. The section would also take care of arranging accommodation for personnel who had discharged from hospital but were not yet fit to return to their units. The second part of the centre looked after what were known as non-effective personnel. This would also include those subject to disciplinary action such as those awaiting Court Martial.

Radar Control Posts, Mobile

    No.1 assigned to No.2 Group

    No.2

    No.3

Radar Navigation Aids, No.72 Wing RAF (60 (Signals) Group)

These units operated radar navigational aids, which provided guidance towards targets in the air or on the ground. By this stage of the war a wide range of such high-tech had been developed such as AI, H2S, OBOE and GEE. The deployment and exact composition of this wing is difficult to ascertain with any degree of precision, but its units were attached to each of the groups within the tactical air force at various stages of the campaign. It is known that the following units were part of the wing during the campaign:

    AMES 102
    AMES 105
    AMES 106
    AMES 108
    AMES 109
    AMES 114
    AMES 117
    AMES 120
    AMES 5369
    AMES 7911
    AMES 7922
    AMES 9000 (also shown as 2/9000)

ALPHABETICAL LISTING OF 2ND TAF SUPPORT UNITS

AMES 9412B
AMES 9431A
AMES 9442

Regiment, RAF

Mobile Wing HQs:

No.1300 landed on 9 June 1944 to B.5 Le Fresne-Camilly

No.1301 landed on 15 June 1944 to B.7 Martragny

No.1302 landed on 8 June 1944 to B.6 Coulombs

No.1303 landed on 15 June 1944 to B.9 Lantheuil

No.1304 landed on 6 June 1944 to B.3 Sainte-Croix-sur-Mer

No.1305 attached to No.83 Group; landed on 6 June 1944 to B.2 Bazenville

No.1306 landed in June 1944 to B.10 Plumetot

No.1307 landed in June 1944 to B.11 Longues-sur-Mer

No.1309 landed in June 1944 to B.4 Bény-sur-Mer

No.1311 landed in August 1944 to B.4 Bény-sur-Mer

No.1312 landed in August 1944 to B.10 Plumetot

No.1314 landed in August 1944 to B.8 Sommervieu

No.1315 landed in August 1944 to Le Neufbourg

No.1316 landed in August 1944 to B.17 Carpiquet

No.1317 attached to No.84 Group; landed in July 1944 to B.7 Martragny

No.1318 attached to No. 84; landed in July 1944 to B.3 Sainte Croix-sur-Mer

Note: the war diary for No.1304 Wing indicates that all RAF Regiment Mobile Wing headquarters were disbanded at some stage during January 1945.

Light Anti-Aircraft Squadrons:

No.2701 Squadron landed in August 1944; initial location unknown

No.2703 Squadron attached to No.83 Group; landed in November 1944 to B.78 Eindhoven

No.2715 Squadron landed in February 1945 to B.65 Belgium

No.2734 Squadron attached to No.83 Group; landed in June 1944 to B.10 Caen

No.2736 Squadron attached to No.83 Group; landed on 18 June 1944 to B.9 Lantheuil

FORWARD AIR BASES IN EUROPE FROM D-DAY TO THE BALTIC

No.2738 Squadron landed in January 1945 to St Omer

No.2741 Squadron landed in January 1945 to B.45 St Omer

No.2760 Squadron landed in February 1945 to B.67 Ursel, Belgium

No.2773 Squadron landed in August 1944 to B.17 Carpiquet

No.2791 Squadron landed in January 1945 to B.51 Vendeville

No.2794 Squadron attached to No.83 Group; landed on 16 June 1944 to B.8 Sommervieu

No.2800 Squadron landed in August 1944 to France; initial location unknown

No.2809 Squadron attached to No.83 Group; landed on 7 June 1944 to B.3 Sainte Croix-sur-Mer

No.2812 Squadron attached to No.85 Group; landed in February 1945 to B.72 Epinoy

No.2817 Squadron attached to No.83 Group; landed in June 1944 to B.5 Camilly

No.2819 Squadron attached to No.83 Group; landed on 7 June 1944 to B.3 Sainte Croix-sur-Mer

No.2826 Squadron landed in February 1945; initial location unknown

No.2834 Squadron attached to No.83 Group; landed on 7 June 1944 to B.2 Bazenville

No.2838 Squadron attached to No.85 Group; landed in February 1945

No.2872 Squadron landed in August 1944 to Normandy

No.2873 Squadron landed in August 1944 to Normandy

No.2874 Squadron landed on 19 August 1944 to B.7 Martragny

No.2875 Squadron attached to No.83 Group; landed in 1944 to France

No.2876 Squadron attached to No.83 Group; landed in June 1944 to B.6 Coulombs

No.2880 Squadron landed in August 1944 to Normandy

No.2881 Squadron attached to No.83 Group; landed in August 1944 to France

Armoured Car Squadrons:

No.2742 Squadron landed in November 1944 to Ghent, Belgium

No.2757 Squadron landed in August 1944 to B.7 Martragny

No.2777 Squadron landed in August 1944 to B.4 Beny-sur-Mer

No.2781 Squadron landed in August 1944 to B.12 Ellon

ALPHABETICAL LISTING OF 2ND TAF SUPPORT UNITS

No.2804 Squadron attached to No.85 Group; landed in September 1944

No.2806 Squadron landed in July 1944 to France

Rifle Squadrons:

No.2710 Squadron landed in May 1945 to Ostend

No.2713 Squadron landed in September 1944 to Rennes

No.2717 Squadron landed in August 1944 to Carpiquet

No.2719 Squadron landed in November 1944 to Horst

No.2724 Squadron landed in November 1944

No.2726 Squadron landed in March 1945 to B.78 Eindhoven

No.2729 Squadron landed in August 1944 to Le Tronquay

No.2731 Squadron landed in February 1945 to Ghent

No.2740 Squadron landed in February 1945 to St Omer

No.2741 Squadron landed in January 1945; initial location unknown

No.2749 Squadron landed in April 1945 to Furnes

No.2750 Squadron landed in November 1944 to Mons

No.2765 Squadron landed in February 1945 to St Omer

No.2768 Squadron landed in February 1945 to Coxyde

No.2770 Squadron landed in October to Ostende

No.2786 Squadron landed in April 1945; initial location unknown

No.2798 Squadron attached to No.21 Base Defence Sector in No.85 Group; landed in July 1944 to France

No.2805 Squadron landed January 1945 to France

No.2807 Squadron dated landed unknown, but to Germany in 1945

No.2811 Squadron landed in November 1944 to Belgium

No.2814 Squadron date of landing and initial location unknown

No.2816 Squadron landed in August 1944; initial location unknown

No.2822 Squadron landed in late May 1945 to Denmark then Germany

No.2823 Squadron landed February1945; initial location unknown

No.2824 Squadron attached to No.2 Group; landed February1945 to B.50 Vitry-en-Artois

No.2827 Squadron landed in July 1944 to France

FORWARD AIR BASES IN EUROPE FROM D-DAY TO THE BALTIC

No.2829 Squadron attached to No.84 Group; landed in November 1944 to Belgium

No.2831 Squadron attached to No.2 Group; landed in October 1944 to Sancourt

No.2843 Squadron attached to No.84 Group; landed in November 1944 to Belgium

No.2844 Squadron landed in May 1945; initial location unknown

No.2845 Squadron landed in September 1944 to Normandy

No.2848 Squadron attached to No.2 Group; landed in November 1944 to Belgium

No.2853 Squadron date of landing and initial location unknown

No.2856 Squadron landed in January 1945 to France

No.2858 Squadron landed in May 1945; initial location unknown

No.2862 Squadron landed in January 1945; initial location unknown

No.2863 Squadron landed in November 1944 to Belgium

No.2865 Squadron attached to No.85 Group; landed in January 1945 to France

No.2868 Squadron attached to No.83 Group; landed in April 1945 to Germany

No.2871 Squadron landed in October 1944 to Belgium

No.2878 Squadron date of landing and initial location unknown

No.2879 Squadron landed in November 1944 to France

No.2883 Squadron landed in April 1945 to Belgium

No.2897 Squadron landed 1944 to France

Repair and Salvage Units

No.403 Unit attached to No.83 Group; responsible for Typhoon aircraft

No.405 Unit attached to No.83 Group; responsible for Spitfire, Hurricane and Mustang aircraft; unit was disbanded on 21 July 1944

No.409 Unit attached to No.83 Group; responsible for Mustang, Spitfire, Mosquito, Typhoon, Hurricane and Auster aircraft

No.410 Unit attached to No.83 Group; responsible for Spitfire, Hurricane and Typhoon aircraft

No.411 (Polish) Unit attached to No.84 Group; responsible for Spitfire and Mustang aircraft

No.412 Unit attached to No.84 Group; Aircraft type responsibility unknown

ALPHABETICAL LISTING OF 2ND TAF SUPPORT UNITS

No.413 Unit attached to No.84 Group; responsible for Typhoon & Auster aircraft

No.416 Unit attached to No.2 Group; responsible for Boston and Mitchell aircraft

No.417 Unit attached to No.2 Group responsible for Mosquito aircraft

No.419 Unit attached to No.83 Group; responsible for Hurricane and Auster aircraft

No.420 Unit attached to No.84 Group; responsible for Spitfire and Tempest aircraft

No.421 Unit attached to No.84 Group; responsible for Spitfire aircraft; unit disbanded on 21 July 1944

Servicing Commando Units, RAF

No.3205 Unit landed on 7 June 1944; returned to the United Kingdom at end of July 1944

No.3206 Unit attached to No.83 Group; landed on 15 June 1944 to Airfield B.6 Coulombs

No.3207 Unit landed on 7 June 1944; provided small detachments and replacements only

No.3208 Unit landed 16 June 1944 to Airfield B.7 Martragny; assigned to No.84 Group from 8 August 1944

No.3209 Unit landed on 7 June 1944; provided small detachments and replacements only

No.3210 Unit landed 7 June 1944; returned to the United Kingdom at end of July 1944

Signals Units, Mobile

No.83 Group:

No.5183W Unit
No.5163U Unit

No.84 Group:

No.5054C (123 Wing)
No.5062J (35 Wing)
No.5063J (131 Wing)

No.5081C (35 Wing)
No.5084C (146 Wing)
No.5086J (146 Wing)
No.5087J (123 Wing)
No.5088J (131 Wing)
No.5091C (131 Wing)
No.5114G (35 Wing)
No.5121J (35 Wing)
No.5406G (131 Wing)
No.5409G (146 Wing)
No.5424J (146 Wing)
No.5437Q (131 Wing)
No.5435Q (146 Wing)

No.85 Group:

No.545K (21 Base Defence Sector)
No.5006H (21 Base Defence Sector)
No.5060T
No.5131A (21 Base Defence Sector)
No.5132C (21 Base Defence Sector)
No.5133C (24 Base Defence Sector)
No.5139H (24 Base Defence Sector)
No.5292J (21 Base Defence Sector)
No.5141Q (21 Base Defence Sector)
No.5142Q (21 Base Defence Sector)
No.5143U (483 GCC)
No.5157T (21 Base Defence Sector)

No.85 Group:

No.5275B (25 Base Defence Sector)
No.5277D (25 Base Defence Sector)
No.5158T (21 Base Defence Sector)
No.5159T (24 Base Defence Sector)
No.5227J (21 Base Defence Sector)
No.5160T (24 Base Defence Sector)

ALPHABETICAL LISTING OF 2ND TAF SUPPORT UNITS

No.5161T
No.5164U (21 Base Defence Sector)
No.5166U (24 Base Defence Sector)
No.5167U (24 Base Defence Sector)
No.5169U (21 Base Defence Sector)
No.5184 (United States Sector)
No.5186W (21 Base Defence Sector)
No.5215N (21 Base Defence Sector)
No.5225J (24 Base Defence Sector)
No.5226J (21 Base Defence Sector)
No.5228J (21 Base Defence Sector)
No.5231P (24 Base Defence Sector)
No.5233P (21 Base Defence Sector)
No.5240Q (24 Base Defence Sector)
No.5241Q (24 Base Defence Sector)
No.5242Q (24 Base Defence Sector)
No.5247Q (United States Sector)
No.5262T (21 Base Defence Sector)
No.5274B (24 Base Defence Sector)
No.5276D (United States Sector)
No.5283G (United States Sector)
No.5288J (24 Base Defence Sector)
No.5289J (24 Base Defence Sector)
No.5290J (24 Base Defence Sector)
No.5291J (24 Base Defence Sector)
No.5293J (24 Base Defence Sector)
No.5316F (21 Base Defence Sector)
No.5317P (21 Base Defence Sector)
No.5318P (21 Base Defence Sector)
No.5319P (24 Base Defence Sector)
No.5372P (24 Base Defence Sector)

No.72 Wing:

No.116
No.7921

Signals Servicing Units, Mobile

>No.307 Unit attached to no.83 Group; landed in France in June 1944
>No.310 Unit

Supply and Transport Columns

>No.309 (with eight companies) attached to No.83 Group
>No.311 (with eight companies) attached to No.84 Group
>No.312 (with eight companies) attached to No.84 Group
>No.313 (with six companies) attached to No.85 Group
>No.314 (with six companies) attached to No.2 Group
>No.317 formed in September 1944 to Malines, Belgium in October 1944

Appendix IV

Composition of 2nd TAF in May 1945

The 2nd TAF order of battle changed several times throughout the campaign as wings and squadrons were added and removed. The following listing shows the order in May 1945.[1]

Headquarters 2nd TAF:

No.34 (Reconnaissance) Wing:

    No.16 Squadron (Spitfire XI)
    No.69 Squadron (Wellington XIII)
    No.140 Squadron (Mosquito XVI)

No.2 Group:

No.136 Wing:

    No.418 (RCAF) Squadron (Mosquito VI)
    No.605 Squadron (Mosquito VI)

No.137 Wing:

    No.88 Squadron (Boston III)
    No.226 Squadron (Mitchell II)
    No.342 (French) Squadron (Boston IV)

No.138 Wing (September 1944 – May 1945):

    No.107 Squadron (Mosquito VI)
    No.305 (Polish) Squadron (Mosquito VI)
    No.613 Squadron (Mosquito VI)

FORWARD AIR BASES IN EUROPE FROM D-DAY TO THE BALTIC

No.139 Wing (September 1944 – May 1945):

    No.98 Squadron (Mitchell II and III)
    No.180 Squadron (Mitchell II and III)
    No.320 (Dutch) Squadron (Mitchell II and III)

No.140 Wing (September 1944 – May 1945):

    No.21 Squadron (Mosquito VI)
    No.464 (Australian) Squadron (Mosquito VI)
    No.487 (New Zealand) Squadron (Mosquito VI)

No.83 Group:

No.39 (RCAF) (Reconnaissance) Wing:

    No.400 (Canadian) Squadron (Spitfire XI)
    No.414 (Canadian) Squadron (Spitfire IX)
    No.430 (Canadian) Squadron (Spitfire XIV)

No.121 Wing:

    No.174 Squadron (Typhoon 1B)
    No.175 Squadron (Typhoon 1B)
    No.184 Squadron (Typhoon 1B)
    No.245 Squadron (Typhoon 1B)

No.122 Wing:

    No.3 Squadron (Tempest V)
    No.56 Squadron (Tempest V)
    No.80 Squadron (Tempest V)
    No.274 Squadron (Tempest V)
    No.486 (New Zealand) Squadron (Tempest V)
    No.616 Squadron (Meteor 1/III)

No.124 Wing:

    No.137 Squadron (Typhoon 1B)
    No.181 Squadron (Typhoon 1B)

COMPOSITION OF 2ND TAF IN MAY 1945

    No.182 Squadron (Typhoon 1B)
    No.247 Squadron (Typhoon 1B)

No.125 Wing:

    No.130 Squadron (Spitfire XIV)
    No.350 (Belgian) Squadron (Spitfire XIV)
    No.610 Squadron (Spitfire XIV)

No.126 (RCAF) Wing:

    No.401 (Canadian) Squadron (Spitfire IX)
    No.402 (Canadian) Squadron (Spitfire XIV)
    No.411 (Canadian) Squadron (Spitfire IX)
    No.412 (Canadian) Squadron (Spitfire IX)

No.127 (RCAF) Wing:

    No.403 (Canadian) Squadron (Spitfire XVI)
    No.416 (Canadian) Squadron (Spitfire XVI)
    No.421 (Canadian) Squadron (Spitfire XVI)
    No.443 (Canadian) Squadron (Spitfire XVI)

No.143 (RCAF) Wing:

    No.168 Squadron (Typhoon 1B)
    No.438 (Canadian) Squadron (Typhoon 1B)
    No.439 (Canadian) Squadron (Typhoon 1B)
    No.440 (Canadian) Squadron (Typhoon 1B)

Air Observation Post:

    No.653 Squadron (Auster IV and V)
    No.658 Squadron (Auster IV and V)
    No.659 Squadron (Auster IV and V)
    No.662 Squadron (Auster IV and V)

No.84 Group:

No.35 (Reconnaissance) Wing:

    No.2 Squadron (Spitfire XIV)

FORWARD AIR BASES IN EUROPE FROM D-DAY TO THE BALTIC

No.4 (Photographic Reconnaissance) Squadron (Spitfire XI)

No.268 Squadron (Mustang II)

No.123 Wing:

No.164 Squadron (Typhoon 1B)

No.183 Squadron (Typhoon 1B)

No.198 Squadron (Typhoon 1B)

No.609 Squadron (Typhoon 1B)

No.131 (Polish) Wing:

No.302 (Polish) Squadron (Spitfire XVI)

No.308 (Polish) Squadron (Spitfire XVI)

No.317 (Polish) Squadron (Spitfire XVI)

No.349 (Belgian) Squadron (Spitfire XVI)

No.322 (Dutch) Squadron (Spitfire XVI)

No.132 Wing:

No.66 Squadron (Spitfire XVI)

No.127 Squadron (Spitfire XVI)

No.135 Wing:

No.33 Squadron (Tempest V)

No.222 Squadron (Tempest V)

No.274 Squadron (Tempest V)

No.145 Wing:

No.74 Squadron (Spitfire XVI)

No.340 (French) Squadron (Spitfire XVI)

No.341 (French) Squadron (Spitfire XVI)

No.345 (French) Squadron (Spitfire XVI)

No.485 (New Zealand) Squadron (Spitfire XVI)

COMPOSITION OF 2ND TAF IN MAY 1945

No.146 Wing:

    No.193 Squadron (Typhoon 1B)
    No.197 Squadron (Typhoon 1B)
    No.263 Squadron (Typhoon 1B)
    No.266 Squadron (Typhoon 1B)

Air Observation Post:

    No.652 Squadron (Auster IV)
    No.660 Squadron (Auster IV)
    No.661 Squadron (Auster IV)

No.85 Group:

No.147 Wing:

    No.219 Squadron (Mosquito XXX)
    No.410 (Canadian) Squadron (Mosquito XXX)
    No.488 (New Zealand) Squadron (Mosquito XXX)

No.148 Wing:

    No.264 Squadron (Mosquito XIII)
    No.409 (RCAF) Squadron (Mosquito XIII)
    No.604 Squadron (Mosquito XIII)

Appendix V

Roll of Honours and Awards to 2nd TAF Support Personnel

This roll has been compiled from data in various war diaries and other secondary sources. It is certain there are many more, but many sources do not show if individuals were 2nd TAF support units. This listing is as accurate as possible but any readers who have additional information or corrections are asked to contact the author via his website at https://www.trevorstonelogistics.co.uk.

Roll of Honour
2nd TAF Personnel Who Died on Active Service

Akass, Charles Richard, Corporal RAFVR (930476). No.2757 Squadron RAF Regiment. Killed on 16 December 1944 during a V-2 rocket attack on Antwerp. Buried at Schoonselhof Cemetery, Belgium, Grave V. D. 73.

Allen, Arthur Foster, Leading Aircraftman RAFVR (1435005). No.2717 Squadron RAF Regiment. Killed on 16 December 1944 during a V-2 rocket attack on Antwerp. Buried at Schoonselhof Cemetery, Belgium, Grave V. D. 44.

Batchelor, Lionel Algie, Corporal RAFVR (1533722). No.2817 Squadron RAF Regiment. Lost at sea on 7 June 1944. Commemorated on the Runnymede Memorial, United Kingdom, Panel 241.

Brookes, Archibald, Corporal RAFVR (869570). Balloon Operator. No.974 (Balloon) Squadron. Killed on 7 June 1944 by a German mine. Buried at Bayeux War Cemetery, France, Grave V. D. 8.

Christophers, Derrick Harold, Flying Officer RAFVR (127570). No.2880 Squadron RAF Regiment. Killed on 16 December 1944 during a V-2 rocket attack on Antwerp. Buried at Schoonselhof Cemetery, Belgium, Grave V. D. 42.

Clotworthy, Harold, Leading Aircraftman RAFVR (1049735). No.2757 Squadron RAF Regiment. Killed on 16 December 1944 during a V-2 rocket attack on Antwerp. Buried at Schoonselhof Cemetery, Belgium, Grave V. A. 45.

Crofts, Jack Henson, Leading Aircraftman RAFVR (1678283). No.3207 RAF Servicing Commando Unit. Lost at sea on 7 June 1944 when his LCI was torpedoed. Commemorated on the Runnymede Memorial, United Kingdom, Panel 241.

Crooks, William, Leading Aircraftman RAFVR (1715907). No.2817 Squadron RAF Regiment. Killed on 1 January 1945 during the Luftwaffe's New Year's

ROLL OF HONOURS AND AWARDS

Day attack. Buried at Eindhoven (Woensel) General Cemetery, the Netherlands, Plot KK, Grave 248.

Doherty, Anthony, Leading Aircraftman RAFVR (1556904). No.2805 Squadron RAF Regiment. Killed on 9 April 1945. Buried at Reichswald Forest War Cemetery, Germany, Grave 17. A. 7.

Dring, Norman Douglas, Leading Aircraftman RAFVR (1483454). No.2817 Squadron RAF Regiment. Lost at sea on 7 June 1944. Commemorated on the Runnymede Memorial, United Kingdom, Panel 241

Fancourt, Albert Henry, Leading Aircraftman RAFVR (862656). No.1 RAF Beach Squadron. Killed in action on 6 June 1944. Commemorated on the Runnymede Memorial, United Kingdom, Panel 242.

Ferguson, John Hamilton, Aircraftman 1st Class RAFVR (1565310). No.216 Fighter Direction Tender. Killed on 7 July 1944 when his ship was torpedoed by a Ju 88. Commemorated on the Runnymede Memorial, United Kingdom, Panel 243.

Finch, William Major, Leading Aircraftman RAFVR (1650137). No.2834 Squadron RAF Regiment. Killed on 6 June 1944. Commemorated on the Runnymede Memorial, United Kingdom, Panel 242.

Francis, John, Leading Aircraftman RAFVR (1452021). No.2717 Squadron RAF Regiment. Killed on 16 December 1944 during a V-2 rocket attack on Antwerp. Buried at Schoonselhof Cemetery, Belgium, Grave V. D. 43.

Gaughan, James, Leading Aircraftman RAFVR (1036266). No.216 Fighter Direction Tender. Killed on 7 July 1944 when his ship was torpedoed by a Ju 88. Commemorated on the Runnymede Memorial, United Kingdom, Panel 242.

Harris, David, Airman 1st Class RAFVR (1143334). No.483 Group Control Centre. Killed on 10 June 1944 during a bombing attack on a dispersed site near Crépon. Buried at Crépon Churchyard, France, Grave 1.

Hartles, Alfred Ernest, Leading Aircraftman RAFVR (1358487). No.2809 Squadron RAF Regiment. Died on 22 October 1944 following a road traffic accident with a Canadian vehicle near Aarschot. Buried at Brussels Town Cemetery, Belgium, Grave X. 18. 55.

Hawkins, Francis Ewart, Flying Officer RAFVR (147413). No.5022 Airfield Construction Squadron. Died on 5 September 1944 following an accident. Buried at Lille Southern Cemetery, France, Plot 5, Row A, Grave 7.

Highfield, Douglas Charles, Flight Lieutenant RAFVR (117492). No.15082 GCI, No.21 Base Defence Sector. Killed in action on 6 June 1944. Buried at Bayeux War Cemetery, France, Grave X. B. 14.

Ingram, William Douglas, Flight Lieutenant (31332). No.1 RAF Beach Squadron (No.102 Beach Flight). Killed in action on D-Day, 6 June 1944. Buried at Hawkinge Cemetery, United Kingdom, Plot O, Row 3, Grave 76.

Lansdowne, Leonard Charles, Leading Aircraftman RAFVR (1384610). No.3206 RAF Servicing Commando Unit. Died on 12 September 1944. Buried at Marissel French National Cemetery, France, Grave 324.

Laytham, John, Leading Aircraftman (1521861). No.1 RAF Beach Squadron. Died on 11 June 1944. Buried at Hermanville War Cemetery, France, Grave 1. E. 22.

Leonard, William, Leading Aircraftman (1682612). No.2809 Squadron RAF Regiment. Killed on 11 November 1944 during an enemy air attack on Airfield

B.80 Volkel. Buried at Uden (Odiliapeel) Roman Catholic Cemetery, the Netherlands, Grave 4.

Logan, George, Corporal, RAFVR (1001089). No.216 Fighter Direction Tender. Killed on 7 July 1944 when his ship was torpedoed by a Ju 88. Commemorated on the Runnymede Memorial, United Kingdom, Panel 241.

Lovat, Joseph, Corporal (1486192). No.2809 Squadron RAF Regiment. Evacuated after being wounded on the airfield in Antwerp on 23 September 1944. He died later on 30 October 1944 at RAF Hospital Wroughton, United Kingdom. Buried at Deighton Methodist Chapelyard and Extension, United Kingdom, Section B, New Ground, Grave 81.

Lynch, Thomas, Leading Aircraftman, RAFVR (1085258). No.309 Supply and Transport Column. Killed on 8 February 1945 following an air attack on his vehicle convoy. Buried at Sittard War Cemetery, the Netherlands, Grave A. 1.

McNaught, Joseph, Leading Aircraftman (1562096). No.1 RAF Beach Squadron. Killed in action on 6 June 1944. Commemorated on the Runnymede Memorial, United Kingdom, Panel 242.

Maxfield, James, Leading Aircraftman RAFVR (1305565). No.4 RAF Beach Squadron. Killed on 15 June 1944 by a mine explosion. Buried at Bayeux War Cemetery, France, Grave XV. D. 1.

Onley, Frank Thomas, Corporal RAFVR (1446612). No.483 Group Control Centre. Killed during bombing attack on dispersed site near Crépon. Buried at Crépon Churchyard, France, Grave 2.

Palin, Arnold, Aircraftman 1st Class RAFVR (2209498). Died on 11 May 1945. Buried at Choloy War Cemetery, France, Grave 2. H. 7.

Parker, James Ronald, Sergeant RAFVR (1541161). No.2817 Squadron RAF Regiment. Lost at sea on 7 June 1944. Commemorated on the Runnymede Memorial, United Kingdom, Panel 235.

Peckham, Ronald James, Leading Aircraftman RAFVR (1434174). No.216 Fighter Direction Tender. Killed on 7 July 1944 when his ship was torpedoed by a Ju 88. Commemorated on the Runnymede Memorial, United Kingdom, Panel 242.

Reah, William Thomas Hedley, Leading Aircraftman RAFVR (1047387). No.2757 Squadron RAF Regiment. Killed on 16 December 1944 during a V-2 rocket attack on Antwerp. Buried Schoonselhof Cemetery, Belgium, Grave V. D. 27.

Roberts, Eric Lloyd, Flying Officer RAFVR (127666). No.2805 Squadron RAF Regiment. Killed on 9 April 1945. Buried at Rheinberg War Cemetery, Germany, Grave 13. C. 18.

Rolt, Thomas Callaghan, Aircraftman 1st Class RAFVR (1681468). No.216 Fighter Direction Tender. Killed on 7 July 1944 when his ship was torpedoed by a Ju 88 aircraft. Commemorated on the Runnymede Memorial, United Kingdom, Panel 243.

Ross, Albert, Leading Aircraftman RAFVR (1471302). No.2809 Squadron RAF Regiment. Died on 23 October 1944 following injuries sustained in a vehicle collision at Airfield B.80, Volkel. Buried at Uden (Odiliapeel) Roman Catholic Cemetery, the Netherlands, Grave 2.

Salmon, Neville William, Sergeant RAFVR (1309425). No.2726 Squadron RAF Regiment. Lost at sea 7 June 1944. Commemorated Runnymede Memorial, United Kingdom, Panel 237.

ROLL OF HONOURS AND AWARDS

Skeet, Leading Aircraftman (1429660). No.2811 Squadron RAF Regiment. Killed on 18 November 1944 during a V-2 rocket attack on London prior to departing for the Continent. Buried Barkingside Cemetery, Ilford, United Kingdom, Grave 2867.

Skeggs, Edward John, Aircraftman 1st Class RAFVR (1460523). No.3209 RAF Servicing Commando Unit. Lost at sea on 8 June 1944. Commemorated on the Runnymede Memorial, United Kingdom, Panel 243.

Wickens, Gerald Arthur Bishop, Aircraftman 1st Class RAF (578579). No.6197 Servicing Echelon, 197 Squadron, No.146 Wing. Killed on 25 October 1944 during a V-2 rocket attack on Airfield B.70 Deurne. Buried at Schoonselhof Cemetery, Belgium, Grave III. H. 14.

Wilkins, Leonard, Leading Aircraftman RAFVR (1047377). No.2757 Squadron RAF Regiment. Killed on 16 December 1944 during a V-2 rocket attack on Antwerp. Buried at Schoonselhof Cemetery, Belgium, Grave V. A. 64.

Awards

These awards have been gleaned from several sources where it is clear that the individuals are 2nd TAF support units. There are probably many more (especially mentioned in despatches) and the author would welcome any comment via his website at www.trevorstonelogistics.co.uk. References to *The London Gazette* (*LG*) are shown by edition number or date promulgated.

Officer of the Military Division of the Order of the British Empire:

Armiger, Brian, Acting Wing Commander RAFO (31364). OC No.2 RAF Beach Squadron. *LG*, 1 January 1945, p.19.

Faulkner, Leonard Stanley Nelson M., Acting Wing Commander RAFVR (75937). OC No.1 RAF Beach Squadron. *LG*, 8 June 1944, p.2583.

Mawhood, David Vere George, Acting Wing Commander RAFO (40314). Wing Commander Operations, HQ No.24 Base Defence Sector. *LG* (supplement), 1 January 1945, No.36866, p.20.

Murphy, John Edward Terrence, Acting Wing Commander RAFO (31287). OC No.4 RAF Beach Squadron. *LG*, 1 January 1945, p.20.

Member of the Military Division of the Order of the British Empire

Lissimore, Frank Eric, Acting Squadron Leader RAFVR (115833). CO GCI Convoy No.15083. *LG* (supplement), 1 January 1945, No.36866, p.23.

Maguire, Patrick, Acting Warrant Officer RAF (965735). No.2874 Squadron RAF Regiment. For brave conduct at Volkel airfield following collateral damage to buildings and vehicles after a V1 attack. *LG* (supplement), 13 March 1945, No.36980, p.1387.

British Empire Medal

Brown, Archibald, Acting Sergeant RAFVR (100239). No.2874 Squadron RAF Regiment. For brave conduct at Volkel airfield following collateral damage to buildings and vehicles after a V-1 attack. *LG*, 13 March 1945, p.1387.

Cheeseman, Eric Franklin, Sergeant RAFVR (905334). No.24 (later No.25) Base Defence Sector. *LG*, (supplement) 1 January 1945, No.36866, p.41.
Northmore, John Leonard, Leading Aircraftman RAF (1249681). No.2831 Squadron RAF Regiment. *LG*, 18 December 1945.
Webb, Stanley George, Leading Aircraftman RAF (1612216). No.2831 Squadron RAF Regiment. *LG*, 18 December 1945.
Whyte, Josiah Weir, Corporal RAF (623786). No.2831 Squadron RAF Regiment. *LG*, 18 December 1945.

Military Cross

Best, Richard Norman, Squadron Leader RAFVR (75523). No.21 Base Defence Sector, 6 June 1944. *LG* (supplement), 14 November 1944, No.36793, p.5210.
Harding, Geoffrey Clarence, Reverend (Squadron Leader) (140848) RAFVR. No.21 Base Defence Sector, 6 June 1944. *LG* (supplement), 14 November 1944, No.36793, p.5210.
Jay, Walter Ross, Acting Flight Lieutenant RAFVR (109231). No.2804 Squadron RAF Regiment. *LG* (supplement), 4 January 1946, p.227.
Millar, John Still, Flying Officer RAF (137840). No.2781 Squadron RAF Regiment. *LG* (supplement), 5 June 1945, p.2849.
Page, Norman John, Flying Officer RAFVR (137852). No.2816 Squadron RAF Regiment. *LG* (supplement), 9 February 1945, p.818.
Rycroft, Richard Noel, Flight Lieutenant MRCS, LRCP, RAFVR (116496). No.21 Base Defence Sector, 6 June 1944. *LG* (supplement), 14 November 1944, No.36793, p.5210.
Trollope, Frederick Joseph, Squadron Leader RAFVR (68965). No.21 Base Defence Sector, 6 June 1944. *LG* (supplement), 14 November 1944, No.36793, p.5210.
Wild, John Reginald Bawater, Flying Officer RAFVR (134955). No.2781 Squadron RAF Regiment. *LG* (supplement), 9 February 1945, p.819.

Military Medal

Adair, Hugh, Leading Aircraftman RAFVR (1570785). No.2876 Squadron, RAF Regiment, 1 January 1945. *LG*, 4 January 1946, p.227.
Davies, Thomas Gwyn, Leading Aircraftman RAFVR (1087956). No.2798 Rifle Squadron, RAF Regiment. October 1944. *LG* (supplement), 27 March 1945, p.1658.
Eckersall, Reuben, Flight Sergeant, RAFVR (978501). No.21 Base Defence Sector, 6 June 1944. *LG* (supplement), 14 November 1944, No.36793, p.5210.
Fones, Cyril James, Leading Aircraftman RAFVR (1407205). No.662 (AOP) Squadron, No.83 Group. *LG* (supplement), 8 March 1946, p.1278.
Greening, Albert Ernest, Flight Sergeant RAF (519679). No.2816 Squadron, RAF Regiment. September–October 1944. *LG* (supplement), 9 February 1945, p.819.
Reid, John Young McGregor S., Leading Aircraftman RAFVR (1550961). No.21 Base Defence Sector, 6 June 1944. *LG* (supplement), 14 November 1944, No.36793, p.5211.

ROLL OF HONOURS AND AWARDS

Toye, George Daniel, Sergeant RAFVR (964295). No.2701 LAA Squadron, RAF Regiment. *LG* (supplement), 13 April 1945, p.1966.

Croix de Guerre (avec étoile en vermeil) (France)

Adair, Muir, Flight Sergeant Fulton. No.21 Base Defence Sector.
Fry, H.C., Acting Flight Sergeant. No.101 Beach Flight.
Woollacott, D., Acting Flight Lieutenant. No.104 Beach Flight.
Harpur, Geoffrey, Flight Lieutenant RCAF. GCI Convoy No.15083.
Godfrey, Kenneth, Acting Squadron Leader. RAF Regiment.

Order of the Crown with Palme (Belgium)

Park, Edward Bennet, Squadron Leader. OC No.2816 Squadron, RAF Regiment. *LG*, 11 July 1947, p.3207.

Croix de Guerre with Palme (Belgium)

Park, Edward Bennet, Squadron Leader. OC 2816 Squadron, RAF Regiment. *LG*, 11 July 1947, p.3207

Mentioned in Despatches

Alcock, J.R., Acting Flight Lieutenant RAFVR (100197). Landing Officer, No.103 Beach Flight. *LG*, 29 December 1944, No.6866, p.71.
Archbold, E.S. Acting Flight Lieutenant RAFVR (105720). Ammunition Officer, No.101 Beach Flight *LG*, 29 December 1944, No.36866, p.71.
Binns, F., Acting Flight Lieutenant RAFVR (104917). Motor Transport Officer, No.103 Beach Flight. *LG*, 29 December 1944, No.36866, p.71.
Bruce, G.L., Flight Lieutenant RAFVR. (117132). Ammunition Officer, No.108 Beach Flight. *LG*, 28 December 1945, No.37407, p.96.
Butler, P.M., Acting Flight Lieutenant RAFVR (79864). Officer in Charge, Assembly Area, No.103 Beach Flight. *LG*, 29 December 1944, No.36866, p.69.
Dobbin, J.N., Flight Lieutenant RAFVR (67773). Beach Flight Commander, No.101 Beach Flight. *LG*, 1 January 1945, p.69.
Driscoll, M., Acting Flight Lieutenant RAF (49166). No.5357 Airfield Construction Wing. *LG*, 8 June 1944, p.2621.
Fry, H.C., Acting Flight Sergeant (644472). RAF Landing Section, No.101 Beach Flight. *LG*, 29 December 1944, No.36866, p.81.
Godfrey, Kenneth, Acting Wing Commander RAFVR. RAF Regiment. *LG*, 8 June 1944, p.2617 (as Acting Squadron Leader) and 1 January 1946, p.91.
Goodrich, A.T., Reverend (Squadron Leader) RAFVR (136148). No.5357 Airfield Construction Wing. *LG*, 8 June 1944, p.2616.
Gould, A.G., Flight Sergeant RAFVR (1605203). Landing Section, No.107 Beach Flight. *LG*, 28 December 1945, No.37407, p.107.

FORWARD AIR BASES IN EUROPE FROM D-DAY TO THE BALTIC

Haines, D.L., Acting Squadron Leader RAFVR (117181). No.5357 Airfield Construction Wing. *LG*, 8 June 1944, p.2617.

Harpur, Geoffrey, Flight Lieutenant RCAF (C14356). GCI Convoy No.15083. *LG* NYHL, 1 January 1945, p.101.

Harvey, G.A., Leading Aircraftman RAFVR (1215060). Landing Section, No.107 Beach Flight. *LG*, 29 December 1944, No.36866, p.93.

Heather, F., Leading Aircraftman RAFVR (1309741). No.2817 Squadron RAF Regiment. NYHL, *LG*, 1 January 1945, p.93.

Herbert, Flying Officer RAFVR (127608). No.2800 (LAA) Squadron RAF Regiment. NYHL, *LG*, 1 January 1945, p.75.

Holgate, J., Leading Aircraftman RAFVR (148384). No.2817 Squadron RAF Regiment. NYHL, *LG*, 1 January 1945, p.93.

House, A.G., Flight Sergeant RAF (366116). RAF Landing Section, No.108 Beach Flight. *LG*, 28 December 1945, No.37407, p.107.

Hughes, T., Warrant Officer RAF (364056). RAF Motor Transport Section, No.101 Beach Flight. *LG*, 29 December 1944, No. 36866, p.77.

Inge, E.G., Sergeant RAFVR (644104). Ammunition Section, No.104 Beach Flight. *LG*, 28 December 1945, No.37407, p.111.

McBride, G., Acting Flight Lieutenant RAAF (287435). Landing Officer, No.101 Beach Flight. *LG*, 29 December 1944, No.36866, p.99.

Morris, J.E., Flight Lieutenant RAFVR (119282). Landing Officer, No.108 Beach Flight. *LG*, 28 December 1945, No.37407, p.98.

Park, Edward Bennet, Acting Squadron Leader RAFVR (85196). OC No.2816 Squadron, RAF Regiment. *LG*, 14 June 1945.

Peckham, R.J., Leading Aircraftman RAFVR (1434174). No.216 FDT.

Rae, H.G., Acting Squadron Leader RAFVR (87603). Beach Flight Commander, No.102 Beach Flight. *LG* 29 December 1944, No.36866, p.67.

Ross, C.E., Sergeant RAFVR (989130). No.2800 Squadron RAF Regiment. NYHL, *LG*, 1 January 1945, p.75.

Sandison, R.A., Acting Squadron Leader RAFVR (89074). Beach Flight Commander, No.103 Beach Flight. *LG* 29 December 1944, No.36866, p.68.

Silk, P.A., Flight Lieutenant (121715). No.2817 Squadron RAF Regiment. *LG*, NYHL 1 January 1945, p.73.

Strong, C., Leading Aircraftman RAFVR (1456206) No.2817 Squadron RAF Regiment. *LG*, NYHL 1 January 1945, p.95

Thorman, N.L., Corporal RAFVR (1007284). Provost Section, No.101 Beach Flight. *LG*, 29 December 1944, No.36866, p.91.

Towers, E., Squadron Leader RAFO (31297). Beach Flight Commander, No.104 Beach Flight. *LG*, 29 December 1944, No.36866, p.65,

Wilson, F., Flight Lieutenant RAFVR (86962). Landing Officer, No.107 Beach Flight. *LG*, 28 December 1945, No.37407, p.99.

Warren, G.C., Leading Aircraftman RAFVR (1404004). No. 3210 RAF Servicing Commando. *LG*, June 1944, No.36544, p.3029.

Wood, W.J., Sergeant RAFVR (909879). Clerk, General Duties, Headquarters. *LG*, 28 December 1945, No.37407, p.113.

Notes and References

Specific acronyms used in the notes: AHB – Air Historical Branch and AM – Air Ministry. All others as per the glossary or as introduced in the narrative.

Preface

1. Orange, Vincent, *Coningham: A Biography of Air Marshal Sir Arthur Coningham* (London: Methuen, 1990), p.237.
2. See Shores, Christopher and Thomas, Chris, *2nd Tactical Air Force*, four volumes. The appendices in Volume 3 does include four pages on the role of some of the support units. See also two earlier works: Shores, Christopher, *2nd Tactical Air Force* (Reading: Osprey Publications, 1970) and Bickers, Richard Townshend, *Air War Normandy* (Barnsley: Pen & Sword, 2015). More specialised works have been published on 2nd TAF's pre-invasion airfields and 2nd TAF's Typhoon Wings – see Jacobs, Peter, *Airfields of the D-Day Invasion Air Force: 2nd Tactical Air Force in South-East England in WWII* (Barnsley: Pen & Sword, 2009) and Thomas, Chris, *Typhoon Wings of 2nd TAF 1943–45* (Oxford: Osprey Publishing, 2010).
3. Guedalla, Phillip, *Middle East 1940–1942: A Study in Air Power* (London: Hodder & Stoughton, 1944), p.167.
4. Air Ministry (AM), 84 Group Second TAF, Royal Air Force, *From Normandy to Hanover June 1944 – June 1945* (London: Air Ministry, Undated), p.44.

Glossary

1. AM, *Royal Air Force (RAF) War Manual, Part I: Operations 1940* (London: Air Ministry, 1940), Chapter V, para. 23.
2. AM, *RAF War Manual, Part II: Organization and Administration* (London: Air Ministry, 1940), Appendix I.
3. TNA, AIR 37/128, Appendix A to AEAF/S.20677/EQ dated 16 March 1944 – Supply of POL to the RAF on the Continent.
4. AM, *RAF War Manual, Part II*, Appendix I.
5. AM, *RAF War Manual, Part II*, Appendix I.

FORWARD AIR BASES IN EUROPE FROM D-DAY TO THE BALTIC

Introduction

1. AM (AHB), The Second World War 1939–1945, Royal Air Force, *Maintenance* (London: Air Ministry, 1954), pp.293–301 and Stone, Trevor, *Sustaining Air Power: Royal Air Force Logistics since 1918* (Exeter: Fonthill Media, 2017), pp.140–147.
2. This framework is as detailed in: War Office, *The Administrative History of the Operations of 21 Army Group on the Continent of Europe 6 June 1944 – 8 May 1945* (Germany: War Office, 1945).
3. Despatch by Air Chief Marshal Sir Trafford Leigh-Mallory, Air Operations by the Allied Expeditionary Air Force in north-west Europe from 15 November to 30 September 1944, in Grehan, John and Mace, Martin (compilers), *Despatches from the Front: Liberating Europe D-Day to Victory in Europe 1944–1945* (Barnsley: Pen & Sword, 2014), p.66. This despatch hereafter referred to as Leigh-Mallory's despatch in any further notes.
4. Norman, Albert, *Operation Overlord: Design and Reality* (Harrisburg, PA: Telegraph Press, 1952), pp.156–157 and 158–161.
5. The work of the RAF beach squadrons is an interesting story and well told in Rogers, David and Rogers, Joseph, *D-Day Beach Force: The Men who Turned Chaos into Order* (Stroud: Spellmount, 2012). Additionally, there is an excellent website created and maintained by Mike Fenton whose father was a member of an RAF beach squadron during the campaign. See: https://www.rafbeachunits.info.
6. Gordon, Edward E. and Ramsay, David, *Divided on D-Day: How Conflicts and Rivalries Jeopardized the Allied Victory at Normandy* (New York: Prometheus Books, 2017), p.310.
7. Lamb, Richard, *Montgomery in Europe 1943–1945: Success or Failure?* (London: Buchan & Enright, 1983), p.216.
8. Terraine, John, *The Right of the Line: The Royal Air Force in the European War 1939–1945* (Ware: Wordsworth, 1997; repr. London: Hodder & Stoughton, 1985; repr. Barnsley: Pen & Sword, 2010), p.668.
9. Natkiel, Richard, *Atlas of World War II* (London: Bison Books, 1985), p.182.
10. Wilmot, Chester, *The Struggle for Europe* (Ware: Wordsworth Editions, 1997), pp.671–673.
11. Montgomery, Field Marshal, *The Memoirs of Field-Marshal Montgomery* (London: Fontana, 1960; repr. Barnsley: Pen & Sword, 2005), p.343.
12. Delve, Ken, *The Source Book of the RAF* (Shrewsbury: Airlife, 1994), p.108.

Chapter 1: A New Air Force

1. Hall, David I., *Strategy for Victory: The Development of British Tactical Air Power, 1919–1943* (Westport, CT: Praeger Security International, 2008), p.xi.
2. Bailey, G.J., *The Arsenal of Democracy: Aircraft Supply and the Anglo-American Alliance, 1938–1942* (Edinburgh: Edinburgh University Press, 2013), pp.28–29.
3. RAF College Library, *Monthly Air Force Lists 1933–1935* (London).

NOTES AND REFERENCES

4. AM, *The Expansion of the Royal Air Force 1934–1939* (London: Air Ministry, undated), p.132. Training Command was further split into Flying Training Command and Technical Training Command in May 1940.
5. Richards, Denis, *Royal Air Force 1939–1945: Volume I – The Fight at Odds* (London: HMSO, 1953), p.26.
6. Provisions for naval air power had been made in 1924 by a Fleet Air Arm within the RAF. This was formally transferred to the control of the Admiralty in May 1939.
7. Shores, *2nd Tactical Air Force*, p.1 and Dean, Sir Maurice, *The Royal Air Force and Two World Wars* (London: Cassell, 1979), p.73.
8. Hall, *Strategy for Victory*, p.149.
9. Delve, *The Source Book of the RAF*, p.100 and Jacobs, *Airfields of the D-Day Invasion Air Force*, pp.4–6.
10. Bickers, *Air War Normandy*, p.xi.
11. Leigh-Mallory had been appointed Air C-in-C in November 1943 (COSSAC Directive (43) 81 dated 16 November 1943), with the specific directive from Eisenhower that he should exercise operational command of the British and American tactical air forces supporting the assault of Western Europe from the United Kingdom. To provide a national 'balance' in the command structure, a United States general was appointed as Leigh-Mallory's deputy.
12. As with most of the senior Allied appointments, Conningham's role as AOC Allied Expeditionary Air Force, whilst still commanding 2nd TAF within it, became embroiled in argument, especially from some of the American air commanders. For a fuller narrative on these issues see Orange, *Coningham*, pp.187–193.
13. TNA, AIR 37/106, Allied Expeditionary Air Force: 2nd TAF: Formation and Organisation. Formation of Tactical Air Force dated 2 August 1943.
14. Browne, John, *Airfield Construction by the Royal Air Force 1939 to 1966* in RAF Historical Society Journal No.51, 2011, pp.14–15 and Higham, Robin, *The Bases of Air Strategy* (Shrewsbury: Airlife Publishing, 1998), p.185. See also Jacobs, *Airfields of the D-Day Invasion Air Force*.
15. Shores and Thomas, *2nd Tactical Air Force*, Volume Three, p.545 and Sturtivant Ray, Hamlin, John and Halley, James J., *Royal Air Force Flying Training and Support Units* (Tunbridge Wells: Air Britain, 1997), pp.187–188.
16. Shores, *2nd Tactical Air Force*, p.4.
17. Jacobs, *Airfields of the D-Day Invasion Air Force*, pp.9–11.
18. Orange, *Coningham*, p.181.
19. AM, *From Normandy to Hannover*, p.8.

Chapter 2: Planning for D-Day

1. TNA, AIR 9/159, Staff Study: Operations on the Continent in the Final Phase, p.8.
2. Morgan, Lieutenant General Sir F.E., *Overture to Overlord* (London: Hodder & Stoughton, 1950), pp.9–10, 39–40 and 41–42.
3. Leigh-Mallory's despatch, p.39.

4. Carlo D'Este, *Decision in Normandy: The Unwritten Story of Montgomery and the Allied Campaign* (New York: E.P. Dutton, 1983; repr. 2001), pp.37–38.
5. TNA, AIR 37/146, Allied Expeditionary Air Force: 2nd TAF: Operation Overlord Directive. Agreed Procedure for Joint Planning for Overlord dated 6 December 1943.
6. Ellis, Major L.F., *History of the Second World War Victory in the West: Volume I – The Battle of Normandy* (United Kingdom Military series) (London: HMSO, 1962), p.66 and War Office, *Operations of 21 Army Group*, p.9. The British and Canadian beaches were further sub-divided into smaller sectors: for GOLD Beach (west to east) these were ITEM, JIG and KING; for JUNO Beach (west to east) these were LOVE, MIKE, NAN and OBOE and in the case of SWORD Beach (west to east) PETER, QUEEN and ROGER. A further sub-division was made in each of these beaches where the eastern half of the beach was named GREEN and the western half RED – in line with the nautical and aircraft lighting convention of red for port and green for starboard. Thus, the eastern edge of KING Beach was known as KING GREEN.
7. Leigh-Mallory's despatch, p.40. This list of tasks emerged from extensive discussions with the Supreme Allied Commander and the respective commanders-in-chief as to the requirements of the army and the navy from the air forces.
8. TNA, AIR 20/10223, Unofficial Account of No.34 (Reconnaissance) Wing, p.13.
9. TNA, AIR 20/10223, Unofficial Account of No.34 (Reconnaissance) Wing, p.10.
10. Leigh Mallory's despatch, Part IV, para. 423.
11. Delve, *The Source Book of the RAF*, p.126.
12. TNA, AIR 37/106, Allied Expeditionary Air Force: 2nd TAF: formation and Organisation. Re-organisation of No.2 Group for Mobile Warfare dated 23 September 1943.
13. TNA, AIR 37/106, Allied Expeditionary Air Force: 2nd TAF: formation and Organisation. Re-organisation of No.2 Group for Mobile Warfare dated 23 September 1943.
14. TNA, AIR 16/1062, Operation Overlord: Administrative Plan: AEAF and RAF. Royal Air Force Administrative Plan, Appendix F.
15. TNA, AIR 37/128, Allied Expeditionary Air Force: Administrative Instructions. Supply of POL to the RAF on the Continent dated 16 March 1944.
16. TNA, AIR 37/594, Allied Expeditionary Air Force: Supply of POL to RAF in the Field: Policy. Notes on Aviation Fuel Storage and Distribution (undated).
17. TNA, AIR 37/128, Allied Expeditionary Air Force: Administrative Instructions. Supply of Explosives to the RAF on the Continent dated 16 March 1944.
18. TNA, AIR 16/1062, Operation Overlord: Administrative Plan: AEAF and RAF. Royal Air Force Administrative Plan dated 19 February 1944.

Chapter 3: The Support Plan

1. In the early days of the Normandy assault, the RAF units involved in this work came under the command of AOC 2nd TAF until the No.85 Group units came ashore to establish the more permanent base organisation.

NOTES AND REFERENCES

2. For a fuller account of the tri-service work involved in Beach Maintenance see Rogers and Rogers, D-Day Beach Force.
3. D-Day Revisited website, Mulberry harbour at https://d-dayrevisited.co.uk/d-day-history/d-day-landings/mulberry-harbour.
4. For a fuller account of the Mulberry harbours see Hartcup, Guy, *Code Name Mulberry: The Planning, Building and Operation of the Normandy Harbours* (Barnsley: Pen & Sword, 1977).
5. TNA, AIR 9/159, Operations on the Continent. Joint Planning Staff to War Cabinet dated 24 December 1941.
6. Shores, *2nd Tactical Air Force*, p.2.
7. TNA, AIR 37/129, Allied Expeditionary Air Force: Administrative Instructions. Transfer of Damaged Aircraft and Equipment from the Continent to the United Kingdom by LCT Shuttle Service dated 2 June 1944.
8. Whilst the Base Aviation Fuel and Ammunition Park was under the administrative control of No.85 Group, it was under the functional control of the Senior Equipment Staff Officer at HQ 2nd TAF.
9. Stone, *Sustaining Air Power*, pp.149–151 and AM, *Maintenance*, p.335. The Supply and Transport Columns were also able to help with the movement of non-mobile units.
10. AM, *Maintenance*, p.334.
11. Stone, *Sustaining Air Power*, pp.309–313.
12. Butler, P., *Air Arsenal North America: Aircraft for the Allies 1938–1945, Purchases and Lend-Lease* (Hinckley: Midland Publishing, 2004), pp.191–193, and Thetford, Owen, *Aircraft of the Royal Air Force Since 1918* (ninth edition) (London: Putnam, 1995), p.151.
13. AM, The Second World War 1939–1945, *Airborne Forces* (London: Air Ministry, 1951; repr. 2017), pp.103–109.
14. TNA, AIR 37/1228, SHAEF (main and rear): Operation CATOR: Airlift for Overlord. SHAEF Administrative Memorandum No.18 dated 30 May 1944.
15. Leigh-Mallory's despatch, p.83 and TNA, AIR 37/13, No.46 Group (Transport Support): Organisation and Operations during Invasion of Europe. An Account of the Organisation, Training and Operations (and lessons learned) of No.46 (Transport Support) Group, Royal Air Force during the Invasion of Hitler's Europe, pp 3–5.
16. AM (AHB), RAF Narrative (First Draft), *The Liberation of Northwest Europe: Volume II – The Administrative Preparations* (London: Air Ministry, Undated), pp.190–191.
17. TNA, AIR 37/13, No.46 Group (Transport Support): Organisation and Operations during Invasion of Europe. No.46 Group. Organisation and Operations during Invasion of Europe and Lessons Learned.
18. TNA, AIR 37/284, No.38 Group (No.38 Wing): Operation *Overlord*: Re-supply. Organisation and Function of CATOR dated 2 June 1944.
19. Each of the Royal Engineers airfield construction groups consisted of two road construction companies and two pioneer companies. They had a wide range of plant including motor graders, scrapers, crawler tractors, rollers, tipper trucks and transporters.

20. AM, *Works* (London: HMSO, 1956), p.465. The army formations with which the RAF wings and squadrons worked were No.16 Airfield Construction Group and No.25 Airfield Construction Group (Nos. 64 and 681 road construction companies, and Nos. 214 and 217 pioneer companies).
21. Higham, *Bases of Air Strategy*, p.187.
22. Kellett, Pete and Davies, Jeff, *A History of the RAF Servicing Commandos* (Shrewsbury: Airlife, 1989) pp.1–2, 8–26, 27–52, 53–74 and 75–80.
23. TNA, AIR 37/161, Chief of Staff, Supreme Allied Command: Servicing Commandos for Continental Operations. Agenda for a meeting to discuss Servicing Commandos in the Tactical Air Force dated 29 September 1943 and TNA, AIR 37/791, 2nd Tactical Air Force: Organisation and Administration. HQ No.83 Group to HQ 2nd TAF dated 15 February 1944.
24. AM, *Maintenance*, p.345.
25. Annon, Fighter Direction Tenders – FDTs Nos. 13, 216 and 217 at https://www.combinedops.com/FDTs.htm [accessed 28 June 2021].
26. TNA, AIR 37/756, Air Commander-in Chief, AEAF, Air Chief Marshal Leigh-Mallory: Operation '*Overlord*': No.85 Group Air Staff Plan dated 13 July 1944. For the duration of the arrangement, the RAF units in the American sector came under the operational command of the US IX Air Defence Command.
27. No.21 Base Defence Sector at OMAHA Beach, 6 June 1944 available at https://rafoverlord.blogspot.com.
28. Throughout the various primary and secondary sources these convoys are often just referred to as mobile radar units.
29. Base Defence Sector at OMAHA Beach, 6 June 1944 on Project *Overlord* – The RAF and the Campaign to Liberate Northwest Europe, 1944–45. Available from: https://rafoverlord.blogspot.com/2019/03/21-base-defence-sector-at-omaha-beach-6.html21.
30. The history of the RAF Regiment in the Second World War is covered in the excellent work by Oliver, Kingsley, *The RAF Regiment at War 1942–1946* (Barnsley: Pen & Sword, 2016).
31. Oliver, *RAF Regiment at War*, pp.104–105.
32. Although a Lincolnshire focused website, the site for RAF Elsham Wolds (https://www.northlincsweb.net/RAFElshamWolds/html/q_sites.html) provides a concise and useful summary of this background.
33. TNA, AIR 37/675, 2nd Tactical Air Force: Concealment and Decoy Organisation. Various documents.
34. TNA, AIR 26/512, Operations Record Book (with appendices). No.5357 Airfield Construction Wing, RAF. Entry for April 1944.

Chapter 4: A Foothold on the Continent

1. AM, *Maintenance*, pp.326–327.
2. Heritage Calling (Historic England Blog) available at: https://heritagecalling.com/2019/06/04/how-the-allied-forces-prepared-for-d-day/.

NOTES AND REFERENCES

3. AM, *Maintenance*, p.329.
4. A good overview of Southwick House (with related web links) and its role in *Overlord* can be viewed at: https://www.portsmouth-guide.co.uk/local/southwick.htm [accessed 25 May 2021]. The now famous wall map had been manufactured in the Midlands by the well-known toy manufacturer Chad Valley. The United Kingdom's Imperial War Museum has an excellent watercolour by the war artist Barnett Freedman in its collection, showing the map room in use during June 1944 and can be previewed at: https://www.iwm.org.uk/collections/item/object/10043.
5. Leigh-Mallory's despatch, pp.41–54.
6. Both accounts from AM, *From Normandy to Hanover*, pp.10–11. Leigh-Mallory's despatch, para 108(a), however, is at odds with these accounts and records that the target was attacked on 5 June by Typhoons on Nos 174, 175 and 245 squadrons. It is not clear if this was a corrected version or if the 5 June attack was a supplementary mission to fully neutralize the target.
7. Leigh Mallory's despatch, para. 107.
8. Leigh Mallory's despatch, para. 419.
9. TNA, AIR 29/110, RAF Regiment Squadrons. Operations Record Book: No.2834 (Anti-Aircraft) Squadron RAF Regiment.
10. Karl Work's diary extracts and other material on the FDTs, reproduced with permission from Geoff Slee (www.combinedops.com). FDT No.217 acted as the master control vessel and was authorised to call in fighter reinforcements when required. FDT No.216 was nominated to take on this role if 217 was lost or disabled. Karl's ship returned to Cowes, Isle of Wight on 23 June for a five-month period of leave and work, having had his first shower in three weeks.
11. TNA, AIR 29/152, Operations Record Book for No.15053 GCI/FDP (No.83 GCC), entry dated 6 June 1944.
12. Cited in Forty, George, Marriott, Leo and Forty, Simon, *Hitler's Atlantic Wall: From Southern France to Northern Norway, Yesterday and Today* (Oxford: Casemate, 2016), p.47.
13. WW2 Encyclopaedia – Belgian Gate at: https://www.skylighters.org/encyclopedia/belgiangate.html [accessed 9 June 2021]. For an excellent overview of the various types of obstacles see Juno Beach Centre website at https://www.junobeach.org/beach-obstacles/.
14. Full text reproduced in Bickers, *Air War Normandy*, p.xii.
15. TNA, AIR 26/40, Operations Record Book, No.21 Base Defence Sector, report on the Landing of the First Echelon of No.21 (BD) Sector on 'D' Day 6 June 1944, p.2.
16. TNA, AIR 26/40, Operations Record Book, No.21 Base Defence Sector Operations Record Book.
17. AM, *Maintenance*, p.343.
18. It is difficult to identify all the specific 2nd TAF losses from the Commonwealth War Graves records, but those that are known have been listed in Appendix Nine.
19. Source: https://rafbeachunits.info/stories/ted-inge/. Reproduced with permission.

FORWARD AIR BASES IN EUROPE FROM D-DAY TO THE BALTIC

20. Hutchinson M.G., Night Fighter Control for (D-Day) Operation *Overlord* available at https://mraths.org.uk.
21. TNA, AIR 27/2324, Squadron No.976, Summary of Events.
22. On OMAHA Beach, 2,000 troops were killed, wounded, or went missing. Across both SWORD and GOLD beaches, approximately 2,000 British troops were killed, wounded, or went missing. On JUNO Beach, 340 Canadian soldiers were killed and another 574 wounded.
23. Promulgated in *The London Gazette* (supplement),14 November 1944, No.36793, pp.5210–5211. Available at https://www.thegazette.co.uk.
24. Account of Leslie Dobinson on Men of D-Day website available at: www.6juin1944.com

Chapter 5: Developing the Bridgehead

1. TNA, AIR 29/110/3, 2834 (Anti-Aircraft) Squadron RAF Regiment, Operations Record Book: No.2834 (Anti-Aircraft) Squadron RAF Regiment.
2. Smith's squadron formed part of the highly important attack on the headquarters of the German Panzer Group West accommodated in the Chateau de le Caine, south-west of Caen. For a detailed account of this operation and its wider significance see The Dinner Raid in Shores and Thomas, *2nd Tactical Air Force*, Volume 1, pp.148–149.
3. The AOC returned to the airfield by air on 23 July 1944, this time in his trademark captured German Fiesler Storch but in the company of Prime Minister Winston Churchill who paid a morale boosting visit, giving a speech at the airfield, and then visiting troops in the area by jeep.
4. Kellett and Davies, *RAF Servicing Commandos*, pp.143–145. On p.92, the authors relate that some personnel of No.3209 SCU served at Airfields B.3 and B.4 (from a veteran's account) but the war diary for this unit cannot be traced in The National Archives, Kew.
5. Hadaway, Stuart, 'Flying from France – Airfield Construction and the RAF Regiment in Normandy', *Royal Air Force Salute - D-Day 70th Anniversary*, 2014, p.52.
6. Ramsey, Winston, (ed.), *Invasion Airfields: Then and Now* (Old Harlow: After the Battle, 2017 – now incorporated by Pen & Sword, Barnsley), p.32.
7. AM, *Maintenance*, p.343.
8. AM, *Maintenance*, pp.63–67 and 333–334.
9. Higham, *Bases of Air Strategy*, p.186.
10. Source: https://www.thememoryproject.com/stories/1326:frank-leblanc/.
11. TNA, AIR 29/1118, Mobile Wings, RAF Regiment, No.1301 Mobile Wing diary.
12. TNA, AIR 37/675, 2nd Tactical Air Force: Concealment and Decoy Organisation. The personnel used for the taskings described were drawn from Nos. 1 and 2 C&D Units, with the army personnel provided by No.556 Field Company Royal Engineers.

NOTES AND REFERENCES

13. Pennington, Hugh, 'The impact of infectious disease in war time: a look back at WW1', *Future Microbiology*, 14 (3) (2019), pp.165–168.
14. Rexford-Welch, S.C., History of the Second World War (United Kingdom Medical Series), *The Royal Air Force Medical Services: Volume III Campaigns* (London: HMSO, 1958), pp.490–491 and 506–507.
15. Rexford-Welch, *The Royal Air Force Medical Services: Volume III Campaigns*, pp.514–515.
16. The 'Queen Mary' trailer is a British semi-trailer combination designed for the carriage and recovery of aircraft. Made by Tasker Trailers of Andover, it could be pulled by either Bedford or Crossley Motors tractors. The trailer could carry five tons, had a very low floor and ground clearance with wheels which were outboard of the load area. The side rails allowed aircraft wings to be carried upright on their leading edges. It is believed that its name relates to its length and rather prosaic comparison to the ocean liner RMS *Queen Mary*.
17. TNA, AIR 37/13, No.46 Group (Transport Support): Organisation and Operations during Invasion of Europe. An Account of the Organisation, Training and Operations (and lessons learned) of No.46 (Transport Support) Group, Royal Air Force during the Invasion of Hitler's Europe, p.62 (outbound and inbound tables).
18. TNA, AIR, 37/594, Supply of POL. SHAEF G-4 Division to SESO, HQ AEAF, 13 July 1944.
19. TNA, AIR 37/594, Allied Expeditionary Air Force: Supply of POL to RAF in the Field: Policy. SHAEF AEAF Staff to SESO, HQ AEAF dated 20 July 1944.
20. AM, *Maintenance*, p.344.
21. For a fuller account of the development of the Embarkation Units see Stone, *Sustaining Air Power*, pp.303–305.
22. Of note are: Edgerton, David, *Britain's War Machine: Weapons, Resources and Experts in the Second World War* (London: Allen Lane, 2011; repr. 2012), p.116 and van Creveld, Martin, *Supplying War: Logistics from Wallenstein to Patton*, second edition (New York: Cambridge University Press, 2004), pp.208–211. Hartcup, Guy raises the point in his *Code Name Mulberry*, pp.140–141, but presents a more balanced argument.
23. Monckton, Sir Walter, Report for the Chiefs of Staff Committee, *The Part Played in 'Overlord' by the Synthetic Harbours* (London: Chiefs of Staff Committee, 1946).
24. Map redrawn from the original in: War Office, *Operations of 21 Army Group*, Appendix F.
25. AIR 29/762, No.50 MFH Operations Record Book, entry for 31 July 1944.
26. No.53 arrived between 17 and 18 August 1944 as part of No.84 Group, becoming RAF Hospital Hamburg in September 1945; No.54 arrived between 21 and 23 August 1944 as part of No.84 Group, becoming RAF Hospital Celle in September 1945 and No.55 arrived between 23 and 28 August 1944 as part of No.2 Group, becoming RAF Hospital Gütersloh in September 1945.
27. TNA, AIR 29/762, No.50 MFH Operations Record Book, entry dated 17 June 1944.

28. Rexford-Welch, *The Royal Air Force Medical Services, Vol III*, pp.502–506. There is a paucity of detail on the formation and operation of the CAEUs and it is possible there was a No.4 and possibly a No.5 CAEU operating in France prior to the formation of No.1, but this cannot be verified at the time of writing.
29. TNA, AIR 29/828, Airfield Construction Squadrons.
30. TNA, AIR 29/828, Airfield Construction Squadrons.
31. Browne, *Airfield Construction*, p.16.
32. Shores and Thomas, *2nd Tactical Air Force, Volume Three*, p.547. R/T denotes communication by speech, whilst W/T is communication by signal such as by Morse code.
33. Shores and Thomas, *2nd Tactical Air Force, Volume Three*, p.548,
34. Warwick, Nigel, from original article in *Centurion Journal*, 2013, reproduced in Royal Air Force Salute 2014, p.52. The rifle squadrons were made up of a squadron headquarters, three rifle flights and a 3-inch mortar flight with four weapons. The armoured car squadrons were equipped with the Humber Light Reconnaissance Cars Mk IIIA.
35. TNA, AIR 29/762, No.50 MFH Operations Record Book, entry for 20 July 1944.
36. TNA, AIR 29/762, No.50 MFH Operations Record Book, entry for 31 July 1944.
37. TNA, AIR 29/762, No.50 MFH Operations Record Book, entry for 31 July 1944.

Chapter 6: Crossing the Start Line – Breakout from Normandy

1. TNA, AIR 20/1593, Operations of 2nd TAF, 6 June 1944 – 9 May 1945, report by Air Marshal Sir Arthur Coningham, p.40. This report hereafter referred to as Coningham's report in any further notes.
2. TNA, AIR 29/828, Airfield Construction Squadrons. No.5022 Airfield Construction Squadron and No.5023 Airfield Construction Squadron. IIM/FV789/1. and AM, *Works*, p.466.
3. TNA, AIR 29/102/1, No.2806 (Armoured) Squadron RAF Regiment, entry for 31 July 1944.
4. Because of the critical need to protect the forward airfields of the 2nd TAF composite groups, much of the Air Technical Intelligence team escort work was conducted by regiment squadrons from Nos. 2 and 85 groups.
5. TNA, AIR 29/102/1, 2806 (Armoured) Squadron RAF Regiment, entry for 7 August and 4 September 1944.
6. HQ Advanced AEAF moved to the Continent on 9 August 1944 and located alongside HQ United States Ninth Air Force, located next to the Twelfth United States Army Group. It remained in the field during the advance from the Cotentin Peninsula to Versailles, near Paris. Main HQ AEAF did not move to the Continent until 8 September 1944, initially to Julouville alongside Eisenhower's headquarters and the also to Versailles on 19 September 1944. Both headquarters (main and advanced) AEAF merged into a single formation on 23 September. HQ 2nd TAF relocated to Amiens on 5 September 1944.

NOTES AND REFERENCES

7. Tucker-Jones, Anthony, *Falaise: The Flawed Victory* (Barnsley: Pen & Sword, 2018), p.174.
8. Coningham's report, p.12.
9. Coningham's report, p.20.
10. Coningham's report, p.21. There were no hard and fast geographical boundaries for airfield locations and the numerical approximation of eighteen sites is taken from an approximation using Map 13, Northern France, 1944–1945 in 'Jeff' Jefford, *RAF Squadrons*, Shrewsbury: Airlife, 1988), pp.212–213.
11. TNA, AIR 29/100, 2798 Squadron, RAF Regiment Operations Record Book entry for 29/30 July 1944.
12. TNA, AIR 29/543/6, 5 Mobile Field Photographic Section Operations Record Book, entry for 31 August 1944.
13. TNA, AIR 29/1118, Mobile Wings, RAF Regiment, No.1300 Mobile Wing diary.
14. TNA, AIR 29/152, Operations Record Book for 15053 GCI/FDP (No.83 GCC) Operations Record Book, entry for 23 to 29 August 1944.
15. Coningham's report, p.22.
16. TNA, AIR 20/10223, Unofficial Account of 34 (Reconnaissance) Wing, p.33.
17. Coningham's report, pp.22–23. The risk of enemy interception of radio communications was judged to be minimal as the speed of advance made it unlikely that the enemy would intercept these circuits and a reduction in the standard of signals security was therefore acceptable.
18. TNA, AIR 29/105/1, 2819 (Anti-Aircraft) Squadron RAF Regiment Operations Record Book, entry for 6 September 1944.
19. TNA, AIR 29/787, Air Stores Parks. Entry for No.404 ASP dated 15 September 1944.
20. TNA, AIR 29/787, Air Stores Parks. Entries for No.404 ASP from 15 to 19 September 1944.
21. TNA, AIR 29/816, Supply and Transport Columns. Operations Record Book for 309 Supply and Transport Column from August 1944 to May 1945.
22. Jefford, *RAF Squadrons*, pp.23–105 and Appendix 11, Maps 13 and 14.
23. TNA, AIR 29/787, Air Stores Parks. Entry for No.404 ASP dated 30 September 1944.
24. TNA, AIR 29/822, Care and Maintenance Parties. Operations Record Book for No.422 AFAP from 2 September 1944 to 30 September 1944.
25. Rexford-Welch, *The Royal Air Force Medical Services, Volume III Campaigns*, p.462.
26. Veeder, Major Timothy A., '*An Evaluation of the Aerial Interdiction Campaign Known as the "Transportation Plan" for the D-Day Invasion, Early January 1944 to Late June 1944*'. Research paper presented to the Research Department Air Command and Staff College (unpublished research paper 1997), p.27.
27. War Office, *Operations of 21 Army Group*, pp.40–41.
28. TNA, AIR 29/920, Base Personnel Centre Operations Record Book, entry for 31 August 1944.
29. TNA, AIR 29/920, Base Personnel Centre Operations Record Book, summary entries for October to December 1944.

30. TNA, AIR 20/10223, Unofficial Account of 34 (Reconnaissance) Wing, pp.22 and 26.
31. Detail from the recollections of Basil Jackson who was a photographer with No.140 Squadron and published online at: https://www.shawbits.co.uk/index.html [accessed 20 May 2021]. An article in the *Commercial Motor* magazine dated 1 December 1944 suggests that other vehicle types were employed by these units including Bedford-Taskers and Thorneycroft Tenders.
32. TNA, AIR 29/543/5, No.4 Mobile Field Photographic Section Operations Record Book, entries from August to December 1944.
33. TNA, AIR 29/543/6, No.5 Mobile Field Photographic Section Operations Record Book, entry for July 1944.
34. TNA, AIR 29/543/6, No.5 Mobile Field Photographic Section Operations Record Book, entry for July 1944.
35. TNA, AIR 29/828. Airfield Construction Squadrons. No.5022 Airfield Construction Squadron. IIM/FV789/1. No.5023 Airfield Construction also contributed to the work at B.19 taking care of outstanding tasks after No.5022 Squadron had moved on.
36. Ramsey, *Invasion Airfields*, p.154. See also AM, *Works*, pp.465–466.
37. TNA, AIR 29/828, Airfield Construction Squadrons. No.5022 Airfield Construction Squadron. IIM/FV789/1.
38. John Buckley, *Monty's Men – The British Army and the Liberation of Europe* (London: Yale University Press, 2014), p.203.
39. TNA, AIR 25/649, Operations Record Book, entry for No.46 (Transport) Group dated August 1944.
40. AM, *Maintenance*, p.348.
41. AM, *Maintenance*, pp.350–351 and TNA, AIR 37/594, Allied Expeditionary Air Force: Supply of POL to RAF in the Field: Policy, Supply of POL dated 16 September 1944.
42. Ryan, Cornelius, *A Bridge Too Far* (London: Hamish Hamilton, 1974), Foreword.
43. Ritchie, Sebastian, *Arnhem - Myth and Reality* (London: Robert Hale Ltd, 2011), p.194. Ritchie provides valuable and enlightening scholarship on the 'air' perspective and tackles many of the myths which have endured and perpetuated by other authors. Not least of these are the facts surrounding the availability of air transport aircraft and how this affected the numbers of Allied airlift used over the three days of the airlift itself. See his chapter 3.3.
44. Coningham's report, p.23. The lessons learned regarding the value of air transport and the need for them to be under the operational control of a tactical air force did feature in the Air Ministry report on the air and administrative organisation of 2nd TAF (see AM, *Report on the Air and Administrative Organization of the 2nd Tactical Air Force 1947* (London: Air Ministry, 1947; repr. 2017), pp.91–92. The rights and wrongs of what happened in 1944 seem to have become a popular topic of debate amongst various authors and historians.
45. TNA, AIR 14/857, Use of Bomber Aircraft for Carrying Supplies, 24 September 1944 and subsequent note entitled Petrol Supplies Flown to 21st Army Group by No.4 Group (Pocklington Base).

NOTES AND REFERENCES

46. TNA, AIR 20/1593, Operations of 2nd TAF, 6 June 1944 – 9 May 1945, report by Air Marshal Sir Arthur Coningham.
47. Data from: TNA, AIR 37/1096, SHAEF (main and rear): No.46 Group Weekly Airlift Returns, Summaries of No.46 Group Weekly Lift Returns (United Kingdom – the Continent) for weeks ending 17 September to 19 November 1944.
48. Coningham's report, pp.90–92.
49. TNA, AIR 29/122/3, No.2874 Squadron RAF Regiment Operations Record Book, entry for 14 September 1944.
50. TNA, AIR 37/247, Chief of Staff, Supreme Allied Command: Captured or Liberated Ports Under British Control: Port Organisation, Minutes of the 1st Port Organization Committee meeting dated 27 September 1943.
51. Higham, J.B. and Knighton, E.A. (eds.), *The Second World War 1939–1945 Army, Movements* (London: War Office, 1955), p. 374.
52. TNA, AIR 29/18, Embarkation Units, Operations Record Book for No.93 Embarkation Unit from September to November 1944.
53. Higham and Knighton (eds.), *The Second World War 1939–1945 Army, Movements*, pp.375–376.
54. Data collated from: RAF Logistics Heritage Centre Archive, Miscellaneous Map Collection – The Development of the Administrative Plan, Map 28 and War Office, Paper on Operational Aspects of Mulberry 'B', p.5, Annexure I and Annex V. The problems encountered by the Americans with the capture and use of the Brittany ports is discussed in Harding, Ganz, A., 'Questionable Objective: The Brittany Ports 1944', *The Journal of Military History*, 59(1) (January 1995), pp.77–95.
55. The reasons for the Great Mistake and its consequences are described in detail in Beale, Peter, *The Great Mistake: The Battle for Antwerp and the Beveland Peninsula, September 1944* (Stroud: Sutton Publishing, 2004), p.1.
56. Love, Robert W. and Major, John (eds.), *The Year of D-Day: The 1944 Diary of Admiral Sir Bertram Ramsay* (Hull: University of Hull Press, 1994), p.152.
57. Montgomery, Field Marshal, *Normandy to the Baltic* (London: Hutchinson & Co Ltd, 1947; repr. October 1948), p.151.
58. Love and Major, *The Year of D-Day*, pp.151–152. The corridor which Ramsay refers to, was the salient running north-east from the Dutch border with Belgium to the Rhine, gained following the Arnhem operation.
59. Coningham's report, p.26
60. Coningham's report, p.26.
61. TNA, AIR 29/122/3, No.2874 Squadron RAF Regiment Operations Record Book, monthly summary entry for September 1944.
62. Leigh-Mallory's despatch, para. 415.
63. Data from Leigh-Mallory's despatch, para. 415.

Chapter 7: Logistics at Breaking Point – The Autumn Crisis

1. See also: https://www.historyofwar.org/articles/operation_switchback_breskens.html.

FORWARD AIR BASES IN EUROPE FROM D-DAY TO THE BALTIC

2. TNA, AIR 29/122/3, No.2874 Squadron RAF Regiment Operations Record Book, entry for 14 October 1944 and summary entry for that month. Maguire and Browne were awarded the MBE and BEM respectively (see entries for these men in Appendix 9).
3. Promulgated in *The London Gazette* (supplement), 9 February 1945, p.819. Available at https://www.thegazette.co.uk.
4. AM, *Normandy to Hanover*, p.28.
5. TNA, AIR 38/121, AEAF: Air Transport Overseas Organisation Operations, Coningham to Main Headquarters AEAF dated 27 September 1944.
6. Moulton, Major General J.L., *Battle for Antwerp: The Liberation of the City and the Opening of the Scheldt 1944* (London: Ian Allan, 1978), p.186 and Coningham's report, pp.34–35.
7. Promulgated in *The London Gazette* (supplement), 9 February 1945, p.819. Available at https://www.thegazette.co.uk.
8. Promulgated in *The London Gazette* (supplement), 9 February 1945, p.819. Available at https://www.thegazette.co.uk.
9. Promulgated in *The London Gazette* (supplement), 27 March 1945, p.1658. Available at https://www.thegazette.co.uk.
10. Saunders, Hilary St George, *Royal Air Force 1939–1945: Volume III – The Fight is Won* (London: HMSO, 1954), p.203.
11. Ellis, Major L.F., *History of the Second World War Victory in the West: Volume II – The Defeat of Germany* (United Kingdom Military series) p.138.
12. Coningham's report, p.35 and AM, *Maintenance*, p.349.
13. TNA, AIR 29/18, Embarkation Units, Operations Record Book for No.93 Embarkation Unit, November 1944.
14. War Office, The Administrative History of the Operations of 21 Army Group, p.71.
15. Detail from The Belgians Remember Them website 'RAF unaccounted Personnel fallen in Belgium between September 1944 and May 1945 – The wreck of the HM LST-420 on 7/11/1944'. Available at: https://www.belgians-remember-them.eu.
16. TNA, AIR 29/920, Base Personnel Centre Operations Record Book, entries for 8 to 11 November 1944.
17. Jefford, *RAF Squadrons*, pp.23–105 and Appendix 11, Map 14.
18. Coningham's report. p.37.
19. AVM John Browne, Airfield Construction by the Royal Air Force 1939 to 1966 in RAF Historical Society Journal No.51, 2011, p.16.
20. AM, *Works*, p.467.
21. TNA, AIR 26/513, Operations Record Books, Wings. Nos. 5352, 5354, 5357 and 5358 (airfield construction) wings. B.78 Eindhoven, Technical Report on Construction Work, 19 September 1944 – 15 March 1945.
22. Coningham's report, p.38.
23. Map redrawn from the original in Ellis, Major L.F., *History of the Second World War Victory in the West: Volume II – The Defeat of Germany* (United Kingdom Military series) (London: HMSO, 1968), p.140.

24. Coningham's report, p.70.
25. Coningham's report, p.38.
26. Coningham's report, p.98.
27. TNA, AIR 20/1593, Operations of 2nd TAF, 6 June 1944 – 9 May 1945, report by Air Marshal Sir Arthur Coningham.
28. AM, *Maintenance*, p.349 and TNA, AIR 20/1593, Operations of 2nd TAF, 6 June 1944 – 9 May 1945, report by Air Marshal Sir Arthur Coningham.
29. TNA, AIR 20/1593, Operations of 2nd TAF, 6 June 1944 – 9 May 1945, report by Air Marshal Sir Arthur Coningham.
30. TNA, AIR 29/110/3, 2834 (Anti-Aircraft) Squadron RAF Regiment, Operations Record Book: No.2834 (Anti-Aircraft) Squadron RAF Regiment.
31. The RAF Regiment's role in the campaign was extensive and saw them being employed in a much wider sense as 1944 ended and well into 1945. For a more detailed account see Oliver, *The RAF Regiment at War*, pp.104–127.
32. Operation *Bodenplatte* 1 January 1945 on the RAF Memorial Flight Club website https://www.memorialflightclub.com/blog/operation-bodenplatte-1st-january-1945.
33. Greater detail of the RAF Regiment involvement in this attack can be found in Oliver, *The RAF Regiment at War*, pp.113–116.
34. TNA, AIR 29/122/3, No.2874 Squadron RAF Regiment Operations Record Book, entry for 1 January 1945.
35. TNA, AIR 29/110/3, No.2834 (Anti-Aircraft) Squadron RAF Regiment, Operations Record Book: No.2834 (Anti-Aircraft) Squadron RAF Regiment, entry for 1 January 1945.
36. TNA, AIR 29/1118, Mobile Wings, RAF Regiment, No.1302 Mobile Wing diary. The airman of No.2817 Squadron who was killed was 21-year-old LAC William Crooks.
37. TNA, AIR 29/110/3, No.2834 (Anti-Aircraft) Squadron RAF Regiment, Operations Record Book: No.834 (Anti-Aircraft) Squadron RAF Regiment.
38. TNA, AIR 29/828. Airfield Construction Squadrons', No.5022 Airfield Construction Squadron. IIM/FV789/1.

Chapter 8: Over the Rhine and into the Reich

1. Coningham's report, p.44.
2. Wilmot, *The Struggle for Europe*, pp.671–673.
3. AM, *Maintenance*, pp.349–350.
4. AM, *Normandy to Hanover*, p.32.
5. TNA, AIR 29/816, No.309 S&TC, entry for 8 February 1945.
6. Saunders, *The Fight is Won*, p.281.
7. Bowman, Martin W., *Air War Varsity* (Barnsley: Pen & Sword, 2017), pp.246–250. See also Lloyd Clark, *Crossing the Rhine* (New York: Grove Press, 2008).
8. Saunders, *The Fight is Won*, p.287.

9. TNA, AIR 29/110/3, 2834 (Anti-Aircraft) Squadron RAF Regiment, Operations Record Book: No.2834 (Anti-Aircraft) Squadron RAF Regiment.
10. Levine, Alan J., *D-Day to Berlin: The Northwest Europe Campaign, 1944–45* (Mechanicsburg, PA: Stackpole Books, 2000), pp.182–183.
11. Coningham's report, p.60.
12. Coningham's report, p.59.
13. TNA, AIR 29/122/3, No.2874 Squadron RAF Regiment Operations Record Book, entry for 16 April 1945.
14. *The London Gazette* (supplement), 5 June 1945, p.2849. Available at https://www.thegazette.co.uk.
15. *The London Gazette* (supplement), 4 January 1946, p.227. Available at https://www.thegazette.co.uk.
16. *The London Gazette* (supplement), 8 March 1946, p.1278. The citation describes Fones as 'starting the engine'. This is most likely to have involved him hand swinging the propeller whilst the pilot was in the cockpit operating the necessary controls. Available at https://www.thegazette.co.uk.
17. Coningham's report, p.65.
18. AM, *Maintenance*, pp.349–350.
19. TNA, AIR 20/1593, Operations of 2nd TAF, 6 June 1944 – 9 May 1945, report by Air Marshal Sir Arthur Coningham.
20. Saunders, *The Fight is Won*, p.291.
21. AM, *Maintenance*, p.351.
22. TNA, AIR 51/376/13, Air Transport Services, various correspondence for April 1945 and TNA, AIR 27/1973/3, Squadron No.512, Summary of Events.
23. Data from TNA, AIR 37/1096, SHAEF (Main and Rear): No.46 Group Weekly Airlift Returns, Summaries of No.46 Group Weekly Lift Returns (United Kingdom – the Continent).
24. Oliver, *The RAF Regiment at War*, pp.117–118.
25. *D-Day to Berlin – Victory in Europe Day by Day* (Barnsley: Pen & Sword, 2013), pp.184–187.
26. TNA, AIR 29/122/3, No.2874 Squadron RAF Regiment Operations Record Book, entry for 2 May 1945.
27. This date probably relates to the initial surrender of all German forces in the Netherlands, north-west Germany, and Denmark at Montgomery's HQ at Lüneburg Heath.
28. TNA, AIR 29/75, No.2717 (Rifle) Squadron RAF Regiment Operations Record Book, entry for 5 May 1945.
29. Jefford, *RAF Squadrons*, pp. 23-105 and Appendix 11, Maps 14 and 15.
30. AM, *From Normandy to Hanover*, p.37.
31. Coningham's report, p.80.
32. Extract from an anonymous piece of verse in correspondence with the author by Mr Jack Hoare who served with No.418 Air Stores Park during the Normandy campaign.
33. Coningham's report, p.100.

NOTES AND REFERENCES

Appendix IV

1. For a fuller account of the development of the RAF beach squadrons see Stone, *Sustaining Air Power*, pp.131–132, 141–142 and 147–154 and Mike Fenton's website at https://rafbeachunits.info.
2. Details on the fighter direction tenders produced with permission from the Combined Operations website at https://www.combinedops.com/FDTs.html.
3. AM, *Maintenance*, p.36 and Shores et al, *2nd Tactical Air Force*, Volume 3, p.549. Initially formed as No.511 in October 1943 and renamed as the Forward Repair Unit (Mobile Aircraft Repairs). In November 1944 the Forward Repair Unit was disbanded with its personnel being absorbed into the BARU which, in turn was renamed No.151 Repair Unit (based at Courtrai). The BASU was also renamed to No.3 Base Recovery Unit. For the first few months of the campaign, the unit remained in the base area, but moved to Airfield B.70 at Antwerp/Deurne in early September 1944 then to Wevelghem in October 1944.
4. Hutchinson, M.G., Night Fighter Control for (D-Day) Operation *Overlord* available at https://mraths.org.uk.

Appendix V

1. Listing based largely on data from Shores, *2nd Tactical Air Force*, Appendices I and II, pp.281–289.

Bibliography

The National Archives, Kew, London
AIR 9 Series – Air Ministry: Directorate of Operations and Intelligence and Directorate of Plans
AIR 16 Series – Air Ministry: Fighter Command
AIR 20 Series – Air Ministry and Ministry of Defence
AIR 25 Series – Air Ministry and Ministry of Defence: Operations Record Books
AIR 26 Series – Air Ministry: Operations Record Books, Wings
AIR 27 Series – Air Ministry and successors: Operations Record Books, Squadrons
AIR 29 Series – Air Ministry and Ministry of Defence: Operations Record Books, Miscellaneous Units
AIR 37 Series – Allied Expeditionary Air Force and 2nd Tactical Air Force
AIR 38 Series – Air Ministry and Ministry of Defence: Ferry Command and successors

Official and Unpublished Sources
Air Ministry (AM), *Royal Air Force War Manual, Part I: Operations* (London: Air Ministry, 1940)
AM, *Royal Air Force War Manual, Part II: Organization and Administration* (London: Air Ministry, 1940)
AM, *Report on the Air and Administrative Organization of the 2nd Tactical Air Force 1947* (London: Air Ministry, 1947; repr. 2017)
AM, The Second World War 1939–1945, *Airborne Forces* (London: Air Ministry, 1951; repr. 2017)
AM (Air Historical Branch (AHB)), The Second World War 1939–1945, Royal Air Force, *Maintenance* (London: Air Ministry, 1954)
AM (AHB), The Second World War 1939-1945, Royal Air Force, *Works* (London: Air Ministry, 1956)
AM(AHB), *The Expansion of the Royal Air Force 1934–1939* (London: Air Ministry, undated)
AM, RAF Narrative (First Draft), *The Liberation of Northwest Europe, Volume II, The Administrative Preparations* (London: Air Ministry, undated)
AM, No.84 Group Second TAF, Royal Air Force, *From Normandy to Hanover June 1944 – June 1945* (London: Air Ministry, undated)

BIBLIOGRAPHY

Browne, John, *Airfield Construction by the Royal Air Force 1939 to 1966* in RAF Historical Society Journal No.51, 2011,

Higham, J.B. and Knighton, E.A., T*he Second World War 1939–1945 Army, Movements* (London: War Office, 1955)

Monckton, Sir Walter, Report for the Chiefs of Staff Committee, *The Part Played in 'Overlord' by the Synthetic Harbours* (London: Chiefs of Staff Committee, 1946)

RAF Lists (various) in the library of the RAF College Cranwell.

Rexford-Welch, S.C., *History of the Second World War (United Kingdom Medical Series), The Royal Air Force Medical Services, Volume III Campaigns* (London: HMSO, 1958)

Veeder, Major Timothy A., *'An Evaluation of the Aerial Interdiction Campaign Known as the "Transportation Plan" for the D-Day Invasion, Early January 1944 to Late June 1944'* Research paper presented to the Research Department Air Command and Staff College (unpublished research paper 1997)

War Office, *Operational Aspects of Mulberry "B"* (Conf. No. 4067) dated 10 May 1945

War Office, *The Administrative History of the Operations of 21 Army Group on the Continent of Europe 6 June 1944 – 8 May 1945* (Germany: War Office, 1945)

Books

Bailey, G.J. *The Arsenal of Democracy- Aircraft Supply and the Anglo-American Alliance, 1938–1942* (Edinburgh: Edinburgh University Press, 2013)

Beale, Peter, *The Great Mistake – The Battle for Antwerp and the Beveland Peninsula, September 1944* (Stroud: Sutton Publishing, 2004)

Bickers, Richard Townhend, *Air War Normandy* (Barnsley: Pen & Sword, 2015)

Bowman, Martin W, *Air War Varsity* (Barnsley: Pen & Sword, 2017)

Buckley, John, *Monty's Men: The British Army and the Liberation of Europe* (London: Yale University Press, 2014)

Buckley, John (ed.), *The Normandy Campaign: Sixty Years On* (Abingdon: Routledge, 2006)

Butler, P. *Air Arsenal North America: Aircraft for the Allies 1938–1945, Purchases and Lend-Lease* (Hinckley: Midland Publishing, 2004)

Clark, Lloyd, *Crossing the Rhine* (New York: Grove Press, 2008)

Dean, Sir Maurice, *The Royal Air Force and Two World Wars* (London: Cassell, 1979)

Delve, Ken, *The Source Book of the RAF* (Shrewsbury: Airlife, 1994)

D'Este, Carlo, *Decision in Normandy: The Unwritten Story of Montgomery and the Allied Campaign* (New York: E.P. Dutton, 1983; repr. 2001)

Edgerton, David, *Britain's War Machine: Weapons, Resources and Experts in the Second World War* (London: Allen Lane, 2011; repr. 2012)

Ellis, Major L.F., *History of the Second World War Victory in the West: Volume I – The Battle of Normandy* (United Kingdom Military series) (London: HMSO, 1962)

Forty, George, Marriott, Leo and Forty, Simon, *Hitler's Atlantic Wall: From Southern France to Northern Norway, Yesterday and Today* (Oxford: Casemate, 2016)

FORWARD AIR BASES IN EUROPE FROM D-DAY TO THE BALTIC

Gordon, Edward E and David Ramsay, *Divided on D-Day: How Conflicts and Rivalries Jeopardized the Allied Victory at Normandy* (New York: Prometheus Books, 2017)

Grehan, John and Mace, Martin (compilers), *Despatches from the Front: Liberating Europe D-Day to Victory 1944–1945* (Barnsley: Pen & Sword, 2014)

Guedalla, Phillip, ***Middle East 1940–1942: A Study in Air Power*** **(London: Hodder & Stoughton, 1944)**

Hall, David I., *Strategy for Victory: The Development of British Tactical Air Power, 1919–1943* (Westport, CT: Praeger Security International, 2008)

Hartcup, Guy, *Code Name Mulberry: The Planning, Building and Operation of the Normandy Harbours* (Newton Abbott: David & Charles, 1977; repr. Barnsley: Pen & Sword, 2011)

Higham, Robin, *Bases of Air Strategy: Building Airfields for the RAF 1914–1945* (Ilkley: Airlife, 1998)

Jacobs, Peter, *Airfields of the D-Day Invasion Air Force: 2nd Tactical Air Force in South-East England in WWII* (Barnsley: Pen & Sword, 2009)

Jefford, C.G., *RAF Squadrons*, Shrewsbury: Airlife, 1988)

Kellett, Pete and Davies, Jeff, *A History of the RAF Servicing Commandos* (Shrewsbury: Airlife, 1989)

Lamb, Richard, *Montgomery in Europe 1943–45: Success of Failure* (London: Buchan & Enright, 1983)

Levine, Alan J., *D-Day to Berlin: The Northwest Europe Campaign, 1944-45* (Mechanicsburg, PA: Stackpole Books, 2000)

Love, Robert. W. and Major, John (eds.), *The Year of D-Day: The 1944 Diary of Admiral Sir Bertram Ramsay* (Hull: University of Hull Press, 1994)

Montgomery, Field Marshal, *Normandy to the Baltic* (London: Hutchinson & Co Ltd, 1947; repr. October 1948)

Montgomery, Field Marshal, *The Memoirs of Field-Marshal Montgomery* (London: Fontana, 1960; repr. Barnsley: Pen & Sword, 2005)

Morgan, Lieutenant General Sir F.E., *Overture to Overlord* (London: Hodder & Stoughton, 1950)

Moulton, Major General J.L., *Battle for Antwerp: The Liberation of the City and the Opening of the Scheldt 1944* (London: Ian Allan, 1978)

Natkiel, Richard, *Atlas of World War II* (London: Bison Books, 1985)

Norman, Albert, *Operation Overlord: Design & Reality* (Harrisburg, PA: The Military Service Publishing Company, 1952)

Oliver, Kingsley M., *The RAF Regiment at War 1942–1946* (Barnsley: Pen & Sword, 2016)

Orange, Vincent, *Coningham: A Biography of Air Marshal Sir Arthur Coningham* (Washington DC: Center for Air Force History, 1992)

Ramsey, Winston (ed.), *Invasion Airfields: Then and Now* (Old Harlow: After the Battle, 2017 – now incorporated by Pen & Sword, Barnsley)

Richards, Denis, *Royal Air Force 1939–1945: Volume I – The Fight at Odds* (London: HMSO, 1953)

Ritchie, Sebastian, *Arnhem: Myth and Reality* (London: Robert Hale Ltd, 2011)

BIBLIOGRAPHY

Rogers, David and Rogers, Joseph, *D-Day Beach Force: The Men Who Turned Chaos into Order* (Stroud: Spellmount, 2012)
Ryan, Cornelius, *A Bridge Too Far* (London: Hamish Hamilton, 1974)
Saunders, Hilary St George, *Royal Air Force 1939–1945: Volume III – The Fight is Won* (London: HMSO, 1954)
Shores, Christopher F., *2nd Tactical Air Force* (Reading: Osprey, 1970)
Shores, Christopher F. and Thomas, Chris, *2nd Tactical Air Force*, four volumes (Hersham: Chevron Publishing, 2004, 2005, 2006 and 2008)
Stone, Trevor, *Sustaining Air Power: Royal Air Force Logistics since 1918* (Exeter: Fonthill Media, 2017)
Sturtivant, Ray, Hamlin, John and Halley, James J., *Royal Air Force Flying Training and Support Units* (Tunbridge Wells: Air Britain, 1997)
Terraine, John, *The Right of the Line: The Royal Air Force in the European War 1939 – 1945* (London: Hodder & Stoughton, 1985; also Ware: Wordworth, 1977; repr. Barnsley: Pen & Sword, 2010)
Thetford, Owen, *Aircraft of the Royal Air Force Since 1918*, (ninth edition) (London: Putnam, 1995)
Tucker-Jones, Anthony, *Falaise: The Flawed Victory* (Barnsley: Pen & Sword, 2018)
Thomas, Chris, *Typhoon Wings of 2nd TAF 1943–45* (Oxford: Osprey Publishing, 2012)
van Creveld, Martin, *Supplying War: Logistics from Wallenstein to Patton,* second edition (New York: Cambridge University Press, 2004)
Wilmot, Chester, *The Struggle for Europe* (Ware: Wordsworth Editions, 1997)

Articles in Newspapers, Magazines and Periodicals
Hadaway, Stuart, 'Flying from France – Airfield Construction and the RAF Regiment in Normandy', *Royal Air Force Salute – D-Day 70th Anniversary*, 2014, pp.48–53.

Articles and Documents from Internet Sources
Annon, Fighter Direction Tenders – FDTs Nos. 13, 216 and 217, Radar, Communications and Intelligence Gathering Ships. Available from https://www.combinedops.com.
Hutchinson, M.G., Night Fighter Control for (D-Day) Operation *Overlord*. Available from Malvern Radar and Technology History Society at https://mraths.org.uk/?page_id=2838.
White, Ian, *A Short History of Air Intercept Radar and the British Night-Fighter 1936–1945*. Available from https://600squadronassociation.com/wp-content/uploads/2014/11.
Project *Overlord* – The RAF and the Campaign to Liberate Northwest Europe, 1944–45 https://rafoverlord.blogspot.com/2019/03/21-base-defence-sector-at-omaha-beach-6.html.
Warwick, Nigel, *Operation 'Overlord' – The Royal Air Force Regiment in Normandy and the Liberation of Europe*, available at: https://www.rafregimentheritagecentre.co.uk/operation-overlord-the-royal-air-force-regiment-in-normandy-and-the-liberation-of-europe.

Websites

Abandoned, Forgotten & Little-Known Airfields in Europe: https://forgottenairfields.com/index.php.
Combined Operations: https://www.combinedops.com.
Commonwealth War Graves Commission: https://cwgc.org.
Men of D-Day: https://www.6juin1944.com/veterans/dobinson.php.
National Army Museum: https://www.nam.ac.uk/explore/market-garden.
Royal Air Force Beach Units: https://www.rafbeachunits.info.
Royal Air Force Bomb Disposal Association: https://www.rafbdassociation.com.
Royal Air Force No.5001 Squadron Airfield Construction Branch Association: https//.www.rafacb.org.uk.
RAF Regiment Heritage Centre: https://www.rafregimentheritagecentre.co.uk.
The London Gazette: https://www.thegazette.co.uk.
The Memory Project: https://www.thememoryproject.com.
The National Archives: https://discovery.nationalarchives.gov.uk.
The Royal Air Force at OMAHA Beach: https://www.therafatomahabeach.com.
Journal Officiel de la République Française: https://gallica.bnf.fr.

Index

Achmer (B.110), 150
Adair, Corporal Hugh, 141
Administrative Plan, RAF, 16–18, 50
Ahlhorn (B.111), 150
Air Ministry, 17, 27, 34, 36, 111, 131
Air reconnaissance, 14–15, 43, 104–109
Air transport/airlift (*see also* supply by air), 29–31, 69, 77, 83, 98, 110–14, 124, 144, 151–2
   No.38 Group, 29, 111, 144
   No.46 Group, 29–30, 78, 110–13, 124, 144
Air Freight Control Centre, 29
Air Transport Operations Room, Combined, 29–30, 111
Air stores parks, 7, 25–8, 100–101, 133, 157 (*see also* Appendix III)
Air technical intelligence units/teams, RAF, 35, 92, 95, 147
Airborne (formations and operations), 14, 30, 45, 48, 98, 112–14, 131, 144–5, 149
Airfield construction, 8, 16, 23, 31, 58–9, 85–6, 91–2, 129–30, 141
Airfield construction wings/ squadrons, RAF, 31, 130–1 (*see also* Appendix III)
   No.5352 Wing, 85, 92
   No.5357 Wing, 31, 38, 50, 85
   No.5022 Squadron, 85, 91, 109, 131, 141
   No.5023 Squadron, 85, 91, 131–2
Airfield HQs, 25, 32–3, 50, 69
Allied Expeditionary Air Force, 6, 14, 18, 29, 34, 42–3, 77, 87, 114, 119, 124
Amiens/Glisy (B.48), 98, 109, 111, 137, 146
Ammunition, 25, 27, 50, 61, 67, 78–9, 89, 100, 111, 119, 139, 142–3, 152
Antwerp, 21, 97, 110, 113, 115–18, 123, 125–8, 134, 150, 156, 162 (*see also* Appendix II)
Ardennes, 36, 128, 133, 135–7, 142
Argentan, 93
Armourers, RAF, 25, 71
Army/RAF support agreements, 17–18
Arnhem, 109, 112, 120, 124, 151, 162
Arromanches, 20, 47, 61, 72, 79–80, 90, 103, 162
Asnelles-sur-Mer (B.1), 59
Atlantic Wall, 11, 49, 102
Auster, AOP aircraft, 8–9, 101, 148–9
Australia, 7
Aviation Fuel and Ammunition Park (AFAP), 18, 27, 101 (*see also* Appendix III)
   No.422 AFAP, 101

Bad Eilsen, 148
Balleroy/Lignerolles (A.12), 109
Balloons, 19, 53–4
Baltic, 145, 150
Base defence sectors (BDS), 33
   No.21 BDS, 33, 49–50, 54, 95
   No.24 BDS, 33, 48
   No.25 BDS, 33
Base personnel centre, RAF, 22,
   103–104, 128 (*see also* Appendix III)
Base signals and radar unit, 22, 128
   (*see also* Appendix III)
Bastogne, 136
Batchelor, Corporal Lionel, 67
Bayeux, 21, 77, 81, 85, 90
Bazenville (B.2), 59–61, 72, 77, 83
Beach squadrons, RAF, 19, 38,
   (*see also* Appendix III)
   No.1 RAF Beach Squadron, 50
     (*see also* Appendix III)
   No.2 RAF Beach Squadron, 50
     (*see also* Appendix III)
   No.4 RAF Beach Squadron 52
     (*see also* Appendix III)
Beauvais, 96, 109
Belgium/Belgian, 7, 69, 81, 85, 90, 93, 97, 104, 109, 114, 119, 123, 128, 133, 135–7, 150
Bentley Priory, RAF, 30, 111
Beny-sur-Mer (B.4), 65, 106
Berlin, 142, 153
Bicester, RAF, 21, 30, 76–7, 102
Bituminised (pre) surfacing, 58, 69, 129
Blakehill Farm, RAF, 23, 29
Blatherwick, Squadron Leader, 123–4
Bluecoat, Operation, 91, 162
Bodenplatte, Operation, 138–41
Bofors Gun, 46, 61, 121, 139–40
Bomb disposal units, RAF, 24
   (*see also* Appendix III)

Boulogne, 78, 95, 115
   (*see also* Appendix II)
Bowhill, Air Chief Marshal
   Sir Frederick, 124
Bowsers, fuel, 28, 72, 78
Bradley, Lieutenant General Omar, 12
Bremen, 137, 145, 150
Brittany, 33, 93
British Army formations
   Twenty-First Army Group, 7, 23, 31, 97, 103, 113, 124, 127, 130, 134, 143, 145, 151, 158
   Second Army, 13, 23, 38, 86, 89, 91, 93, 97, 113, 119–20, 145, 149–50 (*see also* Appendix I)
   Third Infantry Division, 14
   First Allied Airborne Army:
     First Airborne Division, 112
     Sixth Airborne Division, 144
Broadhurst, Air Vice-Marshal Harry, 5, 63
Broadwell, RAF, 23, 29
Brown, Sergeant Archibald, 122
Brown, Air Vice-Marshal Leslie, 5
Bruce, Flight Lieutenant, 52
Brussels, 118, 124, 129, 146, 150, 156, 162
Bulge, Battle of the, 135–6

Caen, 12, 70, 85, 89–90, 95, 162
Calais, Pas de, 12, 43, 97
   (*see also* Appendix II)
Cambrai/Epinoy (A.75), 150
Camouflage and deception, 36–7, 72–3, 100, 120
Canada, 7, 14, 33, 36, 47, 50, 58, 65, 88–90, 97, 114–15
Canadian formations;
   First Army, 4, 86, 93, 97, 107, 125, 145
   Second Infantry Division, 125

INDEX

Third Infantry Division, 14
Air Force, Royal Canadian, 5, 7, 9, 59, 72, 81, 128
Carpiquet (B.17), 14, 85, 92, 95
Casualty air evacuation, 23, 82–5, 111–12, 139
Celle (B.118), 150
Chapman, Squadron Leader B.W.B, 53
Charnwood, Operation, 89 (*see also* Appendix I)
Cherbourg, 13, 20, 43, 79, 81, 116, 162 (*see also* Appendix II)
Churchill, Prime Minister Winston, 12, 145, 158–9
Cobra, Operation, 93
Condé-sur-Noireau, 91–2
Coningham, Air Marshal Sir Arthur, 5, 9–10, 58, 68, 73, 91, 94, 97, 111, 118, 124, 132–3, 145–6, 157–8
Cotentin Peninsula, 12, 20, 91, 116
Coulombs (B.6), 67, 77, 84
Courseulles-sur-Mer, 50, 63
Coxyde (B.71), 129, 146
Crépon, 59
Créton (B.30), 109
Czechoslovakia, 7

Dakota, Douglas DC-3, 23, 29, 64, 69, 77, 83, 109–10, 114, 124, 139, 151
Davies, Leading Aircraftman Thomas, 126
Delden (V.3008), 150
Denmark, 150, 153
Dental units, 7, 22 (*see also* Appendix III)
Deurne/Antwerp (B.70), 107
Deventer, 123
Dieppe, 79, 115, 127 (*see also* Appendix II)
Dobbin, Squadron Leader J.N., 50
Dobinson, Leslie, 56
Down Ampney, RAF, 23, 29
Dring, Leading Aircraftman Norman, 67
Drope (B.105), 150
Dust problem in Normandy, aircraft, 70–1

Eindhoven, 100, 112, 119, 129–30, 140–1, 146
Eisenhower, Dwight D/ Supreme Allied Commander, 5, 12, 49, 97, 117, 125, 142, 145, 154
Elbe, river, 145, 149, 153
Ellon (B.12), 72
Elmhirst, Air Vice-Marshal Thomas, 6, 10
Embarkation units, RAF, 116, 126–7
Embry, Air Vice-Marshal Basil, 6
Ems Weser Canal, 147
Emse, river, 156
Epinoy/Cambrai (A.75), 146, 150
Epsom, Operation, 89, 162 (*see also* Appendix I)
Evère (B.56), 85, 99, 124, 139

Falaise, 93–4, 114 (*see also* Appendix I)
Fassberg, 150
Fighter direction tender, 34, 46–7, 50 (*see also* Appendix III)
Finch, Leading Aircraftman William, 60
Flensburg, 153
Fones, Leading Aircraftman Cyril, 148–9
Forward control posts, 87–8
Forward Equipment Unit, 21, 26, 30–1, 77 (*see also* Appendix III)
Forward Repair Unit, 22, 25, 28 (*see also* Appendix III)
Fuel, petrol/petroleum, 8, 17–18, 25, 35, 50, 67, 75, 78–9, 99–100, 111, 113, 116, 118, 127, 136–7, 139, 143, 148, 151

221

Garratt, Squadron Leader, 92
Ghent, 128, 146
Giles, Sister (Flying Officer) Mollie, 82–3
Gilze Rijen (B.77), 131, 138, 146, 150
Gliders, 30, 44, 48, 66, 112
Glisy/Amiens (B.48), 98, 109, 146
Goch (B.100), 143, 146
Godelmesnil (B.35), 114
GOLD Beach, 13, 20, 33, 45, 47, 50, 52, 56, 59, 63, 72
Goodwood, Operation, 89
  (*see also* Appendix I)
Gosport, 48, 63, 77
Greening, Flight Sergeant Albert, 125
Grenade, Operation, 143
Ground control intercept (GCI), 33, 50, 56
  No.15082 GCI Convoy, 56
  No.15083 GCI Convoy, 47, 52
Group control centres, 61, 87

Hamburg, 115, 137, 151, 153
Hanover, 150, 156
Harding, Reverend Geoffrey, 56
Harrow, Handley Page, 23
Hart, Group Captain R.G, 33
Heesch (B.88), 146
Helmond (B.86), 121, 146
Hospitals, RAF:
  General, 22, 83
    (*see also* Appendix III)
  Mobile field, 7, 22
    (*see also* Appendix III)
  No.50 Mobile Field Hospital, 59, 81, 90
  No.52 (RCAF) Mobile Field Hospital, 81
Hustedt (B.150), 150

Inge, Sergeant E.G, 51–2
Intelligence, 14, 34, 104

Jay, Flight Lieutenant Walter, 147–8
Johnson, Wing Commander 'Johnnie', 59
JUNO Beach, 14, 45, 47, 49–50, 53, 56, 63, 106

Kluis (B.91), 146
Knokke-le-Zout (B.83), 129, 146, 150

Langenhagen (B.120), 150
Lantheuil (B.9), 65
Le Blanc, Frank Flight Sergeant, 72
Le Fresne-Camilly (B.5), 67, 84, 90
Le Havre, 12, 20, 67, 78, 115, 118
  (*see also* Appendix II)
Le Tréport, 25, 116
  (*see also* Appendix II)
Leigh-Mallory, Air Chief Marshal Sir Trafford, 6, 14, 118–19
Leopold Canal, 36, 125–6
Lignerolles/Balleroy (A.12), 109
Lille (B.51), 101, 109, 114, 135, 137, 146
Lingèvres (B.19), 109
Logistics, 11, 21, 89, 101, 109, 115–16, 120, 124, 129, 137, 145, 150, 152, 156
Lübeck, 150, 156
Lüneburg (B.156), 150
Luxembourg, 14, 135
Lynch, Leading Aircraftman Thomas, 143–4

Maas, river, 36, 129, 143
Maguire, Warrant Officer Patrick, 122
Maintenance, aircraft, 24, 32, 65, 69
Maintenance, mobile, 23
Market Garden, Operation, 112–14, 117, 120, 131, 151

INDEX

Martragny (B.7), 65
Melsbroek (B.58), 93, 113, 141, 146, 150
Merville (B.53), 114, 118
Meuse, river, 21, 118, 120, 129, 142
Mill (B.89), 146
Mobility, 5, 16–17, 67, 69, 74, 97–8, 120, 142
Moerkerke, 125
Mont Pinçon, 91–2
Montgomery, Field Marshal Sir Bernard, 7, 12, 23, 31, 46, 97, 108, 112, 117, 120, 137, 142, 144, 149, 155
Morgan, General Sir Frederick, 12
Motor transport, 20, 28, 69–70, 151
Motor transport light repair units, 7, 22, 28 (*see also* Appendix III)
Mulberry harbours, 20, 79–80
(*see also* Appendices I & II)
Munitions, 18, 25, 77–8, 85, 98, 101–102, 116, 137, 152

NAAFI, 65, 134–5, 138
Netherlands/Holland (inc. Dutch), 7, 81, 97, 100, 104, 112–14, 118–23, 129, 130–33, 137–40, 150, 156
New Zealand, 5, 7
Nijmegen, 112, 118, 142
Northolt, RAF, 104, 108

Odon, river, 89 (*see also* Appendix I)
Ogilvie, Sister (Flying Officer) Iris, 82–3
Old Sarum, RAF, 41, 63
OMAHA Beach, 14, 20, 33, 47, 54–5, 79, 95
Orne, river, 13, 73, 89
(*see also* Appendix I)
Osnabruck, 147
Ostend, 115, 128–9
(*see also* Appendix II)
Ouistreham, 50, 54, 90

Padres/chaplains, RAF 7, 56, 65
Page, Flying Officer Norman, 125–6
Paris, 91, 95 (*see also* Appendix I)
Parker, Sergeant James, 67
Perkins, The Reverend T. Gordon, 7
Petit Brogel (B.90), 146
Photographic Sections, Mobile Field (MFPS), 7, 106–108
(*see also* Appendix III)
No.4 MFPS, 106, 138
(*see also* Appendix III)
No.5 MFPS, 96, 107
(*see also* Appendix III)
No.7 MFPS, 134
(*see also* Appendix III)
Pipeline, fuel, 17–18, 78
(*see also* Appendix I)
Plantlunne (B.103), 150
Plumetot (B.10), 65
Plunder, Operation, 144–5
(*see also* Appendix I)
PLUTO, pipeline, 78
(*see also* Appendix I)
Pocklington, RAF, 113
Poland, 7, 142
Ports, 11, 14, 20–1, 23, 33, 41–2, 48–9, 79, 81, 97, 100, 111 115–18, 124, 137, 151 (*see also* Appendices I & II)
Port en Bessin, 14, 78
(*see also* Appendix II)
Portsmouth, 41
Poulton, RAF, 29
Pressed (pierced) steel planking, 58, 129

Quakenbrück, 147, 150
Queen Mary Trailer, 77, 102

Radar (inc.units), 14, 22, 28, 33–4, 42, 52–4, 87, 92, 95, 128, 136
Raggatt, Flying Officer, 92

Railways, 14, 42, 102–103, 137, 151
Ramsay, Admiral Sir Bertram, 117
Rear Maintenance Area, 19, 25, 28, 77–8, 81, 86, 117–18, 124, 128
Reconnaissance, air, 14, 31, 44, 98, 101, 104–107, 111, 131, 146
Refuelling, 16, 24, 32, 50, 57, 62, 78, 89, 99
Regiment, RAF (in general), 35, 67–8, 89, 153
Regiment, RAF wings and squadrons (*see also* Appendix III)
  No.1300 Mobile Wing HQ, 96
  No.1301 Mobile Wing HQ, 72
  No.1302 Mobile Wing HQ, 140
  No.1304 Mobile Wing HQ, 63
  No.1313 Mobile Wing HQ, 125
  No.2703 Squadron, 140
  No.2717 Squadron, 125, 154
  No.2726 Squadron, 126
  No.2729 Squadron, 148
  No.2757 Squadron, 125, 148
  No.2770 Squadron, 136
  No.2773 Squadron, 140
  No.2781 Squadron, 147
  No.2798 Squadron, 95, 126
  No.2804 Squadron, 136, 147
  No.2806 Squadron, 92–3
  No.2807 Squadron, 148
  No.2809 Squadron, 63, 67, 72
  No.2811 Squadron, 124, 136
  No.2816 Squadron, 125
  No.2817 Squadron, 140
  No.2819 Squadron, 67, 99
  No.2834 Squadron, 45–6, 48, 59–60, 67, 71–2, 138–9, 140, 150, 154–5
  No.2874 Squadron, 114, 118, 121–2, 147, 153–4
Reichswald, 143–4
Reid, Leading Aircraftman John, 56
Reinsehlen (B.154), 150
Repair and salvage units (R&SU), 7, 25 (*see also* Appendix III)
  No.405 R&SU, 65
Resupply, 21, 27–28, 77, 85 (bombs by air), 100, 102, 111, 145
Rheine (B.108), 150
Rhine, river, 74, 97, 109, 112, 118, 120, 125, 129, 132, 135, 137, 142, 149, 155
Rocket projectiles (aircraft), 43, 65, 78–9, 89, 93, 114, 131
Rosieres (B.87), 146
Rotterdam, 21, 115
Royal Engineers, 31, 50, 58, 62, 72, 130
Ruhr, 97, 112, 117, 135, 144–5
Russia/Soviet Union, 12, 74, 142, 147, 153, 155, 159
Rycroft, Flight Lieutenant Noel, 56

Saint Nazaire, 33
Saint-Lô, 91, 93
Saint-Aubin-sur-Mer, 50
Sainte-Croix-sur-Mer (B.3), 62–3, 65, 68
Sanitation, 38, 74–5
Scheldt, 117, 120, 125
Schijndel (B.85), 146
Schleswig Holstein, 150, 153
Seine, river, 12, 91, 94–5, 97, 105, 146
Servicing/Serviceability, 70–1, 119
Servicing commando units (SCU), RAF, 24–5, 32–3, 38, 50, 99 (*see also* Appendix III)
  No.3205 SCU, 63, 69
  No.3206 SCU, 69
  No.3207 SCU, 59, 77
  No.3208 SCU, 69
  No.3210 SCU, 63, 69
Sherlow, Sergeant, 50

INDEX

Siegfried Line, 97, 112
Signals units, base, 128
Signals units, mobile, 26, 28, 33, 56, 87 *(see also* Appendix III)
Signals servicing units, mobile, 56 *(see also* Appendix III)
Skeet, Leading Aircraftman, 123–4
Smith, Flying Officer Bill, 63
Sohneverdingen, 150
Somme, 12, 97
Southampton, 63, 77
Southwick House, 42
Sparrow, Handley Page, 23, 111, 139
Spitfire, Supermarine, 8, 16, 43, 45, 48, 59, 62, 64, 68, 70, 78, 102, 109, 157
Squadrons, flying *(see also* Appendix IV):
    No.48 Squadron, 110
    No.69 Squadron, 98
    No.198 Squadron, 43
    No.233 Squadron, 110
    No.245 Squadron, 63
    No.271 Squadron, 110
    No.341 Squadron, 64
    No.349, Squadron 64
    No.401 Squadron, 64
    No.421 Squadron, 72
    No.441 Squadron, 68
    No.442 Squadron, 64, 68
    No.443 Squadron, 68
    No.453 Squadron, 64
    No.512 Squadron, 110
    No.575 Squadron, 110, 124
    No.609 Squadron, 43
    No.662 Squadron, 148
Square mesh track, 58, 69, 109, 129
Stanmore, RAF, 29
Steele, Air Vice-Marshal Charles, 6
Supply and transport column/company (S&TC), 25, 69, 102
    (see also Appendix III)
    No.309 S&TC, 101, 143

Supply-by-air, 27, 29–31, 151
Supreme Headquarters Allied Expeditionary Force (SHAEF), 42, 48
Surgical, teams/services, 22, 59, 83
SWORD Beach, 14, 45, 47, 50, 53, 56, 72, 91

Tedder, Air Chief Marshal Sir Arthur, 5
Telegraphy/telephony, 28, 87
Tilly-sur-Seulles, 85, 109
Totalize, Operation, 93
    (see also Appendix I)
Toye, Sergeant George, 141
Tractable, Operation, 93
    (see also Appendix I)
Transportation Plan, 103
Twente (B.106), 150, 157
Typhoon, Hawker, 8, 16, 43, 45, 63–4, 70, 89, 91, 93–4, 102, 114, 131

United States formations:
    12th Army Group, 97, 151
        1st Army, 14, 97, 145
            2nd Armored Division, 136
            4th Infantry Division, 95
        3rd Army, 132,
        5th Army, 95
        9th Army, 142, 145
    US Army Air Force, 15, 104
    9th Air Force, 6, 13, 31, 45, 133, 151
    IX Troop Carrier Command, 114
    XVIII Airborne Corps, 144
        82nd Airborne Division, 112
        101st Airborne Division, 112
UTAH Beach, 14, 47

V1 flying bomb, 14, 43, 95, 97, 121, 123, 126
V2 rocket, 123, 126
Varrelbusch (B.113), 150, 153

Varsity, Operation, 144
  (see also Appendix I)
VE-Day, 156–157
Veritable, Operation, 142
  (see also Appendix I)
Vierville-sur-Mer, 56
Villiers-le-Sec, 59, 65
Vitry (B.50), 96, 146
Volkel (B.80), 118, 121, 138, 146, 150

Waal, river, 126
Watchfield, RAF, 23
Waterproofing, vehicle, 38, 42
Welfare, 134–35, 138
Wendon, Wing Commander William, 128–29
Weser, river, 145, 147, 156
Wevelghem (B.55), 130
Wilhelmina Canal, 36, 122
Wild, Flying Officer John, 122–3
Wing HQs, 24
Work, Carl, 47
Wunstorf (B.116), 150